Telekhan Yizkor (Memorial) Book
(Telekhany, Belarus)

Translation of
Telekhan

Originally in Yiddish, Hebrew and English

Edited by: Sh. Sokoler

Published in Los Angeles, 1963

Published by JewishGen

An Affiliate of the Museum of Jewish Heritage - A Living Memorial to the Holocaust
New York

Telekhan Yizkor (Memorial) Book
Translation of *Telkhan*, edited by S. Sokoler

Translated by David Goldman
Translations donated by Ray Stone and Rita Krakower Margolis
Copyright © 2013 by JewishGen, Inc.
All rights reserved.
First Printing: July 2013, Av 5773
Second Printing: March 2019, Adar II 5779

Layout: Joel Alpert
Cover Design: Jan R. Fine
Publicity: Sandra Hirschhorn

Published by JewishGen, Inc.
An Affiliate of the Museum of Jewish Heritage
A Living Memorial to the Holocaust
36 Battery Place, New York, NY 10280

Printed in the United States of America by Lightning Source, Inc.

Library of Congress Control Number (LCCN): 2013939697
ISBN: 978-1-939561-07-7 (hard cover: 222 pages, alk. paper)

Cover photograph: Artwork from the original Yizkor book
Back Cover Photo: Image from the original Yizkor book

JewishGen and the Yizkor Books in Print Project

This book has been published by the **Yizkor Books in Print Project,** as part of the **Yizkor Book Project** of **JewishGen, Inc**.

JewishGen, Inc. is a non-profit organization founded in 1987 as a resource for Jewish genealogy. Its website [www.jewishgen.org] serves as an international clearinghouse and resource center to assist individuals who are researching the history of their Jewish families and the places where they lived. JewishGen provides databases, facilitates discussion groups, and coordinates projects relating to Jewish genealogy and the history of the Jewish people. In 2003, JewishGen became an affiliate of the **Museum of Jewish Heritage - A Living Memorial to the Holocaust** in New York.

The **JewishGen Yizkor Book Project** was organized to make more widely known the existence of Yizkor (Memorial) Books written by survivors and former residents of various Jewish communities throughout the world. Later, volunteers connected to the different destroyed communities began cooperating to have these books translated from the original language—usually Hebrew or Yiddish—into English, thus enabling a wider audience to have access to the valuable information contained within them. As each chapter of these books was translated, it was posted on the JewishGen website and made available to the general public.

The **Yizkor Books in Print Project** began in 2011 as an initiative to print and publish Yizkor Books that had been fully translated, so that hard copies would be available for purchase by the descendants of these communities and also by scholars, universities, synagogues, libraries, and museums.

These Yizkor books have been produced almost entirely through the volunteer effort of researchers from around the world, assisted by donations from private individuals. The books are printed and sold at near cost, so as to make them as affordable as possible. Our goal is to make this important genre of Jewish literature and history available in English in book form, so that people can have the personal histories of their ancestral towns on their bookshelves for themselves and for their children and grandchildren.

A list of all published translated Yizkor Books can be found at:
http://www.jewishgen.org/Yizkor/ybip.html

Lance Ackerfeld, Yizkor Book Project Manager

Joel Alpert, Yizkor Book in Print Project Coordinator

JewishGen
Yizkor Book Project

This book is presented by the
Yizkor Books in Print Project
Project Coordinator: Joel Alpert

Part of the
Yizkor Books Project of JewishGen, Inc.
Project Manager: Lance Ackerfeld

These books have been produced solely through volunteer effort
of individuals from around the world. The books are printed and
sold at near cost, so as to make them as affordable as possible.

Our goal is to make this history and important genre of Jewish
literature available in English in book form so that people can have
the near-personal histories of their ancestral towns on their bookshelves for themselves and for their children and grandchildren.

Any donations to the Yizkor Books Project are appreciated.

Please send donations to:
Yizkor Book Project
JewishGen
36 Battery Place
New York, NY 10280

JewishGen, Inc. is an affiliate of the
Museum of Jewish Heritage
A Living Memorial to the Holocaust

Page of the Original Telekhan Yizkor Book

Page of Original Yiddish Yizkor Book

רעדאַקציע־קאָלעגיע :

משה'ל ראָזמאַן, גאָלדע גורשטעל, גרשון גורשטעל
אסתר מילער, שרה רובינשטיין

רעדאַקטאָר: ש. סעקולער

﹏❧●❧﹏

אַרויסגעגעבן פון דעם

טעלעכאַנער יזכור בוך קאָמיטעט

לאָס אַנדזשעלעס

1963

Translation of the previous Yiddish page

Editorial Board:

Mosheh Rozman. Golde Gurshtel, Gershon Gurshtel, Esther Miler, Sarah Rubinshtein

**Published by
The Telekhan Yizkor Book Committee**

Los Angeles

1963

Dedicated to the last
Jewish citizens
of Telekhan

Acknowledgements

Special thanks to the National Yiddish Book Center in Amherst, Massachusetts and the New York Public Library for supplying the high resolution images used in this book.

Note: The original Yizkor book can be seen online at the NY Public Library site: http://yizkor.nypl.org/index.php?id=1314

We wish to acknowledge Ray Stone for his assistance in making this book available in book form. Ray coordinated the translation of the Yizkor book into English so that it could be placed on the Yizkor Book Project web site of JewishGen, Inc. Translations were done by David Goldman and also Ray Stone and Rita Krakover Margolis, who both donated translations.

Map of Belarus showing location of Telkhan

A Short History of Telekhany

Telekhany was founded toward the end of the fifteenth century, during the period when the so-called Tatar Hordes occupied Ukraine, Poland and parts of Russia. The name, from the Tatar language, means "Tomb of Khan". In those days, much of the territory belonged to a benevolent owner, Count Michael Kazimierz Oginsky, who, believing that the Jews would increase his revenue through their business activity, was more than happy to have a Jewish settlement on his estates.

Local peasants soon arrived in town to shop for items they needed. Most business between Jews and peasants were based on a barter relationship. The peasant obtained services from the shoemaker, tailor or other craftsman, and paid with the fruits of his labor – agricultural produce. Gradually, stores started offering merchandise brought in from Pinsk. In the barter exchange, the artisans accumulated surpluses of agricultural products, which the artisan sold on the market. Thus, a small-scale public market developed among the shops, together with new small side streets around the market. The result was the growth of Telekhany.

Count Oginsky owned huge forests and wanted to increase his profits on lumber shipped to Germany. Being a talented man of great energy he undertook to dig a canal uniting the Pripet (near Pinsk) and Shchara (near Slonim) rivers. In order to build the locks needed for the canal, thousands of peasant slaves did the heavy manual work. The project took fifty years to complete, from 1776 to 1826, and thousands of workers lost their lives in the process. Telekhany was a hub of activity during those years. All engineers, artisans and businessmen flourished in the active economy.

The community thrived in all aspects in the ensuing years, until it found itself in the midst of a World War I battleground alternately occupied by German and Russian forces. Following one of its retreats from the town in 1915, Russian soldiers burned the entire town to the ground. All property and wealth that had taken years to build was lost.

At the end of the war, Telekhany citizens returned to rebuild their town, but found themselves again in a border dispute between Poland and Russia which was eventually settled. But World War II soon arrived, and with it Hitler's sadistic forces, who immediately started to bully, rob, shoot and dispossess the large number of Telekhany Jews.

In August of 1941, almost the entire Jewish population of 2000 of Telekhany was annihilated by the Nazis. A stone monument memorializing this horrible tragedy stands at the outskirts of Telekhan.

Telekhan is located in Belarus at 52°31' North Latitude and 25°51'
East Longitude and 119 mi SW of Minsk

Alternate names for the town are: Telekhany [Russian], Telchan
[Yiddish], Telechany [Polish], Cielachany [Belarus], Telechon, Telekani,
Telekhan, Telechan, Tselyakhani, Celjachany

Notes to the Reader:

Within the text the reader will note "*[Page 34]* " standing ahead of a paragraph. This indicates that the material translated below was on page 34 of the original book. However, when a paragraph was split between two pages in the original book, the marker is placed in this book after the end of the paragraph for ease of reading.

Table of Contents in This Translation

2 On the Trail of the Telekhany Tragedy   *Boris Ustinov*

5 A Great Loss for the World   *Esther Miller*

8 How it all began

12 The Tragic Death of Azriel the Mute

14 Introduction

15 Foreword   *Mashele Roseman*

16 The Story of how   *Asher Gursthtel*
    Telekhany was Destroyed

33 The world became poorer   *Esther Miller*

46 The Munich Conference   *Aaron Klitenick*

49 My brother is alive!   *Dina Godiner*

54 Telekhany and World War
    One

63 September 21, 1939

67 My brother Shmuel   *Esther Godiner Miller*

71 The Lives and work of the   *Mina Baron*
    Telekhany Youth

82 Shlomo Landman's Story

86 Also from our birthplace   *Mashele Roseman*
    Telekhany

86 A Eulogy to burned down   *Moshe Bernstein*
    Telekhany

88 The Famous Date -   *Lazer Lutsky*
    Remembered Forever!

93 Memories of Telekhany   *Golda Stolyar*

99 I Remember my Hometown   *Riva Chaim Reuvens*

99 The Power of Goodness   *Chaim Finkelstein*

101 The Oath   *Esther Miller*

102 A letter from Telekhany   *Esther Miller*

102   The Sacred Chain   *Dina Godiner-Klitenick*

105   The Tormented Community   *Yehusha Sklar*
      of Telekhany

107   Telekhany

109   The family of Mordechai
      Gurstal

111   Memories of Telekhany   *Akiva Alevitsky*

121   A Chapter from "From   *Esther Miller*
      Telekhany to America"

126   My Flowers on the Mass   *Laibel Eisenberg*
      Grave

129   A Free Loan Society and   *Golda Bookman-Landman*
      Food Bank for the Poor in
      Telekhany

130   What I remember from my   *Chana Godiner*
      young days in Telechan

131   A letter to the Yizkor book   *Mendel & Kaleh Bernstein*
      committee

132   We had "Sarah-Do-Good"   *Riva Rosenberg*
      in Town

133   A Report from Gershon
      Gurstel

134   Azriel the mute's tragic
      death

137   Pictures and Images of Life   *Gershon Gurstel*
      in Telekhany

141   Yosef Tchernichov Danieli,
      of Blessed Memory

144   A Sacred Memorial to my   *Mashele Roseman*
      Dear Mother, Chaya-Esther

145   Telekhany Burial Society   *Gershon Telechaner*

147   Moshe Vichnes and his
      Family from Telekhany

147   Map of Telechan

148   Map of Polozia

149   The Mitnagdim (non-chassidic) synagogue

149   The Lyubisher synagogue

150   The Stoliner Rebbe and Rabbi Yosef Glick leaving the Stoliner synagogue

150   Telekhany Jews reciting *Tashlich.* The first man with the beard on the left is Alter the carpenter

151   A class from the Jewish religious school. The religious Hebrew school "Horeb"

151   A class from the Polish Public School. 46 of the students are Jews. Three survived and live in Israel.

152   The Telekhaner Drama Club. In a performance of *The Brothers Luria*

152   The last photo of Telekhany Jews. The community attending a performance of the Jewish drama club on a Sabbath evening in 1939.

153   Telekhany youth, members of *Poalei Zion.* With Moshe Grub, a representative of the Central Committee

153   *Hechalutz* movement in Telekhany (1930) [in photo:] The Telekhany Hechalutz Association, 8/10/1930.

154   The Yiddish Public School in Telekhany [Volksschule] (1936). Two of the children survived and are in Israel, 1) Motty Reuven Gurstel; 2) Yaakov Meltzer, son of Moshe the tailor.

154   A group of Chalutzim from Telekhany (1930)

155   The Free Loan Society Committee in Telekhany

155   Moshe Vichnes' family (a description of Moshe Vichnes in on p. 153)

156   The parents and family of Jenny Bloomberg. They all perished except for Golda Buchman (indicated with an arrow). She lives in Chicago.

156   Shlomo Landman

164   Moshe Landman [Moshe Landman helped his family move to Israel.]

157   Shmuel Godiner; a famous Jewish-Soviet writer. Killed fighting the Nazis in World War II

158   "Telekhaner klezmer group" 1908. [Right to left:] [Right to left:] Hershel Melnick, Nissel Melnick, Feivel Arkes Kagan. Feivel Kagan now lives in Hollywood and is a distinguished member of the music world.

159   Yisrael Moshiach with his wife Sarah and neighbors. All perished.

159   Chaim Reuven and his wife Reizel and son Eliezer. All perished.

160   Chaim Yeshayahu Schneidman

160   Gershon Meir Yankels

161   Family of Ezriel the Mute

161   Ezriel the Mute (Ezriel Eisenberg), photographed in 1904.

162   Leibel Eisenberg (when he served in the Polish army).

162   Zvi Eisenberg, son of Ezriel and Minka. Died in a work accident in Israel.

163   Daughter Chaya

163   Shmuel Chaim Eisenberg

163   Son, Motka, (Mordechai). Now an official in Israel.

163   Son, Zvika, badly wounded in War of Independence

163   Son, Yaakov, died in Israel War of Independence

164   Everyone in the photo perished except for Leibel Eisenberg from Brazil, indicated with an arrow. He visited them in 1934.

164   A group of neighbors who perished, except for the partisan Dina Godiner, indicated with an arrow. She lives in Lodz.

165   Malka Kupa (Aharon Moshka's mother) [A member of the Yizkor Book committee. She died in Los Angeles]

165

      Herschel Eisenberg [Hershel Eisenberg edited the original manuscript of the history of Telekhany].

165   Khatsha Bernstein Mendel's mother

166   Introduction

168   The Home of Rabbi Yosef Hakohen Glick in Telekhany   *Mayer Goldsmith*

175   The Gurstel-Gurion Family and the Zionist Movement in Telekhany

177   Jacob Eisenberg, son of Liba and Shmuel Chaim Eisenberg

178   Biography of Laibel Eisenberg, the son of Azriel and Minka

178   Biography of Tzipora Eisenberg, the Daughter of Minka and Azriel

179   Biography of Zvi Eisenberg, the son of Israel

180   In sacred everlasting memory of our martyrs

188   Table of Contents of the Original Yizkor Book

193   Index

Family Notes

Telekhan Yizkor (Memorial) Book (Telekhany, Belarus)

Translation of
Telekhan

Original Yizkor Book Edited by: Sh. Sokoler

Original Yizkor Book Published in Los Angeles, 1963

Originally in Yiddish, Hebrew and English

[Page 3]

On the trail of the Telekhany Tragedy
By Boris Ustinov
Novosti Press Agency Correspondent

1.

Oswiecim, Majdanek, Sachsenhausen, Lidice, Oradour – World War II has made the names of these obscure towns and villages bywords for the ghastly crimes of German fascism. To their number we must yet add another-Telekhany.

Telekhany is a little town located far inland, amidst the woods and marshes of Byelorussia, midway between the towns of Pinsk and Baranovichi, and within nearly sixty kilometers' distance of the nearest railway.

Step by step, speaking to the inhabitants of this little town and neighboring villages, I was able to reconstruct the story of the appalling tragedy which was enacted during the late war.

2.

Before the Hitler armies invaded Soviet territory, Telekhany was a typical little town in the wooded district of Byelorussia,with a large Jewish population. Most of the Jews were artisans and tradesmen, whose sphere of activity extended to the outlying villages. They were tailors, cobblers, smiths, tinkers, watchmakers, harness and cart makers, coopers, butchers, barbers and petty traders.

Disaster overtook Telekhany on June 28th, 1941, when the German Nazi troops occupied the little town. This date marked the beginning of its end.

Telekhany soon remained far in the hinterland of the attacking German troops. On the surface life then seemed to resume its natural course. The inhabitants of Telekhany went on patching boots, sewing garments, tinkering, trading, arguing and praying to God. Many thought that now their greatest fears were behind them and the stories of Nazi atrocities grossly exaggerated.

3.

However, one August morning of 1941, at dawn, Telekhany woke up to hear rumors that the town was surrounded. The terrible rumor was soon confirmed. Telekhany was cut off from the outside world by a chain of guards in green and brown camouflage battledress carrying tommyguns.

Mounted SS soon appeared in the town. With the help of the police they drove scores of the local inhabitants into a wood on the outskirts of Telekhany, making them dig long and deep trenches, the bottom of which was filled with water. No one knew exactly what the Germans needed these ditches for. On the next day, however, which was a Wednesday, the German command issued an order for the entire Christian population to remain at home, not to go out anywhere, and for all Jews of the male sex to assemble at the People's House, as the House of Culture was then called.

Singly and in groups the men went to the appointed place. In front of the People's House a great big bonfire blazed in which the works of Pushkin, Gogol, Tolstoy, Dostoyevsky, Shakespeare, Adam Mickiewicz, Gorki, Mayakovsky, Sholem Aleichem, as well as numerous textbooks, went up in flames.

The half-drunken SS were indulging in a mad orgy around the bonfire, making their victims stand on their knees, beating them brutally with their truncheons, and finally holding a "concert" by dragging a piano out of the building and forcing the cruelly abused, terror-stricken men to sing and dance to the accompaniment of a drunken SS officer.

4.

Mass shooting began on the following day.

All Jews were driven out of their homes, lined up in groups of 30, 40, and 50 persons, and chased into the woods where the ditches had been built.

Men and women, young boys and girls, old folks and little children--all were herded together. No exceptions were made, neither for suckling infants nor for the old and infirm who had to be held up to walk.

This is what Yevgenia Trigenskaya, a native of Telekhany, can recall of that day: "Although we sat at home, we could hear and see a great deal. There is a scene I can remember very well. In one of the groups walked two girls with their arms entwined. One of them I knew a little. Her name was Esther and her surname, if I was not mistaken, was Gotlieb. She was very beautiful and much admired by all of Telekhany's young men. Often she sang and danced at the amateur entertainments arranged at the People's House. She was a merry little thing and a chatterbox. One of the SS convoy, leaning down from his horse, said: "Ah, Judin, why are you so beautiful?" Esther's beauty, however, did not save her. She was shot down with the rest.

The Nazi-Fascist firing squad spared nobody, not the graybearded old men, the pregnant women, nor the babes in their mothers' arms. From the woods came the reports of one volley after another. Those who were shot down were at once covered with earth, even if they were still alive. Upon the layers of earth, running red with blood, new victims fell one after another.

On the next day the SS started a hunt for survivors, combing every barn, shed, attic and basement. The Jews that were discovered were at once dragged out into the street and shot in cold blood.

Leib Brestski, the tailor, had hidden under his stove. He remained there for two days. One of the SS, flashing a light, discovered the poor man, and he was brutally murdered in his own backyard.

It is hard to give the exact number of Jewish victims in Telekhany. However, it is a well-known fact that the Jewish population of the town was nearly 2,000. And all met their death at the hand of the Nazi-fascists. The whole Gurshtel family, for example, which consisted of old Gurshtel, whose first name nobody seems to remember, and his four sons and their families, was wiped out. The-tailor, Srul Gurshtel, his wife Sarah and their two children, 12 and 14 years old, were murdered in their own home. Osher, Yudel and Nisel Gurshtel, their wives and children were shot on the outskirts of the town.

The brothers Vainshtein, together with their own families and their old father, a butcher, were also among those shot, as were the old carpenter, Rubakha, the brothers Esel and Mikhel Kosovsky-two cobblers, Rakhmil Landman, a fish dealer, Mikhel Likhfar, a tailor, the cobbler Beinus, the brothers Motl and Isik Shklyar, and countless others.

Very few managed to escape. Among them were Gdalli Karchmar and Yutsko Chernomoretz, who ran away to join the partisans. No one in Telekhany knows of the fate of the former; the latter, however, is alive, and getting along well today, working in the Ivanovo district of Brest Region.

Aron Rubakha and his brother, the sons of an old carpenter and both workers of the Telekhany district Komsomol, went to the eastern part of the country. Aron now works as a cutter in Tashkent and his brother lives in Kiev. Komadeyev succeeded in escaping from the enemy's encirclement. After the war he continued his education and now works in Leningrad. Five out of two thousand! No more, it seems.

5.

We must not forget those resting in eternal sleep in the countless common graves in Telekhany and its outskirts, the Jews and the Byelorussians, the Russians, the believers in God and the nonbelievers, the Communists and the non-communists, all of whom met their death at the hands of the fascist hangmen.

We must remember the dead for the sake of the living, for there are today walking the earth persons "with two legs, two arms and one head," following in Hitler's footsteps, with their racist rantings and their hands itching to plunge the world into the shambles of an atomic war.

A great loss for the world
By Esther Miller
Translated from the Yiddish by Leah Rosenberg

The Nazis exterminated six millions of our people. They destroyed thousands of cities, towns and villages, including our beautiful little town of Telekhan.

The murderous atrocities perpetrated by the Germans upon the world and the Jewish people in particular, also caused a great loss to the world in general. In the holocaust which Hitler Germany loosed upon Europe in the second World War, five million Jewish adults and one million two hundred thousand Jewish children under the age of fifteen, perished, by various methods, "scientific" and otherwise.

Who were these people? What were their names? They are too numerous for the world to know; the list is too long. The majority of them were ordinary people: artisans, traders, professionals, teachers, etc., who, because of their day to day struggle for subsistence had no chance to develop their special vocations.

But among them were many names known to the world including the names of scientists, inventors, pedagogues, writers, artists, musicians and historians, of great talent and even genius. These were people who had contributed much and could perhaps have contributed still more to the cultural treasures of the world, had they not been killed.

The Nazis tried first to deaden their victims' spiritual and moral capabilities, but despite all the physical tortures, the Jews remained spiritually strong. A Jewish grandfather, just before his death, told his fifteen year-old grandson that he must survive and take revenge. (Quoted from the Ringelblum archives found in the debris of the ghetto after the war. This story was told by that same grandson at the Eichmann trial in Israel).

The heroism of the Jewish children in the ghettos is yet to be fully studied and evaluated. "The aim of the Nazis was to kill the Jewish children, to rob the Jewish people of the younger generation. So, the atrocities toward the Jewish children were of greater ferocity than toward the older generation," said the Israeli judges when they pronounced sentence on Eichmann.

Dr. Dworzhetzky, in his 500 page book, relates: "According to most authentic estimates, the Nazis killed close to one million two hundred thousand Jewish children. During the liquidation of the ghettos, the Nazis used special "children's squads." In Vilno and Kovno, this was done during the 27th and 28th of March, 1944. In Shavel, it was the 5th of November, 1943. In Krakow, it was the 13th of March, 1943, In Lodz, August 1942, and in Bialystock, August 1942.

In Warsaw there were several special liquidations of children. Generally, the first to be exterminated were the children, under the most bestial tortures. Flocks of trained dogs would tear at their delicate little bodies. They split children's heads by swinging them at poles; they would chop their heads off with hatchets, and often throwing the children, still alive, into bonfires. All this was done while the parents were forced to look on.

From all sorts of archives, documents and diaries, found after the war, we find that German doctors conducted the most despicable sex operations and experiments upon Jewish women and children, in the name of "science." After these operations and experiments were completed, the victims were shipped to extermination camps. Very few survived.

Among those killed in the camps was the now famous authoress of the "Diary of Anne Frank." We will never know how many Anne Franks, perhaps in the hundreds or even thousands of highly talented creative people have been lost to the world because of Nazi bestialities.

Our little town of Telekhan had quite a few talented boys and girls who might perhaps, in time, have made contributions to the progress of the world. They fought heroically as Partisans against the bloody enemy. Only a handful survived. Some found refuge in Israel, while some joined the Red Army. The survivors: the two brothers Laibel and Ephraim Klitenik, Eli Sanders, Berl Gieskin, Faivel Lemmel, Aaron Shmuel (Riva's son) who fell defending Leningrad; Laizer Lutzky and Shloime Landman, now in this country. Many teenagers joined the underground, among them my cousin Dina Godiner, who now lives in Lodz, Poland.

There was no ghetto in Telekhan, no crematoriums. The Nazis brought together the entire Jewish population, forced them to dig holes in the earth and fill them with water. They opened fire with machine-guns at point blank range at the Jews who stood at the edges of the holes, and continued to shoot until all were killed. Those who did not die instantly were left to die in agony. The shooting lasted two days. The Nazis also sent out squads of gunmen to hunt down Jewish runaways. This gruesome story was told to Shloime Landman and Osher Gurshtel by the Christians of Telekhan after the war, when they returned to the city.

The same story was related to the Partisan Ephraim Klitenik when he returned to Telekhan. As hardened as he was, Ephraim broke down and sobbed like a child on hearing the story.

The stories of the Nazi bestialities are so fantastic, so gruesome, horrifying and repulsive that the human mind is unable to comprehend them. When we realize that all these atrocities took place in our time, in the civilized 20th century, by the bloody hands of civilized Germans, we become ashamed, and seized with fear for the future.

And there is reason to fear for the future. If the Germans (and biologically they belong to the human race) could degenerate to such cruelties, what assurances do we have that such a holocaust might not be repeated? Shimon Dubnow, the famous Jewish historian who was shot by the Nazis in the Riga ghetto early Sunday morning, November 30, 1941, told the Jewish children of the ghetto: "All the Jewish histories written up till now are meaningless. Jewish history begins now!" We may well add: the history of all mankind is now beginning.

We are still too close to this greatest of human tragedies to comprehend it in all its vastness and ramifications. All we could do in the past two decades was to gather data, materials and facts. And all that which we have gathered so far is only a small part of that which is yet to be unearthed. All we know now is fragmentary. The whole tragedy is yet to be written.

New generations will come and they will have all the facts before them. Then, and only then, when the historians, and the writers and the artists will bring out to the world the full horror of the Hitler story, will the world be able to realize what a loss it sustained.

We could be more at case, breathe more easily again, if we could think of the German people as a nation suddenly gone mad. Then the civilized world could adopt measures to neutralize the German-Nazi pestilence. Or perhaps the world could cure them of their madness, or quarantine them as lepers. But the menace is in the fact that they are not mad, and they were not mad when they threw humanity into the holocaust with their aim of conquering the world.

They mobilized all their scientists, inventors, and all the talents of their nation; they indoctrinated their people with the idea of racial superiority and their claims that the Germans were the only ones destined to rule, and the rest of humanity created to be their slaves, and like vermin, legally fit only to be exterminated. Their professors and doctors experimented on human flesh. Their women made lampshades from human skin. The whole nation became sadists, and fiercest of all was a beast with the title of Doctor, whose name was Mengele. He is still at large somewhere, under an assumed name, in one of the countries of the "free world."

We want to add, however, that with all their preciseness and accuracy, they failed to create a means of eradicating from the human mind the conscience and the faculty of remembering. The world remembers their atrocities. In the slogan: "Not to forget and not to forgive" is the hope and salvation of mankind.

How it all began

The crimes against the Jews in Germany began two months after Hitler's ascent to power, in 1933. First the Jews were deprived of citizenship and their properties were confiscated. They were forbidden to come in contact with non-Jews; they were forbidden to use public transportation; synagogues and all other houses of worship were sacked and burned. Jewish musicians were deprived of the right to play. The works of Jewish composers and writers were burned in public, including those of Germany's greatest poet, Heine. Mobs danced around the fires at the burnings shouting: "Out, Jewish vermin! Jews must be exterminated."

Many German Jews, as the situation worsened, committed suicide. Others tried to escape to other countries but found the gates closed. When the Germans became aware of the indifference of most of the people of other countries to the fate of the Jews, they were emboldened to try extreme measures.

The blame can be laid at the doorstep of the Western democracies, our own United States included. During the years 1933 through 1943, only 190,000 Jewish refugees were admitted into the United States out of the millions who were hopelessly seeking refuge from the bloody hands of the Nazis. Had the hearts and the doors of the Western democracies been open to these unfortunates several millions of Jews might have escaped the crematoria.

In 1939 when the Nazis started the war and invaded Poland, they loosed unheard of persecutions upon the Jews. They were forced to wear the yellow patch. They were herded into ghettos like animals, where hunger and epidemics were rampant. But the Nazis were only warming up to their gruesome work. Since it seemed to them that the process of extermination was too slow as they were then doing it, they began to build the crematoria and gas chambers. In trainloads, Jews were shipped to Maidanek, Treblinka, and others.

Those who could work were used as slave laborers and their extermination was delayed for as long as they were capable of producing. When hunger and exhaustion took their toll, the laborers, too, were sent to the gas chambers. Afraid of the pitiable resistance these wretched people might be capable of, the Nazis used perfidious methods to bring their victims to the gas chambers peacefully. The Jews were told they were being taken to bathhouses, and were even given a towel and bar of soap. But as they entered the gas chambers, the deadly gas was turned on and the victims perished in pain. In one crematorium, Treblinka, there were 13 gas chambers, and every 35 minutes ten thousand Jews were put to death by gas.

After the victims were dead, the Germans extracted the gold from their -teeth. Some corpses were split open, since the Nazis suspected that some of the Jews might have swallowed diamonds. Every week 8 to 10 kilograms of gold taken from the mouths of their victims, were shipped to Berlin, to enrich the Nazi 3rd Reich.

A young man testifying at the Eichmann trial relates: "I grew up in Treblinka. At the age of 14 1 was taken away from my mother. She was shipped to a crematorium with thousands of others. I wanted to commit suicide, but my grandfather talked me out of it. He said, it was my duty to live and help others. And since I was so young, I might yet live to get out of the Hitlerite inferno and be able to tell the world of the German horrors. I performed various duties in Treblinka. One of my jobs was to clip the hair from the dead women's heads and stuff mattresses with it. I also had the job of pulling the gold teeth from the mouths of the corpses. One day I found the body of my sister among the dead."

Another witness tells his story: "In my camp, Chelmna, we did not work on Sundays. The Germans wanted to have fun on that day. They formed long rows of Jews, and had them hold bottles on their heads. They then fired their guns at the bottles. If the shot hit the bottle, the victim was spared. If not, the Jew would be killed. The survivors had the job of clearing away the corpses."

In most places the Nazis succeeded in bluffing the Jews into their death traps, because many Jews did not, or could not believe that the Germans, known as a civilized people, could perpetrate such atrocities. The Nazis stopped at nothing, nor was any trick too perfidious, to prevent resistance from their victims.

However, all the Nazi tricks and tortures notwithstanding, the wretched, starved, physically exhausted and humiliated victims did resist their heavily armed enemy. The heroic resistance of the Jews in Byalistock, Oschwitz, Treblinka, and other camps and ghettos, is still little known to the world. The uprising in the Warsaw ghetto will live on in time as a monument to the courage of the remnants of the Jews of Warsaw and a lesson to future despots.

The mass slaughter of millions of people for the "crime" of being Jews happened in our generation; in the civilized and cultured Twentieth Century. Every man, woman and child on earth should know about it. Mankind everywhere should be on the alert for any manifestation of Nazism, fascism and anti-Semitism, no matter under what guise it should appear. Anti-Semitism appeals to the weak and criminal elements. We may learn from what happened in Germany, for as the virus of Nazism spread, and achieved control of the state apparatus, people were reduced to the status of beasts, and the human traits of justice, truth, sympathy and tolerance, vanished.

We owe it to the future generations to learn an everlasting lesson from the greatest tragedy that ever befell the human race, and particularly our Jewish people. This brief summary, with the lessons it draws of our suffering, and the loss of one third of our people, should be etched onto the minds and hearts of future generations.

Dismayed and disheartened as we are by the indifference of the non-Jewish world to our suffering at the hands of the Nazis, we would not be telling the whole truth, if we did not mention those people in many countries, who, at the risk of their own lives, gave us not only their sympathy, but a helping hand, and in so doing saved many thousands of Jews from destruction.

The noblest example was shown by the Danish people, led by their King. After the Hitlerite invasion of Denmark, the Nazis ordered the Jews to wear the infamous yellow patch. The King, when informed of the order, stated that if the Jews of Denmark would be forced to wear the patch, he would be the first to put it on. As a result the Jews of Denmark never put on the hated patches.

The Danes sheltered older Jews in their hospitals using Christian names. Refusing to accept the Nazi credo of hate and lies against the Jews, they hid Jewish religious articles in their churches. For their warm, humane behavior toward their neighbors in time of crisis, many Danes paid with their lives. Out of a total of seven thousand Danish Jews, only a few hundred were deported to the death camps. When the Danes became aware of the fact that the Jews in the camps were being kept on starvation rations, every Dane, from King to the humblest cobbler, contributed to food shipments to the Jews.

Although not all peoples acted as nobly and freely as did the Danes, yet many peoples in other lands, to a lesser degree, also did what they could to help. It is well to write here of the contributions of the Swedes and the Swiss.

It is important to mention the name of one Swede, Paul Wallenberg, who served in the Swedish legation in Budapest. Wallenberg rented a number of apartment buildings, hoisted the Swedish flag over them, and housed hundreds of Jews, thus keeping them from the hands of the Nazis.

The gates of Luxemburg were also open for Jewish refugees. In Belgium, under the leadership of the Queen Mother and the underground, many Jews were saved from certain death. In Norway, under Nazi occupation, the people risked their lives in freezing weather over rugged terrain, and helped many Jews escape into neutral Sweden.

Our beautiful little town of Telekhan shared the fate of many thousands of other cities and towns where Jews had lived and worked in peace for hundreds of years, side by side with their non-Jewish neighbors. The Jews, with sweat, toil and blood, enriched the lands in which they lived with both material and cultural values. The coming of the Hitlerite hordes put a sudden and bloody end to all this.

We must forever be on guard that such sicknesses as anti-Semitism, racism and genocide can never again rear their heads, and that future generations may be able to live in peace, and with dignity and security.

To this struggle for a better life for the Jewish people and mankind everywhere, we dedicate our modest "Yizkor Book."

The Tragic Death of Azriel the Mute, and
The Fate of the Rest of the Eisenberg Family

It was in the year 1915, during World War I, when the Czarist soldiers were running in panic from the onslaught of the German armies. During the night the demoralized Russian soldiers and their officers wreaked havoc in the Town of Telekhan, especially amongst the Jewish population.

In the morning Azriel the Mute and his brother Chaim, together with their wives, Minka and Libby, ventured into the street to find out how their mother and father had fared in the terrible night. The rising sun did not forecast what was in store for Azriel, his brother and their loved ones.

They found their mother and father unmolested, still in their store. As they came in a peasant also entered and asked to be given change for a rubel. This demand for change was a provocation, since at that time the anti-Semites were reporting a story that the Jews were collaborating with the Germans. Part of the lie was that the Jews had shipped all of their money to Germany, including silver and copper coins. When the father told the peasant that he was short of change, it seemed to lend credence to the story, and the peasant began to beat the father with a stick.

The mother's pleas fell on deaf ears, and it was only after she had bribed the peasant with some merchandise was he willing to stop.

While this was going on, a horde of drunken Russian army officers approached Azriel and Chaim. One of the officers began to molest Azriel's wife, the comely Minka. At the same time he hit Azriel in the face so fiercely that Azriel fell to the ground. Azriel, however, was very strong. He stood up immediately, recovered from the shock and began beating the officer.

As his brother Chaim and two women tried to stop the struggle, the other officers seized Azriel and Chaim, handcuffed them and leaving them on the ground, began to debate the punishment they would mete out to the two men.

In the meantime the German armies were closing in on Telekhan. Fearing that they would be trapped in the town, the officers and the soldiers decided to leave in a hurry, but they took the two brothers with them. While on the run, the officers sentenced the two brothers to corporal punishment. Chaim was given ten lashes and Azriel 15. Azriel did not survive the beating.

Chaim survived, and now lives with his family in Hadeira, Israel.

Luck was not with the Eisenberg family in Israel, where they migrated after the first World War. The first victim was Jacob, the son of Chaim and Libby Eisenberg. (The full story of Jacob's struggle and death is related in the Yiskor Book in a separate article in Hebrew.)

Hershel, the son of Azriel and Minka, was working on a building. A scaffold collapsed and he was killed in the fall. His young niece, Chayele, eight years old, who was bringing him lunch at the time, was injured in the fall of the scaffold and remained a cripple for the rest of her life.

Their son joined the Haganah at the age of fourteen, and at eighteen was accepted for service by the Jewish army. He was given the job of mine detection on heavily traveled Jewish roads. After a year of this work he went to the Negev. Following a year in the Negev, he returned, and while riding in a tank, the tank overturned, and he became an invalid as a result of the injuries.

Chaim's son, Moishe, quit the Haganah in 1944 and joined the British army. The Jewish soldiers were discriminated against by the British. His brigade was sent to the Italian front, and Moishe was wounded. When the war ended he returned to Palestine, and was immediately sent to the front to fight the Arabs.

Chaim's second son, Motke, joined the British army at the age of seventeen. In 1944 he was also sent to the Italian front. He was wounded and hospitalized for six months. On his return to Palestine he settled near Kinereth and began organizing the Sentinels. While at Kinereth he married and now is in the service of the State of Israel.

After Azriel's tragic death at the hands of Czarist officers, his wife Minka settled in Palestine with her two sons, Hershel and Motke. She left behind in Telekhan her daughter Ziporah with her husband and two younger children, who were later killed by the invading Germans. Also left behind was a son, Laibel.

Laibel escaped into Russia and lived in Tashkent during the war. He worked hard there. He was for a time imprisoned, for having used language derogatory to the Soviets. After his release from prison he met and married a daughter of a respectable family. After the war they went to Poland and were scheduled to go to Eretz Israel from there. Enroute they stopped in Germany.

One week before their scheduled departure for Israel, Laibel, together with several other young men, went to see a football game. The truck in which they were riding overturned and Laibel was killed.

His wife, Golde, and their small daughter left for Israel in deep mourning, and there, in Israel, joined Laibel's mother, Minka, and the rest of the family.

[Page 5]

Introduction

With humility and tremendous pain, we are publishing this story as our contribution to the history of the annihilation of a third of our People by the Nazi murderers - may their names and memory be erased forever.

Our little town of Telekhany is only a mere dot on the immense geographical area where the murderers slaughtered, butchered and gassed our brothers and sisters. It is important, however, that our holy martyrs be memorialized in the Book of Remembrance, which in the future will be compiled.

Those of us who are from that generation and who lived through and survived the Holocaust (about which even the Prophet Jeremiah would have no words to describe) are too close to that tragedy to be able to properly evaluate it. Future generations will be amazed at the mystery of how a civilized world could have produced such monsters and their mobs of savage collaborators. In addition, no one will be able to understand how the world could let such a thing happen. However, future generations will be better able to make sense out of the juxtaposition of the decisions and antagonisms existing between the adversaries, and to objectively evaluate how such a catastrophe befell the world in general, and our People in particular.

Therefore, it is essential not to minimize any issue. Every settlement and town should have a detailed description of its own relationship to what occurred in the Holocaust. Although there already exists extensive Holocaust literature, much more is yet to be done. Nevertheless, everything we know, and think we know, isn't even a drop in the sea of what actually took place.

We are therefore adding our own contribution to the "Scroll of Fire" with our Telekhany Yizkor Book.

We ask our dear fellow émigrés from Telekhany to forgive us for any omissions or errors, since they are inevitable under the circumstances in which the book was compiled and published.

The Publishers Committee.

[Page 6]

Foreword
Mosheleh Rozman

Some time ago, Mrs. Esther Miller, Telekhany émigré, and author of "From Telekhany to America" received a manuscript from Asher Gurshtel, a Telekhany émigré living in Tel-Aviv, that he wrote about the founding, and to our great sorrow, the destruction of our dear hometown Telekhany. In his letter Gurshtel stated that because there are very few Telekhany émigrés living in Israel, it was beyond their means to publish the book there, and since there are many more of us Telekhany émigrés living in the United States, it would be easier for us to do it. He also suggested that it be in the form of a Yizkor Book.

This touched the right chord in our grieving hearts, and we immediately established a Telekhany Yizkor Book Committee, and started to collect contributions and appeal to other former residents of Telekhany to assist us in our holy mission. Unfortunately, that appeal wasn't very successful; because of limited financial resources we had to greatly reduce the size of the Yizkor Book.

Thus, we decided, for financial reasons, to do most of the revisions and editing of the material for the Yizkor Book ourselves. The following individuals were appointed to the editorial committee: Golde and Gershon Gurshtel, Esther Miller, Sara Rubinstein, and this writer. Most of us were educated in an old fashioned religious school (*kheder*), as was then the tradition among religious Jews in Russia. Our deep emotional pain provided us with the courage to be able to carry out the Yizkor Book project, even with the baggage of our limited education. Later on, we realized the value of using a professional editor, and our respected friend, S. Sekuler, became the official editor of the Yizkor Book.

Although I left Telekhany 65 years ago, I vividly remember the good traits of the Jewish population, the way they celebrated the Sabbath and holy days with beauty and holiness, and how their lives were filled with acts of goodness. I am sure that Bilaam would have also admired them when he uttered the historical words in the Book of Exodus, "How good are your tents O Jacob, your dwellings, O Israel."

And yet on August 14, 1941 this venerable community was so brutally destroyed by German murderers for the sole "sin" of not being Christians. Even more heartbreaking is the fact that the Jews' gentile neighbors also took part in the destruction because their eternal hatred of the Eternal People "sanctified" the murders they committed.

Now the book is being published; it has not been an easy task. The group of former residents of Telekhany now living in Los Angeles took charge of it and endured its birth pangs. It is therefore entirely appropriate to thank and pay tribute to them for their accomplishments.

First and foremost we wish to acknowledge our respected fellow émigré, Asher Gurshtel from Tel-Aviv, who initiated the book and wrote the manuscript. We would also like to acknowledge the following people: our dear and tireless friend, Herschel Eisenberg, for abridging the manuscript, and for corresponding with many people on behalf of the book; our sincere friend, Gershon Gurshtel, who left no stone unturned, even while ill and bedridden, and who wrote 3-4 letters to the same individual until he received a contribution; dear Esther Miller for her literary contributions, and for hosting most of the committee meetings in her home; cheerful Jenny Blumberg and her husband for inspiring some of our former fellow residents of Telekhany in Chicago to make substantial donations. We also wish to express our immeasurable appreciation to our devoted and wise secretary, Sarah Rubenstein, who is married to a former resident of Telekhany, and to the rest of the committee members in Los Angeles and Israel. May you all be blessed for what you have done to make the Telekhany Yizkor Book a reality.

———

[Page 9]

The Story of how Telekhany was Destroyed
by Asher Gurshtel

Before sitting down to write about the history of our *shtetl* Telekhany and its wonderful Jewish men, women and children, I first have to set out to gather together my memories of so many years ago, open them up and imagine myself back in those days, viewing the annihilation of our brothers and sisters, the martyrs of our beautiful *shtetl* of Telekhany. In my memories I have to bring together all the members of our community who are spread across the globe to share in our terrible tragedy, and to bow our heads in honor of the martyrs of Telekhany who were so brutally exterminated by the murderous German sadists. We must swear never to forget the martyrs, and together pronounce the verse, "May G-d avenge for the spilled blood of your servants." G-d in heaven! Avenge the spilled blood of your children!

I now dip my pen into the blood of our martyrs to record the birth of our *shtetl*, and how it was tragically destroyed

According to what previous generations have transmitted to us, the *shtetl* of Telekhany was founded approximately at the end of the fifteenth century, during the period when the so-called Tatar Hordes occupied Ukraine, Poland and parts of Russia, including our area. In those days, much of the territory around our area belonged a benevolent owner, Count Oginsky. Naturally, the area included a tavern that was leased to a Jewish family. It is also worth mentioning how Telekhany got its name. In Hebrew, the name can sound like the words Tel-Chen – the Charming Hill. However, the name Telekhany is derived from two words, one Russian and the other Tatar.

The story is like this: during the battles between the local inhabitants and the Tatar Hordes, one of the leaders of the Tatar army was called a *khan.* After his defeat, the Tatars didn't know where to find his body. They searched for it throughout the entire area. Wherever they looked, they asked whether anyone had seen their khan, either dead or alive. In Russian, the word *tyelo* means "body;" it was combined with the Tatar word, *khan* to produce the name of the town, Telekhany.

The Creation of the Jewish Community

In those days, there were already some Jewish families living in the area, in villages and settlements, and along the roads. The Jews made their meager living mostly from handiwork: shoemaking, tailoring, carpentry and painting multi-colored linens for peasant women. In addition, there were taverns along the highways that served as a source of livelihood for Jewish families.

Life was hard for Jewish families, especially due to their isolation among their hostile neighbors and the capricious behavior of the landowners, which frequently jeopardized the Jews' meager livelihood and even their physical existence. As ignorant and alienated as the village Jews were from Judaism, they always preferred living among other Jews. Gradually, Jews began leaving the villages and their isolated lives, and settled near the old tavern leased to a Jew by Count Oginsky. Thus, a Jewish community began to develop and eventually grew into the *shtetl* of Telekhany.

Count Oginsky, who owned all the land around the tavern, owned huge tracts of land and dense forests. He was more than happy to have a Jewish settlement on his estates. He believed that the Jews would increase his revenue through their business activity. The Count, therefore, was glad to assist the Jews to settle around the tavern, and even provided lumber for them to build their own homes, which included large gardens that they could cultivate to help them get through the harsh winters.

This is how the community gradually developed. The local peasants started arriving in town to shop for items they needed. Most business between Jews and peasants were based on what economists call a barter relationship. The peasant obtained services from the shoemaker, tailor or other craftsman, and paid with the fruits of his labor – agricultural produce.

Gradually, stores started offering merchandise brought in from Pinsk. In the barter exchange of agricultural products and labor, the artisans accumulated surpluses of agricultural products, which the artisan sold on the market. Thus, a small-scale business with a market among the shops developed, together with new small side streets around the market. The result was the growth of Telekhany.

Count Oginski contributed a great deal to Telekhany's growth. He was a talented man, blessed with energy and was an entrepreneurial person. He undertook to dig a canal, which was named after him, to unite the two rivers Pripet (near Pinsk) and Shchara (near Slonim). His goal was to increase deliveries of his lumber to Germany. The Count owned huge forests and he wanted to increase his profits on the lumber shipped to Germany.

In order to built the canal, and enable the lumber to float down the Shchara, and from there to the Niemen River and on to Germany, it was necessary, however, to build locks in the canal. Since modern machinery was not yet available, the heavy manual labor was performed by human hands. Since the Count owned all the land, with thousands of peasants as his slaves, this "small" undertaking to create a canal did not present a problem to him.

The work was especially hard because the Pripet River covered a very flat, low area, while the Shchara River was much higher. The locks had to be built so that each lock would be higher than the previous one, meaning that the second lock would be higher than the first, the third would be higher than the second, etc. It is difficult to conceive of how difficult and complicated this work was, but the peasant-slaves had to do all the work themselves.

The project took fifty years to complete, and thousands of farmer-slaves lost their lives in the process. The construction of the canal began in 1776, and became ready for use in 1826. During these years, Telekhany was a hub of activity and greatly benefited from the canal construction. Jewish carpenters earned considerable income performing the complicated work around the locks, and were experts in this work. The peasant-slaves, although very poor, also benefited from time to time, as did the engineers, contractors. Various businessmen provided a living for the artisans, shopkeepers and small merchants of Telekhany .

As the city continued to grow, more Jews from the village were attracted to it, and Telekhany became a nice place for Jewish families (cobblers, shoemakers, tailors, blacksmiths, businessmen, shopkeepers and lumber and grain merchants). When the canal opened and navigation began, some Jews became ship owners. They had their own small boats that transported cargo and passengers from Telekhany to Pinsk and back, bringing back merchandise with them. The first ship owners were the Gurshtel brothers. When the first steam ships arrived with passengers, its whistle announced its arrival; the Jews were extremely pleased, and thanked G-d.

Our little town of Telekhany was blessed by nature: it was surrounded by hills full of tall pine trees as well as valleys seeming to grow out of the earth. The beauty of the environment and the healthy climate created by the pine forest, made Telekhany a beautiful resort place. Many people from the larger cities came to our little Telekhany to enjoy the fresh climate and divine beauty, and provided a source of income for Telekhany.

Years went by, and the canal's use for transporting goods and people expanded Telekhany's economy. Many offices with clerks, contractors, and engineers brought a new type of Jew to Telekhany, a more worldly Jew. In one office there was a Jewish engineer from Pinsk who worked on the Sabbath. Although this created a problem with deeply religious Jews, people considered it as a sign of newer trends, and no one seemed to object to the change. The main representative of the general contractor for the canal was a Jew named Leib Tureck, who inherited the job from his father-in-law, Joshua Eisenstadt, who in turn inherited it from the previous generation. Leib Tureck was also a great scholar, and he owned the entire Talmud and many other religious books. Although he was a Lubash chassid, and prayed in the Lubash synagogue, he was involved in the city issues, and was a very generous and worldly man. Among many religious books in his home, one could find all types of books of modern Hebrew literature representing the Enlightenment.

The people in the *shtetl* lived like one big family: where there was happiness, everyone was happy; when (God forbid) there was sorrow, everyone shared that also. Intellectual life in Telekhany developed with *kheder* schools for children, where they studied everything from the alphabet to the commentaries of Rashi and the Tosefot on the Talmud. Eventually, modern Hebrew schools were started, and used the modern way of teaching. Our little town of Telekhany also acquired a rabbi, a great scholar: Rabbi Eleazar Olivitsky, who served in his position at the highest level, and was much appreciated by all classes of Jews.

There were also study groups in town, such as groups that studied the Talmud together, the Mishnah, the *Eyn Yaakov* compendium or the Bible with the Rashi commentary. The simple Jews had their own group for reciting Psalms, and on Saturday afternoons in the summer, people studied Ethics of the Fathers. All these studies maintained a Jewish spirit, and gave the Jews enough strength and courage to withstand life's difficulties and the gruesome decrees of the dark Czarist regime and the landowners.

And so the people of our little town, like their counterparts in so many other towns in Western Russia, Poland, Lithuania, the Ukraine and Galicia, lived and worked hard to earn a meager living. In Telekhany, as elsewhere, there were a handful of well-to-do families, but the majority were poor craftsmen, merchants and just plain poor folks who worked hard the whole week, barely living from hand to mouth to be able to have extra for the Sabbath.

As long as our *shtetl* existed, life focused on the religious/cultural sphere, with its assorted religious functionaries, synagogue caretakers, superstitions, with its chassidim and opponents of chassidism – just like in other towns. There were a number of "battles" between a rabbi's supporters and others, and between the chassidim and their opponents. People in Telekhany bickered about ritual slaughterers, cantors, and rabbis' assistants. Since we had three different chassidic synagogues – one each for the Lubash, Stolin and Yanov chassidim - and one for the non-chassidim, there were different sides of various issues. However, as mentioned earlier, life was oriented to culture and religion. Any Jews that could spare time would go into a synagogue or house of study to hear religious words or to open a religious book. The materialistic life was not primary. A Jew would manage to get along on very little. His main concern was his spiritual life.

So years went by and generation after generation carried on the same way, and people assumed that this was the way the world was created and that's the way it will remain.

Telekhany Becomes a Factory Town

This is how Jews in Telekhany and other cities and towns thought, but the world does not stand still. Even backward Czarist Russia, after freeing the slaves, began to develop industry, and it reached Telekhany too. Three Chernichov brothers from Slonim, Shmuel, Leima and Abba, arrived in Telekhany to build a glassworks factory. The town was overjoyed since people would have work. They'd have a way to earn a living. The city would expand. People said that the glass factory would employ 5,000 people, and this actually came to pass. In the past, a factory would open, and would then close down shortly thereafter. The three brothers, and especially the middle brother, Shmuel, were great scholars, talmudists and familiar with modern Hebrew literature and language, and therefore nationalists. The brothers mainly sought to employ Jewish workers, artisans and various specialists from Germany, Austria and Russia.

The Telekhany Jewish population came to life. The Jews couldn't figure out what was happening. Every Jew developed strength and encouragement, and saw the factory as the end of poverty. In 1895 the construction of the factory was completed, and began a new page in the history of Telekhany.

Let us now evaluate what influence the factory, with its various types of Jews who settled in and around town had on the cultural, social and political life in Telekhany, and how the cultural and community life started to be transformed from a lifestyle from the Middle Ages, and started creating new groups among the Jews who came to town because of the people who arrived from the outside world, and who settled in Telekhany because of the glass factory.

In the latter part of the 19th century, two new movements appeared in Jewish life: political Zionism and the Bund. Under the influence of anti-Semitic pressure in France brought on by the sad Dreyfus trial, a large part of the assimilated Jewish intelligentsia in Western Europe suddenly realized that assimilation was not the way to solve Jewish problems. Nationalism dominated a large part of the Jewish intelligentsia in Europe, and through the work of Dr. Herzl political Zionism was born.

In Russia, Poland, Lithuania and Latvia, the battle against the Czar's reactionary regime became more intense. The working class organization began to challenge the despotic and capitalistic exploitation of the Czarist regime. Influenced by the freedom movement, the Jewish labor movement organized the Bund. These two new Jewish movements stirred and aroused the Jews to engage in cultural and social activity in the heavily religious cities and towns. These two elements – Zionist and the Bund – would have sooner or later found their way to Telekhany, but the people from the outside world who came to work in and around the glassworks factory had an impact on our community, and especially on our youth, a little earlier than elsewhere.

The Telekhany Jewish youth came to life because of these new ideas that came to town. The Jewish youth organized groups to study Yiddish and Hebrew literature, and Jewish history. A library was opened. They even organized a defense unit to protect themselves against pogroms.

At first the youths were impressed by the Zionist ideal. Meetings were held, and the Jewish flag was always present. Shekels were sold to raise funds for the Jewish National Fund, and Zionist activity was quite prominent. The main leaders of the Zionist movement were

Hershel Rosenberg and myself. But since the Czarist regime was always on the alert to organized activities, it also started persecuting the Zionist movement. Hershel Rosenberg was sent from Pinsk to Czenstechow, and worked there as an assistant to Dr. Aharon Singalovsky.

The Bund, however, slowly began to have an impact on the youth, especially the poor working youth, and thus became the strongest movement in town.

Telekhany became divided into various ideological camps. The religious community consisting of chassidim and non-chassidim continued to retain the older generation. The youth, however, were divided between two ideological camps: Zionism and the Bund. Zionism stressed Zion, and maintained that, in the diaspora, Jews could expect only persecution and pogroms. Therefore, the Jews should concentrate on securing a homeland and state in the land of Israel, and thus there was no need to join other freedom-loving organizations to fight the Czarist regime. The socialist Bund, which considered itself a part of the Russian working class, emphasized the struggle for a free and democratic Russia, which would release the entire working class from the yoke of capitalism, and introduce socialism.

In the first few years after 1897, when both political Zionism and the Bund were created, Zionism was a monolithic organization. With the beginning of the 20th century, however, the Zionist movement began to divide into different factions. Due to the influence of the general Russian freedom movement, the Jewish proletariat element wanted a synthesis between Zionist ideology of the ingathering of the Diaspora and the Marxist proletariat ideology. This was the Poalei Zion [Workers of Zion] orientation, which acknowledged the struggle for freedom in the countries of the Diaspora. This is how a third movement developed among the youth.

This is how life was in the *shtetl*. The older generation stuck to its previous lifestyle, but quietly complained about their children's new directions. This led to constant arguments between parents and children. The parents were in constant fear of their children being dragged into the revolutionary movement and eventually falling into the hands of the Czar's police, something, which did happen to some young people.

The older generation concentrated its life around the synagogue; praying, and studying Judaism in the synagogues. During the day they were busy earning a livelihood. In the evenings they forgot about their problems when they opened religious books. Many Jews in town were devoted to their religious studies and didn't work, their valiant wives worked instead, being glad that their husbands could sit and study while the wives could look forward to being their husbands' footstools in Paradise. The younger generation, a large portion of whom worked in the factory twelve to fourteen hours a day for low pay, spent the evenings discussing political, cultural and social problems. They also spent time in the library reading and studying until late at night. They were hungry for knowledge.

The Outbreak Of World War I

This was what life was like in Telekhany until the outbreak of World War I. It would take many volumes to describe in detail what Jews in the war zone and in Telekhany went through during the war years. Suffice it to say that as soon as the Germans started pushing the Czar's army eastward, Russian soldiers set fire and burned to the ground all the towns and villages they passed through. In order to justify their defeat and treachery, the Czarist commanders tried to accuse the Jews of being German spies.

The gentile population, inflamed by propaganda, and seeing unprotected Jewish property, plundered, beat up and attacked the Jews. There were many agitators and hucksters who had been waiting a long time for an opportunity to fabricate all kinds of lies about the Jews in town. For instance, they claimed that Jews sent all their gold, silver and copper to the Germans. In one case, they sent a peasant to buy something from a Jewish shopkeeper; the peasant wanted change for a large bill. The shopkeeper didn't have change for such a large amount of money, which "proved" to the agitators that the Jew had sent his money off to a German. This gave them what they needed to attack Jews.

The worst came along, however, when they set fire to Telekhany from all sides, and the Jews were forced to flee, or more correctly, were chased into the nearby forest. It takes a lot of effort and talent to describe the heartbreaking scenes: Jews fled into the forest and watched their property, which took years of hard work to accumulate, be horribly ravaged and go up in flames. When nightfall arrived the Jews were standing in the forest with their children under the open sky, and the crying of the parents reached the heavens. Having survived, they realized it was the eve of Yom Kippur, the holiest day of the year, and a day of forgiveness and atonement, and yet here were the Jews of Telekhany in the wild woods of a world gone mad, among people gone mad. The sun isn't a sun anymore, and the sky isn't a sky anymore; the earth is a huge fire burning under every Jew's feet. Prayer was impossible; one man hugs a tree instead of his Yom Kippur prayer book and cries out: "God in heaven, where are you? Why are you silent?" The man holds onto the tree and talks to it. "You've got it good. You live with the other trees in peace, while men destroy each other for no rhyme or reason." The man said to himself, "Wouldn't it be great to be a tree?" The man was Josef the Ritual Slaughterer.

When the Germans occupied our area, a few Telekhany Jews immediately moved to locations near Telekhany. Some families from Telekhany settled in the village of Motele, approximately three miles from Telekhany. They moved into the homes of peasants who fled from the Germans deeper inside Russia, while the Jews took over their abandoned farmland. At that time the Germans prohibited Jews from engaging in business, and permitted them only to engage in agriculture to earn a livelihood.

Many Jews from Telekhany and neighboring cities and towns moved to Russia. This is how the first destruction of our hometown of Telekhany ended during World War I.

The Town is Rebuilt

At the end of the war, some Telekhany Jews came back to town and tried to rebuild their lives empty handed. They were all poor, worn down and hungry. There was a rumor that an American Jewish committee came to Pinsk with help for the Jewish population. A respected man in town, Asher Gurshtel, traveled to Pinsk hoping to get some for our town. The trip from Telekhany to Pinsk was a difficult one, and it took him a long time until he finally got to Pinsk. He arrived on the very day when the Poles showed their savage anti-Semitic murderous face; on that day, they Polish authorities shot thirty-seven of the most distinguished Jews in Pinsk.

The story was as follows: a group of the most eminent Jews in Pinsk gathered to decide on a plan how best to distribute the aid from the American committee to the needy Jews in Pinsk and nearby communities. Somebody reported them to the Polish authorities in Pinsk, accusing them of holding a meeting of Bolsheviks. Without any evidence or information, the Poles surrounded the meeting place, arrested the participants, took them to the large monastery and shot them all. Asher Gurshtel reported on the impact, fear and wickedness of the event, which was impossible to describe.

Asher Gurshtel did manage to meet the committee, and brought back some financial assistance for the Jews of Telekhany. Despite the deep sorrow and despair of the Jews in Telekhany when they found out about the misfortune that occurred in Pinsk, the small amount of assistance that Gurshtel brought with him lifted their spirits, and they realized that their Jewish community was not abandoned, that there were Jews abroad who didn't abandon their brethren.

After that, however, the real problems began. The government administrations changed every other Monday and Thursday: first the Poles were in charge, and the next day the Bolsheviks kicked them out and took over, and thereafter the debtors took over and threw out the Bolsheviks. Whenever the Poles or the debtors took over, there was either a larger or smaller pogrom against the Jews, and following the pogroms new decrees were issued, each worse than the previous one, and which gave no respite to the survivors. Whenever the Bolsheviks took over, there were no pogroms, but Jews were classified as businessmen and self-employed artisans. If an artisan had an assistant, he was, from the days of the Bund, considered to be a member of the "petty bourgeois," and the Bolsheviks arbitrarily confiscated anything and everything. Thus, the situation of the Jews in town was very bitter, but at least their lives were spared.

A tragic-comic situation developed among the non-Jewish population. Whenever the Soviet authorities decided to confiscate property for the new administration and for the needs of the army, they did so indiscriminately, confiscating from Jews and gentiles alike. The poor peasants couldn't understand what was going on, and considered the Soviet regime to be very strange, since the regime expropriated equally from everyone. The peasants had been used to the idea that only Jewish could be robbed and plundered, and yet now the Soviets did it to everyone equally.

People were more or less content with the Soviet administration as long as the Red Army was in the area. The officers were self-conscious about their status, and they knew the rules of the game. They knew whom they should confiscate from, whom they should leave alone, and whom they should keep their eyes on. In other words, there was law and order. However, as soon as the army left Telekhany and installed inexperienced local authorities and unqualified individuals who had questionable reputations but who were devoted to the so-called struggle for proletarian justice, they started their sadistic work. Pretending to look for spies, they searched homes everywhere, grabbing whatever they liked: watches, rings, cushions and blankets. They were even satisfied with taking any type of merchandise they could find.

Even this was bearable, but the worst tragedy was the mistrust among people, the suspicion, and there were already people whose hands were dirty. If someone bumped up against someone else, he was simply reported to the authorities, complaining just about anything. The procedure was that all complaints had to be resolved locally, so people got sent to Siberia, thrown in jail, or many times just "put up against the wall."

It was like Sodom and Gomorrah between Jews and gentiles in town. Property was confiscated in the name of nationalization, and punishments were decreed in the name of strengthening the "class struggle." Rightfully or not, all local leaders and Zionists were deemed "enemies of the People." When there was a decree, the Jew suffered more than anybody.

After the changes of the various authorities during the chaotic period, the Polish regime finally took hold, and life in Telekhany began to more or less return to normal. Half-ruined houses and the Chassidic synagogues (of the Chassidim of Lubash, Stolin as well as the non-Chassidic one) were rebuilt. The Polish authorities allowed the Oginsky Canal to reopen and operate as before. Count Paslovsky, who inherited Count Oginsky's estate, built a sawmill at the location of the glassworks to process timber from his forests, and the mill was equipped with the newest machinery. He also built a power plant, providing the town with electric lighting.

With the assistance received from the American Jews an apartment building was built that provided 16 apartments for impoverished Jewish families. The young people got a library, and a firehouse, concert/theater auditorium were also built in Telekhany. A new public bath and ritual bath [mikvah] with running water were constructed. The community also provided a hostel for poor out-of-town visitors and a doctor for sick poor people free of charge. The town survived, and even the tiny railroad built by the Germans during their occupation, began operating between Telekhany and Pinsk.

Jews who fled Telekhany during the war returned to town. Among the returnees was Yosef the Ritual Slaughterer, who resumed his position as community slaughterer, and since there wasn't a Rabbi in town yet, he also served as the town rabbi.

People wanted to forget past troubles, and hoped for a brighter future. The Polish authorities made it mandatory for Jewish children to attend Polish public schools every day until noon. From the rest of the day they were free to attend the Jewish kheder school. This wasn't such a bad regulation. People gradually started making a better living. The Polish authorities re-organized the Jewish community in an open democratic manner. It looked as if everything was getting back to normal, and you could start seeing a smile on Jewish faces; people felt safer.

However, as the saying goes, "Jews have no lucky star." [Trans. comment: The Yiddish author uses a pun on a Talmudic saying that expresses the idea that the fate and fortune of every nation in the world is governed by a planet, except for the Jews, who are overseen directly by G-d himself and not by the astrological signs. The writer's pun is to wryly interpret the saying to simply mean that Jews have no lucky star and are therefore unlucky.] An economic crisis hit Poland that put an abrupt end to Jewish livelihoods. The Polish currency, the zloty, lost its value. It didn't take long for hunger to show up again in

Jewish homes. Young people started asking the old question: "What will be? What can we expect?" In a flood the young people started leaving Telekhany, some to America, others to the land of Israel. The Polish authorities now started showing their sneaky anti-Semitic faces. Anti-Semitism became so thick you could cut it with a knife. They started pulling out the last piece of bread from Jewish mouths.

It's worth describing one case where the Telekhany Jews taught the Poles a good lesson. During those difficult days the arrogant Polish administration decided to build a few locks over the Oginsky Canal. The Jews were overjoyed because it would create a few jobs. The anti-Semites totally ignored the Jewish workers of Telekhany, who for generations were experts in building locks. The Polish authorities didn't want to employ any Jews, and held a parade for the engineers and workers they brought in, together with all kinds of machinery, and began construction.

However, neither the engineers nor the workers that the Poles brought in were qualified to do the job. They built the locks, and then had to take them down again. They tried a second and a third time, and were still unsuccessful. Finally the Poles realized their error, and pleaded with the Jewish carpenters to take over the job. When the Jewish carpenters went to work, they built the locks perfectly, without engineers and officials with fancy epaulets. The most amazing thing was that the supervisor of the construction project, a Jew named Shlomo Blumberg, could hardly sign his own name. However, he was an outstanding artisan. The Jewish carpenters were almost all great master craftsmen in the construction of canal locks. They inherited this from their grandfathers and great-grandfathers, who built the first locks in the eighteenth century.

It should be noted that there were Jewish casualties during the construction of the locks. Shimon Gurshtel, father of Nissel the boatman, was crushed to death by a falling gate during the repair of a lock. There were Jewish casualties here and in other cases in Poland, and yet Jews remained strangers.

And now? And now? The Jewish "now"? The greatest danger for the Jews of Telekhany suddenly arrived when Telekhany was born a few times and then died a few times. In 1939, Hitler arrived in Poland with sadistic Germans, who were full of hate for the Jewish People, and who immediately started to bully, rob, shoot and dispossess Jews using their guard dogs. Numerous Jews were torn to pieces on the roads by the guard dogs. The Nazis were able to carry out their extermination work better in the ghettos.

Even before the Germans came to our area, and even before they declared war against the Soviets, the savage Nazi treatment of the

Jews began. Jews fled to the forests, and along the way, some peasants took Jews in their homes at a good price, of course. However, as soon as the Jew no longer had any money to give them, the peasants sent the Jews back off into the forest, and it was impossible to go back. The Germans closed off the roads around Telekhany, and most Jews stayed in town. The Jews who remained in Telekhany hoped that the Germans wouldn't consider them to be a dangerous element. Since among the Jews there were enemies of the Soviets, the Jews assumed that the Germans wouldn't do them any harm or persecute them.

At first things were pretty quiet. The Germans didn't harm anyone, and they even left Telekhany for a short time. However, as soon as the peasants found out that the Germans had left, the local gentiles, together with peasants from surrounding villages came into town and robbed whatever they could. It looked as if a fire had spread through town, with people carrying as many household possessions out of the houses as they could. According to those who lived through those events, the savagery of the peasants could not even be described. Peasants who had lived with Jews for many years were now unrecognizable. They beat people, broke open locks, doors and gates. The savagery went so far as to even throw a child out of a crib and steal the crib. The Nazis, who had retreated for a short time from Telekhany, had told the peasants through their collaborators among the local population that as far as Jewish property and life was concerned, it was open season. Life became so bitter that people hoped the Germans would come back. The situation continued this way for six weeks. People hoped for the return of the Germans, and indeed they did return and start going about their thievery.

The Germans put all Jewish men women and children on the road to the glassworks heading towards the village of Voulka. They then dug three deep pits, and with their guns and hands, they forced the Jews to undress and sit on their knees facing the pits, so that after being shot, they would fall straight into the pits. If someone tried to escape, the peasants chased him down, shot him, and made off with his clothes and anything else they could find.

Future generations should know that the peasants from town and surrounding villages stood around watching what was going to happen to the Jews. Some went to search for dead and living Jews in the forests to take from them anything they could find.

Our beloved and dear brothers and sisters had to live among such wild animals in human form. Why did they have to be exterminated? Why?

Our Telekhany martyrs were covered over in three large mass graves. They were covered over with dirt and sand that turned red from their blood. From reports of people who were in hiding and watching from a distance, the earth remained over the graves for a long time. Many of the martyrs didn't die immediately from the bullets, but were buried alive. Only when they breathed their last, did the ground fall silent.

This was what happened to our dear and beloved *shtetl* of Telekhany, which met the same fate as all Jewish communities where the accursed Nazis passed through.

Living Greetings From Telekhany

Now the first living greetings arrived from Telekhany, but not from our Telekhany.

In 1944, when Poland was already liberated by the Soviets who chased the Nazis out of Poland, Shlomo Landman and I, both of whom had escaped to Russia, decided that we should go back to Telekhany, even without waiting for the Soviets to send us back as Polish citizens to Poland in transports. We didn't think too long, and went off to the Polish border. We didn't have much money with us, but the desire to see Telekhany with our own eyes was more valuable than money. We decided to travel to Lvov/Lemberg; we knew that from there we could get to the center of Poland much more easily. Both Shlomo Landman and I arrived in Lvov at the end of January, 1945.

In Lvov we found out that in order to travel to Telekhany we had to receive special permits, and we learned that the trains weren't operating normally. We were exhausted from our difficult trip, and I wanted to give up the visit to Telekhany, but when my friend Shlomo told me that he knew where his parents were killed by the Vyhanochsh peasants, he wanted to go to bring their remains to the cemetery in Telekhany. I found the courage to go along with him.

We started on our way; it was a harsh winter, with snowstorms and blizzards. We had to travel by foot; we walked, stopping to rest, and then continued on. We were dreaming of getting to Telekhany. We figured that it would take us more than a week; in fact, it took us sixteen days to get to Pinsk. We were out of money, and continued walking to Telekhany as we conjurcd up pictures of our old hometown and its wonderful people. For a brief moment we breathed easier, but it was only for a brief moment, since we were once again seized by all sorts of thoughts. We continued. A wagon or car came by and took us for a couple of kilometers, and we then continued by foot.

We finally got to the village of Ozoritz, and a peasant took us by wagon to Telekhany. No words could possibly describe our state of mind when we arrived at the Telekhany bridges. I suddenly started shaking uncontrollably, and my friend Shlomo couldn't make me stop. We then came into town. The electric lights were on, including in some houses, but for us it was total darkness. All the houses were still standing; we were traveling and traveling, and yet had nowhere to go. We were strangers in our own town. Our wagon driver understood that we had nowhere to go, so he decided to take us to his brother-in-law, Kolia Sinevitz, who lived in the forest beyond the Polish cemetery on the way to Voulka and Bobrovetz. We knew the brother-in-law, and went into the forest to see him.

As the driver continued, we didn't realize that on the road we were on we would come across the three large mass graves of our Telekhany brothers and sisters and their children.

We spent six days – six mournful and dark days – in Telekhany, and morning and night we stood by the holy graves, saying the mourner's kaddish prayer in a flood of tears. During those six days that we spent in Telekhany, we searched for information about everything that happened, but no one wanted to tell us anything. They remained silent. I went to my own house, a house I built myself, but I couldn't go inside. My feet wouldn't move; they dug into the ground and wouldn't move.

Now we come to the horrific picture we saw: three huge mass graves – one for men, one for women, and the third one for the dear children. Each group was shot separately. The graves are located on the side of the glassworks in the direction of Voulka, across from the Polish cemetery. At the very edge of the road is the grave of the men. The little trees that the German bullets shot through still stand there. The trees tremble, as if they wanted to tell us something. About a hundred and fifty kilometers [sic – probably meant meters] are two mass graves close to each other. One was for the women, and the other for the children. We wanted to find out which was for the women, and which was for the children. However, none of the residents wanted to tell us; they were afraid to be implicated in the massacre.

We also found a large number of individual graves of Jews who escaped the Germans, and who were subsequently captured and killed on the road. Many who managed to escape were captured by peasants of the surrounding villages and shot. It was very difficult to find out who were buried in the individual graves. In one case we were able to find out who was buried in a particular grave: not far from the sawmill and the glassworks, over the canal where the small railway used to go through, is the grave of Yisrael Schwartzberg and his wife.

Filled with sadness about our terrible catastrophe, we decided to visit the large village of Vyhanoshts. We walked there, looking at the ground soaked with the blood of our sisters and brothers. We arrived in Vyhanoshts and started looking around to determine the fate of Shlomo's family. There were no Jews in the village; we started asking people about the grave of Shlomo's parents who were killed by the peasants, who stole their property. No one wanted to say anything. We went into a house, and Shlomo recognized his mother's candlesticks, but we had to keep quiet. We bit our lips so hard and kept quiet that our lips started bleeding. After several inquiries, one of our old acquaintances showed us where the location of Shlomo's parents was. We opened the grave and removed the martyrs; we took them to Telekhany and buried them in the Jewish cemetery.

Upon our return to Telekhany we decided to pay a visit to the local Christian priest in Telekhany. When we arrived at his house, Shlomo immediately recognized his beautiful buffet table. He recognized it right away. The priest noticed Shlomo, and started stammering that he had bought the buffet from the Germans. The priest offered to pay for the buffet, and spent several hundred Soviet rubles on it.

It should be mentioned that our arrival in Telekhany created a storm among the peasant population in town and in the nearby villages. First, they didn't believe that there were still any living Jews, because they were sure that Hitler had already killed all the Jews. Secondly, they were terrified that the Soviet authorities would punish them for collaborating with Hitler's devils in the massacres. They were sure that we had arrived with the assistance of the new authorities, to search houses for anything that had been stolen from Jews.

Peasants arrived from surrounding villages to find out if it was true that two Jews had suddenly appeared in Telekhany. Shocking events took place when the peasants saw us. A few even started kissing us, screaming in Ukrainian, "Who do I see?" But we tossed back at them in their faces, "A demon should possess your fathers! You are crying now? If the Germans were here now, you would certainly turn us in to them to be murdered, the way you did it earlier with our brothers and sisters.!"

A few peasants swore that they had never done that, but how could they be believed? The horrific murder was so gruesome and heartless, that they had become wild beasts. There were most certainly some peasants who hadn't been directly involved with the horrific murders. However, they were so few, that it wouldn't even be worth considering that all of them weren't involved in the murderous activities.

Finally, I would like to briefly describe what happened to our – your – beautiful town of Telekhany. Total destruction hovered over the houses that stood like orphans, covered in black, darkness, and which burned out the eyes of those who had lived there before. Such dear parents, grandparents and children, in a place where everyone lived together like one big family, and who shared their joys and sorrows. The Germans destroyed it all. We must always remember the "verse" of "Remember that which Hitler did unto you....!" [This is a pun on the Jewish tradition of remembering what the Amalekites did to the Israelites in the biblical account of the Exodus from Egypt. The verse states "Remember what Amalek did unto you during your departure from Egypt."]

Almost all houses were still standing; only about ten were missing. Some were burned down, and others stand in disarray, without doors or windows. A large number of houses were taken over by the Soviet authorities for institutions, offices and stores. Nothing remained of the Stolin and Lyubash synagogues. The Germans took them down, and built protective trenches in their place. The non-Chassidic synagogue was spared, and the Germans used it as a warehouse for grain that they brought from the villages. Now the Soviets are using the synagogue for the same purpose. On the other hand, the Christian church and the *kostsholl* were left untouched, as if there had been no war. The Jewish cemetery was in total shambles, and here we could see the effects of the wild animals. The destruction was so great, that we wanted to scream out, "Woe, happened to the Jewish dead who had to suffer a second death?!"

The fence around the cemetery was in disrepair; none of it was still standing. The brick grave structure that had stood for years was completely taken down, and not a single brick remained. The graves and gravestones were in such condition that it was grievously heart-breaking to see just what the evildoers were capable of doing to Jewish graves and the dead.

The graves were dug up by the evildoers as they looked for Jewish gold. They thought that the Jews were burying their gold. They also took the gravestones home, and some of the stones were used as sharpeners to sharpen their scythes and knives. Other stones were used for milling wheat and rye – evildoers milling their bread using the gravestones of holy Jews who never harmed a fly, not shedding a tear as they ground their bread!

We stood at the cemetery filled with sorrow, pain and rage, asking G-d in heaven where his judgment, justice and truth was. We bowed our heads to the martyrs and went further. What did we see? Bones and limbs of the dead were thrown about like pieces of wood; we only wished that we had been blinded before seeing such things.

We went to the Soviet authorities in Telekhany to request a fence to be placed around the mass graves of our murdered martyrs located on the road to Voulka. We told him that if they wanted to do that, we would remain in Telekhany to help with the work. They responded that we were a hundred percent correct and that they were willing to do it. However, since all the men were still in the army, this work could not be done yet. As soon as the men returned, they would proceed to build the fence.

This is what our beloved and dear town of Telekhany was like, the place where the dearest and most beloved people any person can have remained in death. Our parents, our grandparents, our brothers and sisters, children, friends and neighbors. We'll never join them in their place of rest.

We should all now recite the prayer, G-d of Mercy, and swear that we always remember the "verse": "Remember what the Germans did unto you...."

[Page 28]

The World Became Poorer
by Esther Miller

With the Nazis' annihilation of a third or our Jewish population, the World became poorer. The Nazi murderers destroyed cities and towns in Europe including our Telekhany. This was not only a Jewish, but also a general disaster.

Our History for the last 2000 years is full of catastrophes. But the Jewish people never experienced such horrendous, inconceivable disaster as they did the last 25 years, since the rise of Nazism in Germany. During the Nazi-German plague, 5 million adult Jews and 1,200,000 children were killed. Who were they? What were their names? It is too long a list for the world to know. The majority were plain hardworking people, who because of poverty and pressure didn't have the time and finances to develop their natural intellect and talent that Nature gave them. But there were also many names well known to the world. They shone like a beacon at night: scientists, inventors, teachers, writers, poets, educators, artists, musicians, historians – great intellectuals that the world needs so much. With their destruction the world became poorer.

Not in every generation are people born who are able to rise above the time and circumstances they are living in. "The Nazi murderers killed the body before they managed to kill the spirit." We read in the archive of Dr. Emmanuel Ringelblum, and other diaries found in the ground of the ghettos and other "holding places."

A mother died blowing her last breath into the mouth of her dead child. Lovers died in each other's embrace. A grandfather dying of illness and starvation, blessed his 14-year-old grandson and encouraged him to get out alive and fight the Nazi murderers. (The grandson bore witness in Israel, at the Eichmann trial.)

Also my brother Shmuel Godiner from Telekhany, a Soviet Yiddish writer, a partisan, with a broken body, died with intellectual greatness, declaring to the Nazi face, "We will win".

"Avenge our deaths against the bloody enemy!" sounds my brother Aaron's voice in the Warsaw ghetto. You hear the voices of his children and children's children. Also among the children were some with enough spiritual strength to fight empty handed against the heavy equipped enemy, against its newest tools of destruction. The heroism of the little Jewish children has yet to be evaluated.

"The goal of the Nazis was to kill the Jewish children first. The brutal limitless savagery against little children, was supposed to uproot the Jews, one couldn't spare a new generation, who eventually could secure the renewal of the Jewish people." This was said by the Prosecutors in Israel, who found Eichmann guilty of crimes against humanity.

The scientific work of Dr. Dvorszetsky of 400 pages was published in Yiddish and Hebrew. Dr. Dvorszetzky estimates the Nazis murdered 1,200,000 children. He says: When the ghetto's liquidation neared, "children *aktsias*" began. In the Vilna ghetto on March 27, 1944; Kovno, March 27-28, 1944; Shavel, November 5, 1943; Cracow, March 13, 1943; Lodz, August 1942; Bialystok, August 1943; Tarnow, November 7, 1942; Warsaw, July-September 1942 and many more not mentioned. That's how we count "scientifically" our loss, our great misfortune our children, for whom the Jew always lived.

The first led killed were children from the orphanages. The killing was done in the most gruesome manner, using specially trained dogs, crushing their heads on poles, cutting heads with an axe, throwing them alive into wells, burning them alive, often before their mother's eyes.

Dr. Dvorszetsky tells further, that after the war it became known from the trials, and other archives documents and diaries, that the German doctors performed the most heinous experiments and sex operations on Jewish women and small children. Finishing his book, he says: ... most of those children who survived after the experiments were brought to the concentration camps. Not many survived.

Among the children brought to Auschwitz and then Bergen-Belsen, was the 15 years old Anne Frank, who left us the high-spirited Diary of Anne Frank.

In the Therezin ghetto in Czechoslovakia the Nazis killed 15,000 children, mostly Jewish. In Riga they slaughtered 40,000 children. They were under 15 years old.

Some 12 to 15 year old children left us a huge legacy of spirited literature; literature of pain, fear, sadness, but also hope and dreams, hopes embodied in many diaries. They left 4,000 drawings and songs about their life in ghetto, kept in the Jewish State Museum in Prague.

One child by the name of Teddy writes in a song

> To a new arrived child
> Everything seems so strange to him
> Life in Therezin is like hell
> And when I go home
> I won't be able to tell.

The 13 year old Hanush Hochenberg from Prague, killed December 18, 1943 in Auschwitz expressed the change he had undergone, what happened to him:

> I was once a small child
> Just three years ago
> The child dreamed of other places
> But here I am no longer a child
> Because I learned how to hate
> Now I'm a grown man
> And know the taste of fear

An unidentified child tried in 1943 to encourage himself and other children, and wrote poems entitled "Homesickness". The child wrote:

> But nobody should give in,
> The world turns and times will change.
> We all hope that time will come,
> When we will return home.
> Now I realize how dear home is
> And I remember it often.

The belief that there are other people in this world whom one can live with together and befriend is expressed in seven short lines, by the young Alena Sinkova, who survived. She wrote:

> I will take off and go alone
> Where other people are, better people,
> To an unknown place
> Where nobody kills each other
> Maybe many of us
> a thousand, will reach the goal
> Pretty soon.

Under the title "Fear" 12 year old Eva Pikova describes the horror in the Therezin ghetto and cries out:

> No, no my God, we want to live,
> Not see how our number shrinks,

We want to have a better world,
We will work --- we shouldn't have to die.
Another child killed in Auschwitz in October 28, 1944 wrote in the Thereszin ghetto, a little poem, "The Garden"

A small garden
Filled with unusual fragrance and roses,
A narrow path
And a little boy walks on it
A little boy, a sweet boy
Like the blossoming flowers.
When the flowers will wilt
The little boy will not be anymore ....

Like Anne Frank in her hiding, and other children who wrote diaries, the children from the Therezin ghetto also had the awareness and courage to praise life and live bravely. An unidentified child from Therezin, verbalized it in the following lines:

Hey, try to open your heart,
Make a garland of beautiful memories.
Go sometimes to the woods,
And if tears block your way,
You will know how wonderful it is ----
To be alive.

A boy named Friedman from Prague, killed September 29, 1944 in Auschwitz, expressed pain and heroism when he said Goodbye to the last butterfly. He ends his song with these words:

.... butterflies don't live
in the ghetto.

In the resistance movement in the Riga ghetto, 12-13 year old children took part. A little boy, Avremke, was killed by the Gestapo after his interrogation, but he did not utter a word! Heroic episodes of carrying guns to the Riga ghetto writes a boy named Hoffman. One episode when Rene, a boy not even ten years old, hid from an *aktsia*. When caught by the Nazis, threw himself out from the fifth floor, shouting: "Alive I don't give myself up to my murderers".

These Jewish child-heroes who carried out the most risky actions, spilled their blood on the battlefields against Hitler's hordes. These promising, talented children, were killed by the Nazi beasts, and the world became poorer. The world became poorer, but the Jewish roots are still here.

In my motherly mind and heart an image there is engraved the picture that a writer painted of a small 7 year old boy killed by the Nazis in September 1943 in the Plashev camp. Before the execution he asked his mother: "Mama, is dying painful? No, just a little."

The wounds of Jews from Telekhany and the world are yet too fresh (only 21 years old) to be evaluated properly by our generation of writers, artists and playwrights to be able to assess and describe the world's great tragedy. A new generation needs to objectively assess the Nazis' horrors, and assess the colossal loss of human life and worldly value that the Nazi murderers, the beasts in human form brought to the world.

These are the children of Galicia that the Nazi murderers killed, and the world thus became poorer. However, the root remained, that the Jewish people live.

Our Telekhany also had talented children, creative idealistic youth who would have contributed much to human progress. They fought bravely in the underground movement against the bloody German enemy as partisans in the thick White Russian forests. Their memory will live forever in our hearts. Very few survived Hitler's hell. Some left in time for Israel. Some joined the Russian Army. The brothers Leibl and Efraim Klitenick (who survived to contribute much to the cause of peace), Eliyahu Senders, Berl Zuskin, Feivel Lemel, Aaron Shmuel (Rivka's son, was killed defending Leningrad), Leizer Lutsky, Shlomo Landman and many others. Many young children left with the Partisans, among them my cousin, the energetic, talented Dinah Godiner. She survived and lives now in Lodz.

There was no ghetto in Telekhany, no holding places, crematoria or special "children's *aktsias*." The date of our tragedy was August 4, 1941. The Nazi murderers herded the entire Jewish community – men, women, children of various parents, and the elderly, and told them to dig three long graves along the broad Glass Factory Street. They ordered local gentiles (including those of surrounding villages who committed a pogrom against the Jews six weeks earlier) to shoot them. The ignorant gentiles, poisoned with hatred of Jews, shot them all – to the last Jew, the last child. Some didn't die and were set afire.

The former Red Army soldier and partisan, Ephraim Klitenick, who was shaped and hardened by the horrible war, broke down and cried like a child, when he visited his hometown of Telekhany several years later. Sol Landman, who now lives in the United States, was also there. It sends a shudder up your spine to read Ephraim's letter and listen to Sol tell what the sadistic beasts in human form – the Nazis – did to the Jews. Even now, 21 years after the great tragedy, Telekhany still remains deadly silent. Jewish homes, that were more or less closed up were taken over by peasants, who boarded up the doors and windows because of fear from others (or living Jews?). "No one sees any people on the street or hears the sounds of children's laughter" writes Ephraim. "The healthy peasant shook like a leaf when he showed me what he took over in our house" recounts Sol Landman.

The horrors committed by Nazis (and local gentiles who were afraid not to follow Nazi orders) against Jews that the peasant told Sol about, were so dreadful, so hard to believe, that they are inconceivable by the human mind. The question arises whether this is possible. What century are we living in? When we realize that all these horrors took place in our times in the civilized 20 th century, we are frightened and ashamed of mankind – not only for humans of our generation, but for those of future generations as well.

There are reasons to feel shame and fear. If human beings (biologically the Nazis were human) could sink so low and commit acts that only wild animals could commit, what makes the world so sure it couldn't happen again? This is not only a question regarding the destruction of a third of the Jewish People at the bloody hands of the Nazis, it is a question for the entire world. The entire world stands in danger of becoming poisoned by anti-Semitism and participating in racism.

Simon Dubnow, the great Jewish historian who was shot by the Nazi executioners on Sunday morning, November 30, 1941 in the Riga ghetto, was correct. In discussions with children in the ghetto, he said, "Everything written about Jewish history until now is nothing. Jewish history begins now." We can say that human history is beginning now.

It would be an intellectual relief for us Jews, and for the world at large, to know that the German people lost their minds – that something in their brains had broken down, that the Nazis were different from other people. Then civilization would take measures to make sure that the Nazi epidemic didn't spread. Mankind could then heal or quarantine them. However, the danger is greater, since the Germans were clear-thinking, organized, scientists and inventors who put their talents to use, and invented killing machines for the total extermination of the Jewish People. Their professors and doctors experimented on the bodies of women and children. Their "ladies" made lampshades from human skin. The Germans practiced inhumane experiments in various death camps. Dr. Mengele, the head doctor in Auschwitz was the greatest sadist of all. He is still alive, hiding out somewhere in the western hemisphere.

Dr. Mengele isn't the only murderer alive and in hiding. There are other former outright and covert mass murderers who are alive and in hiding (we don't want to contaminate our Yizkor book with their names). The world must be alert to the deadly Nazi microbes.

The beginning of organized criminal behavior against the Jews in Germany

Two months after Hitler came to power in 1933, the Nazis began persecuting Jews. They were robbed of their citizenship and property, and were placed outside of German law that was applicable to everyone else. They weren't allowed to work with or for gentiles; they were prohibited from entering stores, cafés, restaurants, public transportation, factories or theaters. The synagogues were desecrated and burned; Jewish musicians were prohibited from performing Bach or Brahms; Mendelsohn's music was prohibited. Later, the Nazis burned their compositions together with works of the finest Jewish writers, including Heinrich Heine. Mobs danced around fires, screaming " *Heraus mit die jüdische Werm!"* [Out with the Jewish vermin!]; " *Araus von reinem Superman"* [Get away from the pure Aryan supermen!]; "Jews should be thrown out of Germany or be exterminated!"

Many of the robbed and persecuted Jews committed suicide, while others desperately looked for some other country to go to. The Jews ran up against the closed doors of neutral countries. The Germans saw the indifference of the democratic countries to the homeless and persecuted people, and assumed that no one wanted the Jews. The Jews were a burden to the country and worthless on the "market" – it made no difference what happened to them.

Part of the guilt lies with the western countries, especially the United States. From 1933-1943, the United States opened a crack in the "golden door" to European Jews, allowing in 190,000 out of millions of Jews doomed at the bloody hands of the Germans. If hearts and doors had been open wider to the hapless Jews in their desperate situation, a couple of more million could have been saved from the gas chambers, deportation camps and crematoria.

The Nazis soon began their bloody work, and they worked with precision, devilish efficiency and wickedness against the Jews. Jews were compelled to wear a yellow star on their chests, and were treated like livestock in the overcrowded ghettos, where disease, hunger, filth and typhus raged. The Nazi cannibals were still not satisfied. This way of dying was too slow, so every day Jews in the tens of thousands were sent in death trains to the crematoria of Auschwitz, Maidanek, Treblinka and other gas chambers.

Those who were still able to work were used for slave labor in the ghettos. Their deaths were temporarily suspended until they became useless due to the difficult and inhumane work. They were then sent off to the crematoria, and on the way were beaten. Anyone unable to go on fell to the bullets of the murderers. There were more beatings and lashings, and their bodies were broken. Their spirits, however, maintained their humanity: the dead bodies of mothers were founding holding on to their children, trying to protect them until the last minute; the young and the elderly affectionately held on to each other.

The Nazis, meanwhile, were enjoying themselves. No one worked on Sundays in Chelmno, and the Nazis wanted to have some fun on that day. They put the Jews into long lines, placed bottles on their heads, and shot the bottles. If the bullet hit the bottle, the Jew wasn't hit, but if the bullet landed a little lower, he was finished. The lucky survivors of this game were forced to clear away the dead.

Chelmno was a primitive extermination camp. Prior to when mass murder experiments were made using Cyclon B, lethal cyanide crystals were used in the gas chambers. People were fooled into thinking they were going to be taking showers. In Chelmno the Nazis used heavy trucks for transportation. They gave the Jews towels and soap, and told them they were going to have a shower, see a doctor and get fresh clothes. The sealed trucks were taken into a forest, where carbon monoxide was pumped into them. This was a long death, but killed too few people; the death machines had to be improved.

Until 1943, large cars of gas victims were put directly into mass graves using shovels or lifts. After Himmler's visit, it was decided to employ more precise and efficient methods, and this resulted in the use of pyre bonfires to burn the bodies. In Treblinka there were 13 gas chambers, and 10,000 Jews were killed every 35 minutes. Every week, eight to ten kilos of gold (removed from the dead) were taken out of the gas chambers and put into suitcases to be sent to Berlin; the gold was used to enrich the Third Reich.

One man testified at Eichmann's trial in Israel as follows: "I grew up in the Treblinka death camp. At 14 years of age I was torn away from my mother. The Nazis sent her to the crematorium with thousands of other Jews. The Germans called it 'Heaven's Street.' I wanted to commit suicide, but my grandfather wouldn't let me. He blessed me and said that I would survive to help others. Since I was still young, he thought I would survive Hitler's hell, and I could tell the world what the Nazis did to the Jews. I went through various experiences in Treblinka, from shaving the heads of dead women to stuffing mattresses with the hair. One day I found my dead sister's body in a heap of dead corpses." The man looked around with wide-open eyes, as if he was horrified by his own voice.

In Salonika, Greece, the Germans gave permission to the non-Jews to seize Jewish stores and as much merchandise as they wanted. They would cynically tell the Jews that they would pay them back for the merchandise. The robbed Jews were put into ghettos, where typhus soon spread (the Nazis were scared of typhus, and quickly deported all the Jews, including the healthy ones).

As usual, the Nazis spread lies to give the Greek Jews the false hope that they would be traveling to Poland, where they would begin new lives. With their last bit of money, they bought worthless Polish zlotys. The Nazis then packed 78 people into a freight car that was built only to hold 40. The Jews started suspecting what was in store for them. They spent long days and nights together with what the Germans called transport equipment. Children choked from thirst, dirt and sickness. The freight cars always arrived with a large number of dead. The Jewish population of Greece was 56,000, and after the war, only 1,950 remained alive.

The Jews were not sheep who let themselves be driven to the slaughterhouse. They were civilized people for whom it was hard to believe that the Germans, a high cultured world-renowned nation was capable of such barbarous savagery. The Nazis took advantage of the Jewish naivety. They lied, spread false hopes and calming news; they then fooled people and murdered them, wherever the bloody Nazi beast stepped. The soap in Auschwitz gas chambers, supposedly showers, were made of stone. On the trains transporting the Jews to their death, illustrated postcards were given out with the imaginary "Waldsee;" the victims were forced to send cheery postcards back to the remaining Jews in the ghetto (from where they were transported to the crematoria).

The Nazis did everything to prevent possible riots and resistance. And yet, the starving, physically broken, tortured Jews stood up to the heavily equipped enemy, the Nazis. The historical heroism of the Warsaw, Bialystok, Auschwitz, Treblinka, Solibar, Riga, and other ghettoes has yet to be told.

The uprising of the Warsaw ghetto will remain for generations, a monument of courage, and a warning to murderers and despots, that the Jewish people are strong and will overcome victoriously -- Nazism, fascism and anti-Semitism.

Some people make a mistake in believing that the scope of Yizkor books and Holocaust literature is limited. The truth is to the contrary. Keep in mind the extremely valuable informative books and documents that have been written about Hitlerism and his extermination of the Jewish People: *The Rise and Fall of the Third Reich* by William Shirer; Hilllberg's *The Extermination of Jews in* Europe; Rotlinger's book, *On Jewish Extermination*; Hersh's *The Wall, Mila 18* and many others. All of the books have been warmly received by readers, discussed and read. Critics have given positive reviews, showing that we aren't alone in our pain and sorrow. The whole world is starting to understand how poor it became by virtue of the murder of six million Jews – one third of the Jewish People – including famous Jews in the literary world such as Yitzchak Katznelson, Yisrael Stern, Hillel Zeitlin, K. Liss, S. Gilbert, Y. Prager and Zalman Sokolov; Hebrew writers such as Yakir Warshavsky and H. A. Kaplan; columnists such as Aharon Einhorn, Benzion, Khilinovitch and Yanosz Kortchuk; historians such as Shimon Dubnow, Shimon Huberband, Lipman Zamber, Yechiel Lehrer, Natan Eibeschitz, N. Sternberg, Yitzchak Bernstein, Mordechai Gebirtick and other promising talents. Two generations (parents and children) of builders and creators of Jewish literature died in the death camps – people representing the Jewish press, scientists, teachers and performers. The world has been shamed and has become poorer because of it.

The mass murder of millions of innocent people at the bloody hands of the Nazis just because those people were Jews took place in our lifetimes – in the educated 20th century. We have to know everything about it. This knowledge has to be our ammunition to be used in the struggle against Nazism and fascism. We must be alert and learn how to recognize all the signs of public or hidden anti-Semitism, racism, genocide (extermination of peoples), no matter what mask it hides behind, in order to assure that this never happens again, no matter where and to whom.

To ignore it, and close our eyes to anti-Semitism and racism is as dangerous as to ignore cancer. To say: What is there to do? It's a punishment and must end with death. Anti-Semitism is cancer. It befalls the weakest members of mankind who have criminal instincts. The earlier it is recognized, the more chances for a cure. We have seen what has happened in Germany where the cancer cells spread and took control over the political, social and economic body. People turned into wild beasts. Not only Jews die, everything human dies. Justice, truth, decency, mercy, sympathy, tolerance and civilization itself dies.

We are obligated to learn from the worst tragedy, the most disastrous catastrophe happened to us at the bloodstained hands of the Nazis. We owe it to our conscience, to our people, to fight the Nazi cancer, to clean the world of Nazism so that we can live in peace, security and integrity, and to be able to deserve to be called -- a Mensch.

It would be impossible for us Jews as a nation, to maintain our balance, faith in humanity, if it wasn't for some shining exceptions (regrettably they are the exception rather than the rule) of human goodness against Nazi wickedness, shown to us by a part of the gentile world during the Hitler era. Many times they endangered their own lives to rescue a Jew, a Jewish child from the bloody fingers of the Nazis. Not only will our generation remember our non-Jewish friends with affection and reverence, they also will be remembered by future generations as well.

A noble human example was demonstrated by Denmark. The Danes, led by King Christian, rescued their Jews in spite of the wild anger of the Nazis. "If you will force my citizens to wear 'yellow stars' I will be the first to wear it", he said. The Jews of Denmark never wore the yellow star and were never driven into ghettoes.

The Nazis, as usual, tried in many ways to slander the Jews, with dirty implications spread in leaflets, to scare the Danish people. But the Danes didn't give in to those provocations. They transferred Jews to Sweden. They hid elderly Jews in their hospitals under Christian names. They concealed religious articles from the Synagogues in the Lutheran churches. Not one Dane lowered himself or his people by denouncing Jews to the Gestapo. Many Danes paid with their lives for this act of humanity.

A couple of hundred Jews, out of seven thousand living in Denmark, were caught by the Gestapo and sent to Theresienstadt, the mildest of all camps. When the Danes learned that the people were starving there, everyone, from the King to the cobbler sent money to sustain them.

Sweden was neutral in the war, but not so concerning humanity. They gave shelter to anyone who reached their shores, and even warmly offered citizenship to the Jews. This fact motivated the Nazis to issue a special order: "Jews with neutral citizenship have to be sent to the East to the gas chambers." It was found after the war, Sweden also produced a great warmhearted, conscientious man -- Raul Wallenberg, a counselor to the Swedish Ambassador in Budapest. The Nazis daily sent 12,000 Hungarian Jews to death. It was in the summer and fall of 1944, and the Germans were obviously losing the war. Raul Wallenberg rented houses in Budapest, displayed the Swedish flag, and filled the houses with Jews who then called themselves Swedes. Although there were no more wagons, Auschwitz was closed, the Red Army was on the offensive, but the SS continued their mission to destroy the last Jews. They ordered a winter death march for Jews from Hungary to Austria. It was such an outrageous public act of murder that Himmler ultimately ordered it stopped. Raoul Wallenberg rode along the walking and falling Jews and gave them food, blankets and medicine.

The gates of Luxemburg were open for all hunted Jews. In that small defenseless country, they could think of themselves as persons, not tormented animals. The friendliness of the people gave them hope and encouragement. After some time, many received visas to neutral territories. Under the moral guidance of Elisabeth the Queen mother of Belgium, the Archbishop and the Belgian underground helped Jews to derail the death wagons and to escape death. The punishment for helping Jews was death!

We salute every one of our nameless Christian friends. The brave, beautiful spirits, who didn't close their eyes to Jewish sufferings, who risked their lives in helping Jews instead of helping the Nazi barbarians or looking for somewhere to protect themselves or closing their eyes to Jewish suffering. They not only helped Jews survive, they helped to maintain our love and faith in mankind. The brought honor and hope to mankind that Man will overcome all evil connected with the sadistic cancerous Nazi ideology. These were isolated and exceptional cases. If millions more had behaved this way, the world would be totally different – richer and happier.

Norway also showed a noble example of human solidarity against cruelty. When the Nazis threw themselves like vultures to finish off the last remaining Jews, the Norwegians and their underground hurried with their rescue mission. They led a large number of Jews over snow-covered mountains in subzero temperatures to Sweden, through strictly guarded borders, under a shower of bullets. Many of the starved, emaciated Jews didn't make it. Yet the people of Norway, with their underground, did their best to save half of the Jews.

The people of Holland organized a general strike to protest the cruel treatment of their Jews. The strike was suppressed by a German "firing-squad." Although the Nazis increased the reward for denouncing Jews, the Dutch preferred to hide them. "The Dutch refused to sympathize with the German tactics" complained a German document presented to the Eichmann trial.

Even Germany produced a "saint" named Foster Grober. He believed the teachings of his Lord, and openly helped Jews in Germany. For his faith he was incarcerated in the Dachau jail. His friends in Germany helped him quietly in his noble, human work. Their names must still remain secret.

In 1938 after the Nazi organized pogroms in Germany, Foster Grober went to Switzerland to appeal for more foreign visas for the oppressed Jews. At every official institution and embassy, everyone turned a deaf ear. Nowhere could he find understanding and sympathy for the dark misfortune of the Jews. He and his committee left filled with bitterness and shame. "Had the ministries of foreign affairs shown the slightest bit of interest toward the homeless, hunted immigrants, it would have been possible to rescue millions of Jews."

(From Foster Grober's report.) All above are documented facts from authentic sources, brought out at the Eichmann trial.

Thousands of miles away from the murder machines and gas chambers, in the protected and well-fed USA, there lived other noble friends of the Jews in addition to the ones in Europe. One of them was John Williams, a minister. One day he knocked on my door: Look, read what they do to people, they make soap of them. And with dread in his eyes he handed me Life magazine. We were speechless. Pain and shame strengthened our friendship. In the evening we went to his church together and joined by his congregation, we prayed for the suffering and persecuted.

"What does all this have to do with the destruction of Telekhany, with the death of our families and countrymen?" some readers may ask. There is a strong connection. We are just a small segment of a bloody chain. The same Nazi murders who killed the other European Jews, also killed the Jews of Telekhany. But here the wound is more painful, if such a thing is possible, because the executioners were our own neighbors. Our native gentiles spurred on by the Nazis, accomplished their murderous job, and the beautiful little town with its nice Jewish community was reduced to a heap of corpses.

Time cannot heal, cannot release the enormous pain over the loss of our dear families, landsman, and martyrs whose lives were taken in such a horrible way at the hands of the Nazis. In their sacred memory, we open our wounds in the Telekhany Memorial Book. Through it we address our generation and generations to come. Again and again we repeat the message left by our martyrs: Remember the crimes committed upon the Jewish people! Remember and remain on guard. Do not let such a horror happen again! Fight racism, Nazism, anti-Semitism. We owe this to our deceased and to ourselves. It is our obligation to the exterminated Jews and to ourselves. This is the order of the day, and the reason for this Yizkor book.

As great and painful the agony and martyrdom of innocent Jewish people is, we must do it. We must all realize and face the horrible truth, and enter deeply into the wounds of the Jewish People and our destroyed hometown of Telekhany and its honest inhabitants and age-old way of life. We must remember and not be afraid of talking about our past. A people that has no past has no present and, of course, no future.

We hope that our Yizkor book will influence many people to be on guard and fight Nazism, racism, reaction and anti-Semitism, and to make sure that the horror of Nazism is never repeated for a world of freedom, peace and fraternity. Then our Memorial Book will have been worth all the effort we put into it.

[Page 43]

The Munich Conference
by Aaron Klitenick

Silent and sad was Telekhany in 1938. The town wasn't alive, it was vegetating. Many young people had immigrated to Palestine, the USA, Brazil and other countries. Many were incarcerated or expelled for political activities by the Polish-Fascist government. The remaining were elderly, children, and the young who couldn't yet decide what to do.

Cultural life came to a stop. There wasn't anyone to talk to. People feared their own shadow. In the West of Poland, Hitlerism spread rapidly. Poland -- with her Motshizky, Ridz-Shmigli, Beck and his mob imitated Hitler, dancing to his tune.

The Munich Accord between the Great Powers was properly understood by the Telekhaner. A world war was coming.

The elderly Jews wrapped themselves tighter in their prayer shawls and begged God to cancel the terrible decree. They attended meetings with Rabbi Glicks, president of the "Aguda" movement. They believed his speeches, that the stubborn communists, who didn't want to give up, but wanted to carry on their underground activities were responsible for all of it.

The financial conditions in Telekhany at that time were disastrous. The recession in Poland was tangible. The shopkeepers, tradesmen etc. worked tirelessly to provide their families with food. Jewish businessmen toiled the earth for potatoes, cabbage and other vegetables. Our people had never had great wealth, but they always had their dreams and hopes.

Jews In The Army

[In Poland, as in many European countries, army service at a certain age, was mandatory. Translators note.]

Autumn was the time for recruiting new men to army service, which was for two years. Then mothers, sisters, wives saw them off with lamentations and tears. They waited impatiently counting days, weeks, months till the two years passed and the children came home. The young men then told of humiliation they had suffered, how they were made fun of for being Jews. But the joy in being home let them forget past troubles.

The recruiting in the fall of 1938 was larger than in previous years. They made no exceptions for only children, providers of families, etc.

Everyone had to go. They didn't discharge those whose time was up either. It became obvious that a Second World War was nearing.

A number of our Telekhaner youth were drafted: Aaron Landman's son, Michael Landman; Chaim Yuszick's (the Bathkeeper's) grandson, Alter Yuszick. Michael Leifer's son Yasha Leifer. Asher Gurshtel's son Neoma Gurshtel. Alter Kristal's son, Grushka's son, and many others.

Not discharged were Aaron Godiner's only son, Alter Godiner, Golel Grushkin, Pinie Feldman and many others.

The distress worsened in the spring when they drafted older Jews as well as gentiles. The media wrote widely about Hitler's intention to do away with the so-called Polish Corridor and to stretch his paws further into Polish territories.

The Polish leaders clicked their heels and proudly declared they would not give up even a button. The situation then, though a dangerous one, could maybe have been saved if the lordly and capitalist rulers had been more realistic. Unfortunately, because of racism and class hatred, they refused the help offered by the USSR. The Second World War approached rapidly.

The Polish-German War

On Friday September 1, 1939, the sound of gunfire and bombs shocked all of Poland.

The Hitler beast displayed its dreadful face. The Polish people got to experience the taste of all-out war. The cruelest air bombing was launched against the civilian population -- men, women and children.

People ran for their lives, leaving all their possessions behind; tens and hundreds were killed along the way. The survivors were driven out of their minds by fear and despair.

Even earlier, in August 1939, the people of Telekhany organized a self-defense group. Facing the oncoming danger, the various elements united under the leadership of Rabbi Glicks to provide aid to the victims of the war; his closest associates were Zionists and communists as well.

Within the first days of the war in September, Telekhany filled with refugees from central Poland. They were taken in and helped as much as possible. They told horror stories of what the Hitler murderers do. The situation was of great despair. On the 6th of September, the Polish government fell apart. Government officials and military personnel fled to the East, to the Soviet border.

The most senior officials and military officers fled to Romania, creating a vacuum behind them. The military heroically defended the fatherland. But they were poorly equipped and abandoned by senior authorities who were like rats abandoning a burning ship. The Germans were stopped at the Warsaw gates. They surrounded Warsaw and marched farther eastward.

Part of the Telekhaner youth fled, but only one choice was available: to head east to the borders of the USSR where they could find refuge.

Happy Days

On the 17th of September early morning, the radio brought the happy news. The Soviet Army was crossing the border of former Poland to free its brothers and sisters in West Byelorussia and West Ukraine. This meant that Hitler's army wasn't going to get to Telekhany.

The news spread through town like lightning. The whole town spilled out of houses into the streets. Even during market days you couldn't see that many people at once.

They looked ecstatic, and greeted each other joyfully. Jews and White Russians embraced and kissed each other. Rabbi Glicks hugged and kissed Jews and gentiles; men and women hugged and kissed each other, wishing each other mazel tov. The orthodox priest did the same thing, and everyone in town followed their example.

Just then in the early morning hours of September 17, when everyone in town were so overjoyed by the happy news, a group of friends gathered to organize a local leadership to secure order and well being for our town: they were Yisrael David Kagan, Ephraim and Leibel Klitenick, Yisrael Bernstein, Motya Roshchiner, Zinovy Bolodovitch. It was decided to call upon everyone, regardless of party, Jew and gentile, to join the militia and with the permission of the authorities, to hand over any weapons that they might own. Many laborers and peasants signed up.

During those crucial hours, Rabbi Glicks came to this writer, and offered his cooperation. He handed me a pistol given to him by the former Polish authorities. He joined the organizing committee, but soon thereafter had to resign because of his position as rabbi.

Great courage and self-sacrifice was shown us by our longtime sympathizer, Shlomo Landman, who put himself at the disposal of the new administration and was actively involved with it for a long time.

The Soviet army entered Telekhany on the 21st of September, and in four days a well-equipped militia and local administration were already set up. With great sacrifice they were able to keep the peace and avoid bloodshed.

A few weeks later elections were held, and representatives from the people were elected to the new local administration. Among those elected were individuals who had worked for years for a new system.

Life was peaceful and calm for 21 months. Telekhany slowly adjusted to the new situation, and believed that Hitler's Germany would never dare to attack the Soviet Union.

The Great Catastrophe

Terrible was the news on the radio on June 22, 1941. It reported that Hitler attacked the USSR. We knew then that the war would be very costly for mankind. However, the final number was much more horrifying: six million Jews, three million Poles, ten million Soviet citizens as well as millions of people throughout Europe were murdered. This was the outcome of Hitler's war.

A few weeks after the arrival of the Hitlerian authorities, the Jews of Telekhany were herded together in one place and shot down with machine guns. All the martyrs were buried in mass graves a few miles from Telekhany.

Many of those who fled perished under unknown circumstances.

Only in 1957 did I have the possibility of visiting Telekhany and the mass graves. They were shown to me by my former friends, gentiles who fought with the Partisans and survived.

Telekhany became free of Jews [*Judenrein*], as Hitler wished, and regretfully there is no one to put a gravestone on the graves.

[Page 47]

My Brother is alive!
by Dina Godiner

Daybreak. The town was in a deep, restless sleep. I closed my eyes and opened them again. My heart ached. I hadn't slept the whole night. In my ears I still heard the scary warnings, "Attention, attention, it's coming!" It meant that the enemy bombers were on their way to unload their deadly cargo on us.

I was thinking of my only young brother who had been taken away somewhere into the trenches to defend the fatherland. I lived with just one desire, to see him alive, to hear his voice. I'm also thinking with great concern about Alterke, Chaim, the bathkeeper's grandson, and about Aaron Landman's son, Michael, and about many other precious Jewish boys from Telekhany, who were taken from their homes and thrown into a hellish fire .... But life goes on, hope comes on wide wings and brings back life and joy .....

I was standing at the window with eyes full of tears, looking into space. I imagined seeing my brother; here he was, haggard, he pulled himself out of the fire and is coming .... Suddenly I heard "Mazel Tov" and a delicate hand embraced me .... Asher was coming. Asher Godiner was alive, walking now on Sventovolier Street ....

Never before had fantasy and reality been so interwoven like this. My eyes were fogged, but I saw how my dear father tried to get up to meet him, but could not move. He hardly believed in his great luck. So it was true, my brother was alive. Here he came, wrapped in rags, darkened and exhausted, but with restless, shining eyes as if the horror of the war fire was mirrored in them.

The whole town knew the news, and many walked him to our house. Like an arrow the news flew over the town. Mothers and fathers who weren't as lucky as us, and to our great sorrow will never be, came to our house. Slender Alterke was killed as was Chaim this writer's grandson. Handsome, good Michael Landman, and many others of the dear beloved names were no more.

So there we were, enjoying our brother and mourning the dear others at the same time.

My brother told us how he succeeded in avoiding death. He was lucky. A friendly Polish family took him in, changed his military uniform for these rags, thanks to which he could save himself. He looked very young and those rags transformed him into an abandoned youngster who wandered the world begging. He walked from town to town, from village to village. His way was long, tiresome, accompanied by fire, sword and bombs.

I wanted to be joyful, I had my dear brother back. But there was a weight pressing against my heart, the sky was heavy as lead .... Was it a foreboding that my joy is a fleeting one, and that something horrible was about to happen, that a Damocles sword was hanging over the heads of my beloved ones, over my little town, my cradle, Telekhany?

Luck Came Unexpectedly

The night was dark, I was afraid to go to the shore. Shadows scared me at every corner. Be courageous, be courageous, I said to myself, feverish with angst.

Efraim and Leibl, Israel Bernstein, Israel David and some White Russian friends, had a meeting on the beach to decide what steps to take: to run away or to desert. No, they were fighters, they will not quit. It was decided to take part in the battle, to fight the world's worst enemies, the Nazis, together in the Polish army. We moved like ghosts in the nighttime darkness. The town was breathing heavily and hopelessly. Who would shine light into the darkness? From where will come the rescue? Unexpectedly, hope arrived. A bright sun promised the "Garden of Eden" on earth. Mazel Tov! Mazel Tov! Young and old, Jews and Christians alike, embraced, hugged and kissed each other. The war ended, the Red Army was coming to free White Russia/Byelorussia. They brought joy and songs.

Ephraim travels to search for the Red Army

Where were they, our liberators? None of us had seen them yet, and we were suddenly seized by doubt. So many Polish officers traveled through Telekhany –they were running through like chased animals, but left many victims in their wake. They just landed in town, bringing with them civilian members of the regime. Chaos struck Polesia, and Telekhany ended up alarmed and forlorn like an orphan.

Then a committee was formed, and the following people were selected: Ephraim, Leibel, Motke Roshchiner, Yisrael David, Yisraelikel Bernstein, Leiba Eisenberg and a few Byelorussian friends, and then Shlomo Landman joined voluntarily. He demonstrated his readiness to face any danger that happened to lurk and threaten us.

Ephraim, Leibel and Shlomo Landman were always on guard. I dreamed in vain to see Ephraim staying at home. I became jealous of the new regime, and missed Ephraim. I wanted to talk about things with him, and tell him so many things. However, he was involved in more important things than his personal life. In a strange way I laugh and cry at the same time: laughing and crying are like two brothers who are willing to give up their lives for peace, for a nicer and better world.

Agreeable and happy about my fate, I was always nervous about them, my loved ones. Every minute a new danger threatened their lives. Everyone in town was in a mess; many lost hope that the Red Army was really on its way to improve our situation. The evil forces were together, ready to attack us, to rob and murder, and so far help was far off. There were rumors that the Red Army was already in Hontzevich, but people were impatient, and didn't believe it; danger increased every day.

Then it was decided that someone would have to risk their life and travel to Hontzevich to meet up with the Red Army, and thereby bring someone to Telekhany. Ephraim and two other brave Byelorussian friends were selected. No one could imagine what I thought and felt at that time. Legends were shaping in my mind, each one more dreadful than the last. Death lurked over the roads, and here, my neighbors, my father were warning and appealing to me:

"Don't let him do it. Don't let him go! It's doubtful if you'll ever seem him alive again." However, a car was waiting for him, filled with people, as if they were going to a funeral. And me? I didn't want to stay alone, no! I couldn't stop him, I couldn't do such a thing! What about going along with him? Who would stop me?

Unfortunately, to my great surprise, as I was begging them to let me go along, with tears running down my face, I ended up alone. It was too dangerous to take a woman along. I tagged along after the car, ready to die, but just to be together with them. However, Leibel pulled me back, afraid to let me stand there alone.

The situation was so intense, more than ever. Earlier, we had been able to listen to the radio report that the Poles were coming back. We were very nervous, and didn't even know what kind of a world we were living in. Now, suddenly, as I talked with Leibel, a gunshot whizzed by –it seemed very close by, and Leibel fell to the ground, and the sky fell to the ground. We were sure that the shot came from the open window. Leibel stood up, he was wounded, but wasn't afraid of danger. He started shooting with his own revolver that he had on him. The bullet flew by me, and luckily missed me, though I was somewhat dazed, feeling like I was going to become unconscious. I was going through so many experiences all at once. Ephraim was somewhere in danger, Leibel was wounded, and the situation of the community was so unclear.

Leibel was taken to a doctor; Gittel and I were together with him. The night was an autumn night, and our hearts were like the season too. We wondered what the secret tomorrow had in store for us.

Darkness Always Precedes The Sunrise

It was no small task for them to go on the trip to Hantzevich, where they had never been before. On the road they ran into many Polish soldiers, and there were many victims who fell along the road in those days. The group found out that the Red Army wasn't in Hontzevich, and no one knew anything about them coming there at all. They were told that the Red Army was on the wide dirt roads and not throughout the forests. It was entirely possible that the Red Army was going to return to where they came from. There were so many versions of events, with no consolation in the group's disposition as they returned from their difficult trip back to Telekhany at dawn.

The entire population was waiting impatiently, looking for the truth through their tired and sleepless eyes. "The end justifies the means," so they decided to lie in order to calm the population and to scare off those waiting to commit robbery.

The Red Army was in Hantzevich, and was moving rapidly through White Russia. They would arrive shortly in Telekhany; everyone breathed easier. A heavy stone was removed from my heart as well (I was among those who were fooled), and that night I slept more soundly than ever before.

The next day, well rested, I ran over to my "dictator." I wanted to see a happy smile on his face, but all I found was a pall of gloom and of sleepless nights, and who knows how much suffering in his heart.

I found Shlomo Landman deep in thought and feeling very sad; Leibel was lying sick in bed following the shooting incident, and I felt as though something was wrong. They were hiding something from me.

That evening was calm, but filled with dread. On the day after Ephraim's return with his two friends, accompanied by fearsome shooting of wild gangs approaching from Sventevolia Street were a group of Polish officers who arrived with clattering of horses and countless gunshots that broke the silence of the night. It was like an omen of cruelty and destruction. It was as if they wanted to disprove the fact that the Red Army was really here, and that the liberation would arrive tomorrow, the next day or soon thereafter.

My father was awake; his troubled eyes looked at me. I could tell what he was feeling in his heart. I was half-dressed; I grabbed a coat and opened the door. Someone pulled me back with warm but nervous hands. My father begged me with teary eyes: "Where are you running now, when there's all that shooting??"

Where did I have that strength? I pulled away from his hands and ran breathlessly. On the one hand I was just a kid, and on the other hand, like black shadows galloping and soaring high, shooting. Boy, did my heart pound! I didn't delay, and warned them on time. I knew them, those heroic fellows. They would fanatically stand on guard and wait. They were just a group who would try to stand up against so many officers who were running to the ends of the earth and who were scared of their own shadows, and yet who could kill so many innocent people.

I got there on time! They were standing outside: Ephraim, Shlomo Landman and a Russian friend. Their goal was to go to check on the guard that was set up for the whole town. However, now they were arriving on horses, shooting breathlessly.

We were standing next to the tether in the narrow alley where Michel Laufer lived. Ephraim and Shlomo Landman broke out in battle with unusual strength! Nothing would be left of them.

Fortunately, they ran as fast as lightning fearlessly, taking along a few young people who were standing guard (at their guard posts), without confusion, doubt or fear.

———

[Page 52]

Telekhany and World War One

On the banks of the Oginski Canal, which has two rivers, the Fina and Shchara, right near the border of Polesia and not far from the Pinsk swamps, there is the town of Telekhany.

Telekhany signifies that it was there that the body of a Tatar khan was hidden; this khan was expanding his realm as far as the beloved town, where he ended his accounts with the world. This is what grandfathers said, and this is what their grandchildren would transmit.

The town was small and poor, but it played a very important strategic role in later events, both during the First World War and the Second World War. Telekhany, surrounded by villages and towns, was always the pride of Polesia, and always excelled in its youthful growth. Even before the 1905 Russian revolution, Telekhany already had widespread freedom organizations that participated in breaking down the fortress of ism. The youth of Telekhany took part in bringing down ism in 1917. When a new colonial government headed by Pilsudski was established, the youth of Telekhany, guided by unseen strength and educated in sacred traditions of freedom, were once again carried into the mass struggle for a new life. In following chapters, we will write about a whole series of struggles.

Solar Eclipse

It was 1914. The town of Telekhany slept soundly. Grandfathers groaned in their sleep, and grandmothers quietly wept. Mothers clasped their children to their hearts and called them by tender names.

At dawn fathers prayed with great feeling, asking G-d for livelihood and peace –for peace in the world. However, the sky was dark, and the sun was short of light. Gray spots floated around, and ominous black clouds covered the sky –it was a solar eclipse. Soon the sun would be covered up, and everyone knew that it would reappear with radiant light. However, something else was approaching from afar, and disturbed the hearts of young and old.

It was a bad sign. War was hanging in the air, and it wouldn't spare the town of Telekhany either. A solar eclipse. It suddenly became dark. From the darkness a black bird flew around, and went back and forth from east to west. It climbed over the Jewish cemetery, and with its wings warned of an impending war.

Get ready for battle! The bad news arrived soon enough. Somewhere people were fighting, and since the Germans, who were rolling through from the west, crushed the Czar's army, the town of Telekhany became very nervous upon hearing the military announcements of "nightingale, nightingale, little bird." The walls of the wooden shacks shook and swayed with the beat of the song. The retreating cavalry and infantry, the large regiments of various peoples.... The dark images frightened the Cossacks with their wild cruel whips. They all harassed the Jews, and pursued Jewish women. They were Circassians, Georgians and Tatars. The Czar's army was huge, but it was weak and lacking in strength. It didn't have the right equipment.

The retreat of the regiments lasted a long time, and it was a frightful time for the town of Telekhany. One Friday night, when Jews were on their way home from the Lubosher synagogue, they noticed a huge fire burning on Volostno Street in the courtyard of Berl, the Hatter, and were seized by panic. It looked like it was the end: the town was on fire, and with their last bit of energy, they managed to cry out "Fire!" Cossacks jumped out of the shadows like menacing demons, and lurched out at the unlucky Jews with their whips. Evidently, they had started a fire to roast a pig.

It was Rosh Hashanah, 1915. The Jews of Telekhany were all at the synagogue, where the walls were trembling from fear. They sky was again dark, without any blue showing through. The eve of Yom Kippur was also frightful for the Jews of Telekhany. The Russian authorities quickly ordered that the town be evacuated. The deadline for the evacuation was short, and the Jews scarcely had enough time to gather up some of their hard-earned possessions and move to the other side of the bridge. Many Jews went out hardly dressed, carrying babies in their arms. They all made strong efforts to escape out to the forests along Hartela, Samana and Viehonoshcha roads.

The evacuation order reached them there too. The 1st army pushed them further, deep inside Russia. Only a small number remained, and they hid out in the forest. When the German forces arrived, they returned to Telekhany.

Unfortunately, there was no town left. It was viciously burned down, and only a few houses remained standing. The returnees had to move west, and remained in Polish towns such as Lomza, Makovo, Ostrolenka for several years.

After the outbreak of the Karensky revolution, the Jews of Telekhany returned to town. Even the Telekhany Jews who remained in nearby towns such as Motele returned home. Telekhany was totally destroyed, and only the barracks that served as homes for the glassworks workers remained. However, the glassworks itself was also burned down. In 1921, a sawmill was built in its place.

Among those who returned to Telekhany were: Alter Gurshtel, the carpenter, with his sons and two daughters; Nisan Gurshtel, the shipper, with his sons: Asher, Yudel, Velvel, Michel, Motel and a daughter Sima; David Klitenik, the shoemaker and his two sons and daughter; Aharon Feldman and his daughter Itka; Gershon Kagan and his children; Avraham Chaim Kamadeyev and his family; Asher and Riva Kagan and their children; Gershon Klitenik and his family; the brothers, Yisrael and Aharon Godiner and their families; Yisrael Schwartzberg (known as Yisrael Mashiach) and his wife Sarah; Reuven Gurshtel and his family; Avraham David Eisenberg and his beautiful daughters; Isser Backelman and his family; Rachel Meltzer and her children; Chaim Yeshayahu the teacher, with his children; Hershel Rotkovsky, the teacher, with his daughters and sons; Moshe Feivel Klitenik; Yitzchak Landman, Mendel Landman, Aharon Landman and their families (the Viehonoshcha ones); Aharon Abramovich (Gotshnitsa) and family; Yossel David Eisenberg and his sons and daughters; Shalom Shalachman, with his son, Motel, and their families; Makha Dondik, his wife Dina Rivka and their daughters; Cherna the widow and her daughters; the ritual slaughterers Yossel and Aharon Kobrik and their families; Chaikel the butcher; Sender the tailor; Hillel Eisenberg, the tailor; Chaim, the bathhouse attendant; Yozshik, Leiba and Chananiah Mozrirer, and their families; Mordechai, the shoemaker (Basha's); Shama and Esther Kruptshik and their family; Feivel Rubacha (Khasha Leah's son); Freidel Lutsky (Aharon Lutsky's wife) and her family; the widow Eisenberg (Krupnick) and her daughters and son, Itshe Meir, Bashka, Sarah and others.

Everyone didn't arrive at once. Slowly but surely, the Jewish residents of Telekhany reestablished their hometown and rebuilt their homes.

Telekhany Jews were never helpless

In 1917, the Jews of Telekhany who were living in the Polish towns around Warsaw found out that they could return home, and the German authorities gave out permits. No one could have imagined that the town had been burned. The German authorities provided transport assistance, and people were happy to return to Telekhany. However, when they arrived, they found the town to be covered with overgrown weeds, bushes and small birch trees. They had no choice but to move into the barracks that the Germans had built in the forests, around three kilometers from town. However, the returnees still had to live and eat –where were they supposed to get that? Fortunately, it was summertime, and they could find berries, raspberries, mushrooms, and especially lisitsas, which were small, medium and large mushrooms. The Jews collected these fruits, cooked and ate them until the end of the autumn.

When winter arrived, the situation became quite serious. However, even then the Jews didn't give up. Some traveled to the Motele and Kossovo area and bought potatoes, grain, flour and cereals. Others engaged in business, and still others turned to begging. In the spring, people engaged in some work. How Telekhany Jews learned peasant work so quickly is still too hard to explain. The first of several impulses in this direction was simply hunger. In addition, during the war remaining residents had learned these skills from local Motele and Yanovo peasants.

Slowly but surely, people started getting settled, and the Jews thanked G-d that they had returned home to Telekhany and were able to eat enough bread and potatoes, which enabled them to forget about the frightful war.

However, while the Telekhany Jews were involved in their day-to-day concerns, far away there were important events going on. The Russian Revolution liberated all peoples from the huge Czarist empire. The winds of freedom also blew through Telekhany. Jews felt safer and more hopeful; they forgot about their day-to-day troubles, and became deeply involved in their labor. Young men and women in Telekhany, dressed in their best clothes, traveled to Pinsk and Luninetz to welcome the new regime. Even children were proud to think about new pastimes. The fearsome Czar Nicolai no longer scared anyone, and now served as a target for games in which each "soldier" would shoot at the target, thereby relieving his anger and hatred; the children's games would thus provide opportunities for "revenge" for the suffering and worries of their parents, grandparents and great-grandparents.

Unfortunately, the holiday atmosphere quickly dissipated. The Balachov gangs and Petlura's heidemaks were engaged in a struggle with the Bolshevik regime, attacking a whole series of towns in Ukraine and White Russia. They robbed and started pogroms against Jews. Fortunately, these gangs never reached Telekhany.

The situation reached its climax when the Bolsheviks crushed a part of the gangs, and the battles moved far to the eastern, southern and western parts of Russia. In the winter of 1918-1919 Telekhany was like a bear in hibernation, having stored food in their "dens" in order to get through the winter peacefully. What awoke them from their hibernation and disturbed them from their peace was a new army that entered Telekhany in March, 1919. These were Pilsudski's forces, which were dissatisfied with the freedom of the revolution, and which sought to grab territory so as to eject Bolshevik forces from the west.

In the spring of 1919, life for Jews in Telekhany became especially difficult. The new rulers brought the news about the 39 martyrs in Pinsk, taxes and lashes. These events also brought along marauding soldiers who pillaged the forest barracks, and stole the last bit of bread from the Jews. Such attacks on Jewish homes would occur 2-3 times a week. The Jews were powerless and helpless.

The Polish army was able to hold on to Telekhany for months through the peasant partisans in villages such as Hartal, Ritchka and others. Powerless against the peasants, the new regime administered every kind of method to terrorize the local population. They even employed lashes. This type of punishment from the Middle Ages didn't spare Yudel Gurshtel, Nissel's son, Aharon Abramovich (Nochnitsa) as well as some local peasants. Anyone who even protested against the regime was subject to a whipping.

Telekhany lived through a dreadful short period of time. Jews became even more involved with their agricultural work, plowing and sowing –as if they wanted simply to forget the troubles of the new taxes, which were regularly afflicted upon them by new local commanders. In 1920, Telekhany tried to escape the Polish army by moving deeper into the forest, thereby hiding horses, livestock and the last little bit of property from the forest thieves.

There was an exchange of gunfire, and an hour after the retreat of the Polish forces, the first scouting party of the Communists arrived, followed a few hours later by the Red Army. There were regiments of both men and women, as well as units of young people. They hurried westward in order to reach "Warsaw and Berlin."

Telekhany then came to life again. A local government was established, and Jews participated in it. Simcha Zilberstein, Michael Gurshtel, Yankel Klitenik and others were outstanding members of the militia. This didn't last long, however. A few months later, the Red Army had to move eastward again as they were being pursued by the Polish army, which brought with it horrors and whips.

There were horrors of Jewish beards being cut off. The first one to get hit was Leizer Dinovitz, who had been peacefully on his way to prayers at the house of Alter the carpenter (Gurshtel). There weren't any synagogues yet, so people would gather for services in private homes. Leizer didn't expect to run into units of the Polish army on his way to prayers, but suffered a beating for it. How dare a Jew go to prayers carrying his tallith and tefillin when the Polish forces were retaking Telekhany!!

A couple of hours later they captured Alter Gurshtel, and for his "arrogant behavior" on the street, they cut off his beard, but didn't use scissors. Then there were taxes, taxes ad infinitum. The year 1921 was much better. Yaakov Tsirinsky came to Telekhany and built a sawmill on the place where the burned down glassworks stood.

Once again Telekhany came back to life. Jews started turning the forest into lumber, went into construction and started working in the sawmill. Some started baking bread for sale, while others sewed clothes and made shoes for the sawmill workers. Jews started opening retail stores of manufactured products. The first four involved in this were Avraham Chaim Kamadeyev, Gershon Kagan, and Asher and Yudel Gurshtel, who opened grocery stores where Jews dealt with Christians, providing Aharon the Slaughterer (Nachum Perlstein's son-in-law) the monopoly on candles, yeast and kerosene. Whenever a visitor from the United States arrived in Telekhany with letters from friends and relatives, as well as dollars, the joy in town was immense. Jews came back to live. Everyone became involved in rebuilding the town, making it more beautiful and better than it was prior to the war. There was no shortage of building material. Wood was available from the sawmill, and if it was necessary to steal some, well....

There was also no shortage of brick. Part of it was available by digging up the basements in the barracks, and more was available from the "empty brick house," which no longer frightened children as it had their grandparents. More brick was purchased from local peasants.

The town of Telekhany grew. A few people gave up on the town and moved to Russia. They were: Isser Kegelman's two sons and two daughters; Simcha Zilberstein (the Yanover's); Isser and Moshe Shalachman; one of Khasha Leah's grandchildren, and others. They didn't break up the unity of Telekhany, which had forged its population from generation to generation.

The Attack on Telekhany in 1924

It was an autumn day. The town was going about its peaceful day-to-day life, and became accustomed to the new regime, which slowly became established, and which divided businesses for its industry, offering certain discounts for local citizens and wealthy peasants, and providing government institutions with police. Children were forced to attend Polish schools, and people believed that things were being administered better. The Polesia peasants did not forget that they had been separated from their nation and kingdom, and a new regime had been established in their midst, and which with difficulty was proceeding toward a new way of life.

Many villages were incited to rebellion, and their hatred and anger was directed into partisan separatism that lasted from 1919 to 1924-25, when international stability caused them to disband. One of their last acts was the attack on Telekhany, when the partisans captured the entire town. The goal was to attack the police and disarm them, and to capture the local Polish administrators, arrest them, and shoot them and the police.

However, something else happened. Unknown covert operatives appeared in groups of three or four on the streets of Telekhany. Their unexpected arrival frightened the Telekhany residents. It was clear that the unknown visitors were armed, and that on one fine autumn day they were preparing for a dreadful attack.

The armed groups, surprised by the easy victory went to collect money from the wealthy local residents and, facing slight resistance from Sarah Gurshtel (Nissel the shipper's wife), they shot her. They also shot policemen, the local administrator and Yaakov Klitenik, and a son of Zavel the butcher.

The attack made an awful impression on the residents of Telekhany – such a dreadful night, and so many innocent lives. It is difficult even to describe it. Why did the partisans shoot two Jews who weren't even part of the government administration? It took the Telekhany Jews a long time to forget that unlucky night. Even the slightest rustle was a frightening warning that the attacks may be continuing.

The youth of Telekhany get organized

It was now a few years after the peace agreement between the Bolsheviks, and Poland was on a volcano that rumbled from time to time. The workers felt the force of the government, which had to invest all of its energy to controlling the progress of the working class, and to suffocating every liberation movement in rivers of blood. However, the guns of the Polish nobility's gendarmerie and the police didn't stave off economic crisis, which grew worse by the day. Inflation was growing so fast that the monthly earnings of a worker amounted to millions of marks, which could only purchase a few bags of mushrooms.

The youth of Telekhany was devoted to its progressive traditions, and in 1922 the youth established their first organization, although it was far from being a full-fledged movement. Everyone felt the necessity to create the bases for broad cultural activity that could be expressed by a wealthy library. The youth involved were: Pinya Mazrirer, Michel

Tshizh, Rivka Abramovich, Itka Meltzer, Doba Rotkovitsky, Yehoshua Eisenberg, Riva Levin, Toiba Schneidman and many others. At the same time, Mordechai Bromberg, a progressive and leftist activist, came to Telekhany. He provided significant assistance in organizing the library, and showed the young people broad perspectives in their project. Everyone agreed that it was most important to first organize the young people, and they would then find their proper course of action.

Among those who were the first of the young people in the organization that was first known as Hashomer Hatsa'ir [the left-wing Zionist movement, "Young Guard"], were: Yossel and Shetel Schneidman, Dovka Klitenik, Yoel Mazrirer, Ephraim and Leibel Klitenik, Golda Stolyar, Khaytshe Lutsky, Yisraelik Bernstein, Yisrael David Kagan, Rosa Abramovich, Nekhka Meltzer, Nechemiah Levin, Yehoshua Sklyar and others. They were mostly youth around 15-16 years of age, and were already involved in workshops where they worked for 15-16 hours a day, and therefore experienced the heavy yoke of the nobility's capitalist Poland.

With tremendous energy and desire, the young people got to work. They became known to their friends, and very rapidly the small group grew into two strong youth organizations: Left Poalei Zion [socialist non-Marxist "Workers of Zion"] and the Left [appears that the name of an organization may be missing]. They continued the work of building the library, and its reading room, where a lot of cultural activity took place. Each one of the aforementioned organizations made its ideological platform clear, and worked for its program. Professional organizations that included practically all the working youth were also created.

In 1926, the Left called the first strike among the sawmill workers. Several hundred workers went on strike. The workers demanded an 8-hour workday, higher wages, recognition of the worker's union, and a whole list of other demands. The strike was a success. Several weeks later, a second strike was called. This one included all local artisans and workers: shoemakers, tailors, carpenters, locksmiths and blacksmiths. They demanded an 8-hour workday, higher wages, and recognition of their professional organization.

The strike developed slowly, with the participation of increasingly more workshops. The determination of the strike leaders and their pronouncements inspired the entire youthful population to participate in the struggle. Business owners started their own counter-action, even threatening to bring in the government authorities, but the unity of the strikers forced the business owners to offer concessions. The strike committee was composed of Ephraim Klitenik, Yosef Schneidman, Hershel Kagan, Leibel Chernomoritz and Shimon Yaakov

Gurshtel. The monolithic position of the strike committee influenced the entire young working population. It was a long time since Telekhany had witnessed such a strongly unified strike action.

In the autumn of 1926-27, a series of demonstrations were organized in Sventovalia and Kossovo against Pilsudski's fascist regime; the party and youth of Telekhany also played an active role there. Their march forward spread to the nearby towns of Kossovo, Yanovo, Motele, Lahishin, Sventovalia and others. The Polish nobility capitalist regime kept track of these activities, and started to take repressive measures.

In the spring of 1927, Mordechai Bromberg, Leibel Eisenberg and Mordechai Bobrow were arrested, as were a whole group of their White Russian friends. In the summer of 1927 contacts were established, and the activity of these young people spread to many areas where there were working youth.

This activity included a whole host of issues: labor culture, the library and the reading room. The administration included Yisrael David Kagan and Yisrael Bernstein; the professional work was handled by Ephraim Klitenik, Yosef Schneidman, Yoshka Meltzer, Shimon Yaakov Gurshtel, Leibel Klitenik and Yisrael Begin. The illegal activities were undertaken with the extraordinary activity and assistance of Yisrael Bernstein, Leibel Klitenik, Shimshon Landman, Yisrael David Kagan and others.

Their work lasted until 1928, at which time Ephraim and Leibel Klitenik were arrested. Gedaliah [last name missing] went into hiding, and eventually left Poland. The activities of the young people was interrupted for a short time, but in 1929 it was continued by Shimshon Landman, Yisrael David Kagan, Yisraelik Bernstein, Motke Roshchinder, Berl Rubacha, and was led by Leibel Klitenik, who was released after a year's stay in jail. This time their work lasted until 1931, when new arrests were made, and some of the aforementioned were arrested. The following received jail sentences: Mordechai Bromberg, 6 years; Leibel Eisenberg, 4 years; Ephraim Klitenik, 6 years; Leibel Klitenik, 5 years; Yisrael David Kagan, Shimshon Landman and Yisraelik Bernstein, 4 years. The increased repression led to the emigration from Poland of a large number of young people. Then the influence of the Left spread and drew in young people from other organizations that sympathized and collaborated with it. These people included Golda and Beiltshe Roshchinder, Mina Gurshtel, Rivka Feldman, Shaul Ber, Levi Laufer and others.

The fascist regime devoted all its attention to the youth of Telekhany, and dealt a harsh blow to any attempt to rebuild the leftist organization, but it was unable to stifle the desire for freedom. The work of the young people was driven deeply underground, but all contacts were maintained.

At the outbreak of World War II in 1939, the young people of Telekhany did not disperse, but on the contrary got organized, and by September 17, 1939, when the Red Army broke through its borders to liberate western White Russia and western Ukraine, there were organized authorities in Telekhany that were able to maintain law and order in Telekhany and surrounding areas until the arrival of the regular Red Army forces.

In the newly elected committee, the following people were members: Ephraim and Leibel Klitenik, Yisrael David Kagan, Yisraelik Bernstein, Motka Roshchinder, Berl Rubacha and others.

————

[Page 62]

September 21, 1939
by Dina Godiner

The day came when we were finally convinced that the Red Army was really about to arrive in White Russia, and Telekhany was also expecting the new "guests." On September 21, 1939, a dozen or so Red Army soldiers arrived in Telekhany from Pinsk, and the entire town went out to meet them. A large meeting was held at which many Jews and Christians came out to greet the honored guests and liberators. Telekhany then gradually relaxed, without fear of fleeing officers or the specter of war.

In October, local government elections were held in Telekhany, and were based on a secret ballot. A large and fiery meeting was held at the Folks Club, and everyone was in a holiday mood. Many candidates appeared, and the Jewish candidates elected were: Yisraelik Bernstein, Yisrael David Kagan, Ephraim and Leibel Klitenik. For the first time a woman was elected chairman, and her deputy was Ephraim Klitenik, who a while later was elected People's Judge, and who performed his duties wisely and appropriately. Frequently his father, David Klitenik, would visit his son at work; Ephraim was thoughtful, quiet and proud. David, with his fine happy eyes was a proud father who understood his crusading son well. Yisraelik Bernstein was later nominated as director of the sawmill. Many good White Russians were also elected to the local government.

Both Jewish and White Russian schools were started. Asher Pelach from Pinsk, a wonderful person and a fine psychologist, stood out among all the teachers. He won over the children and connected them to him with his clever approach and ability to penetrate deeply into the children souls. The young people in Telekhany mirrored their teacher, who loved and gave his students so much; the students grew up proud, fine and exalted.

Unfortunately, the pleasure and calm enjoyed by Telekhany parents didn't last long. No one could have ever imagined that blooming flowers like the Jewish children of Telekhany and their worthy teacher, Asher Pelach, with his dreamy black eyes, would soon be killed so horribly.

Telekhany, a Shtetl known for its Hospitality

Never before had Telekhany seen so many new faces –so many fine young men and women. These people had fled Warsaw, Lodz, Katowitz and many other Polish cities captured by the Nazi murderers. Telekhany was well known for its hospitality, and all the refugees appreciated this and loved Telekhany.

Aharon Godiner didn't have large rooms, and he put a bed in his dining room for Yoliek, a quiet and refined refugee boy from Warsaw. Yoliek didn't lack anything, and felt right at home. Godiner shared his morsels of food with him and was very kind, even kinder than to his own children. For a time, Yoliek was thoughtful but lonesome. He missed Warsaw and his friends and sisters who he left behind, and who were now in such grave peril.

Among the refugees there were very gifted young people who had to escape from home with empty hands. Thanks to an initiative of Ephraim Klitenik, Jews in Telekhany collected money and other things for the refugees. The local Jews provided them with jobs and even work permits. Many of the intellectuals worked as teachers, accountants and employees, and many tailors from Warsaw created their own joint workshops. Ephraim provided them with his own sewing machine, press iron, and quilts. For many months, they worked and made money. With great joy, Telekhany Jews often heard the refugees' happy laughter and singing.

We flee from death

Only twenty-one months later our peaceful and carefree lives were interrupted, as was our pleasure in helping the lonely Warsaw refugees; our satisfaction in getting to know so many new strangers who now became so close to us was also affected. The Jewish children in Telekhany were growing, studying and making progress. There were dances and successful performances at the Folks Club; we met new children and got to know new places. Then suddenly, everything turned upside down. The sun set so unexpectedly, and darkness overcame us.

June 23, 1941. Ephraim was at work; he had shift duty, and as usual I waited impatiently for him. He was standing watch, and wouldn't come home that night. The next day the Germans made a surprise attack on the Soviet Union. They crossed the Bug River and bombed every town. As they advanced they saw death and destruction everywhere.

Rumors circulated in town that our army was holding its positions, and that the war would not last long. Almost all the men were to be mobilized, and it appeared that the wooden shacks were weeping along with the women, who were saying their goodbyes to their husbands and sons as the men left for parts unknown.

It was a dark night. I peered through the window and saw bright flames, like fiery flashes of lightning, from the direction of Pinsk. There were also frightful sounds like thunder in a bad storm (this demolished the Pinsk Bridge). Then came a soft knock at the door. My heart trembled with dread and a premonition. It was Kizelstein, the director of the White Russian school. He fled alone from Warsaw and lived through a terrible tragedy in Telekhany. He said he didn't want to run away any more –he didn't have any more strength or courage, but encouraged us to leave Telekhany as quickly as possible. He had just seen how all the officials and their families were getting ready to flee.

Kizelstein's little gentle wife died, and his newborn baby lived a short time and then Kizelstein was left alone. I ran breathlessly to get dressed, and I was barely able to convince him to abandon his guard duty, and that we should save ourselves and escape Hitler's fire.

Together we ran over to Leibel's house. Leibel had just returned from Pinsk by foot. (He was in Pinsk for a conference, and the war impeded his return). He was now asleep like a dead man. We woke him up and told him the terrible news, and then all went on our way. My father was in a fitful sleep, but my beautiful, good but very ill little sister Beila couldn't sleep.

"Father, get up, let's go!" He raised his tired head, "What's wrong? Where and to whom are we going?" He motioned with his clean but resolute and overworked hands. "Do you see? With these hands I built everything my whole life. Every drop of my blood is inside every brick and corner of my house. How can I just leave it, and suddenly start wandering around?"

My good and holy father! The best and most decent man in the world. In a short time the German bandits came around with guns. They came to my him, my step-mother, Itka, her young grandson and my poor little sister, Beila, and pointed a gun at them, ordering them to leave the house as fast as possible. To this day there is a living witness who was at our home – my father's White Russian partner at work. We quickly said goodbye to each other, and to this very day I can still feel my father's tears on my face.

We carefully woke up Ephraim's parents and his sister Necha and her family, who were sound asleep. Ephraim's mother, Leah, opened her eyes and asked, "Efroyka, what do you want? Cheese and cream (She knew what her son liked)? It's in the kitchen on the table."

"Mother, we have to say goodbye." Her nearsighted eyes started to brighten but showed fear. "Say goodbye? I have rarely said goodbye in my life. We have rarely ever been separated, so tragically separated."

Ephraim's father, David, always remained a hero. He awakened calmly, got dressed quickly, and turned to us, "Children! You have to get out of here as quickly as possible, and I'll go along with you with Yossel's horse for a short distance (Yossel, Ephraim's brother-in-law and Necha's husband, had been drafted).

After a tragic goodbye to all of our loved ones, we left town in a hurry. Ephraim's father, David, accompanied us for a few kilometers, and then he started feeling sad and already missing us. "I am going to take the horse along, and we'll all escape together my children." He left, and didn't come back. We waited a long time on the road, and every minute was a frightening moment to have to wait in the forest, but we hoped that they would come back. We still didn't know what happened to David. It's possible that the peasants had already killed him on the road since there were plenty of murderers among the local peasants who were lying in wait to pounce on any Jew with the help of German murderers.

We ran through fields and forests without a moment's rest. We wouldn't spend the night in the same place we spent the day. We met many Telekhany Jews who unfortunately returned home –it wasn't easy to run away through an unfamiliar country without even a piece of bread or hope. Airplanes droned ominously and frightfully in the sky, and here and there a bomb fell. The sound reverberated from the distance, and it felt the earth was shaking. Then we heard shots being fired over our head –some German airplanes were firing at a heavy Soviet aircraft. We almost became deaf from the sound of the bangs. We saw the aircraft burning with the Soviet pilots. This was the first fire we saw so close to us.

Day in and day out –eight uninterrupted days we traveled by foot. During the day the sun beat down on us, and at night we shivered from cold.

Where should we go? Minsk was burning, Bobroisk was under occupation, and German mechanized army units were on all the highways.

A powerful feeling gripped our hearts. As we continued, we came upon a small town called Kopshevitch, which still had a Soviet government. We didn't arrive alone, since along the way we met my brother Asher and many people from Hortzevich. The representatives of Kopshevitch treated us very well. They took us to a clinic, where a nice nurse bandaged our bloody and swollen feet. They also gave us food and drink, and we felt like we were in an oasis in the middle of a desert. We slept the whole night, and departed the next day feeling very grateful to our warm hosts.

Once again we felt like hunted animals with wounded and beaten feet. We were accompanied everywhere only by the sounds of bombs and anti-aircraft fire as we tried to repress the pain and longings for home and loved ones, whom we left, and about whom we had no idea that they would be brutally murdered and buried in mass graves forever.....

[Page 66]

My Brother Shmuel
by Esther Godiner Miller
(Los Angeles)

My brother Shmuel Nissen Godiner was born in 1893 in the little town of Telekhany, Minsk gubernia [district]. Our parents were very religious and also very poor. Our family believed that our name, Godiner, was derived from the Yiddish expression, Got-diener, meaning servants of G-d, pointing to fear of G-d. Our father, Israel David, and grandfather, Moshe, leased a piece of land in the village Viade; they were very religious, and Father was a great scholar. He was supposed to become a Rabbi, but became a teacher instead. From early morning until late evening he stuffed his pupils' little heads with Torah. He had great respect for scholars, but disdain for Rabbis. Perhaps this was because the rabbi in our town played a decisive role in my father's divorce of his first wife. I once overheard him saying: "I begged them not to separate a body from its soul"; his appeal didn't do any good. The Rabbi said that since the woman was barren, he had to divorce her.

My father then married a woman from Pinsk who was a totally different kind of person: our mother, Fradel, came from well-to-do parents, and had a relatively modern education by the standards of those days; she also knew foreign languages. She was very energetic and well built. As a single woman she worked, not because she needed to, but to show that women were able to work as well as men, and that there was nothing to be shamed of in working.

Coming from parents with various traits and talents, since early childhood my brother Shmuel Nissan adopted our father's reverence for Torah and tradition, and mother's inclination for modern education, her energy and common sense. Shmuel was the fourth and last child of our parents. When he was born, the oldest, Aaron, was 12 years old. The other two were girls: Chana and Esther, the writer of this story. Due to our poverty, everybody had to be somewhat of a provider –if not to earn money, then at least to get rid of an eater. The oldest, Aaron, attended a trade school in Pinsk and boarded with relatives. The girls also found places without earning anything for three years, and then in the fourth year they earned 10 rubles. But the biggest provider was Shmuel starting at age 1 week.

It happened that the wife of a well-to-do shopkeeper died at childbirth. Her husband gave the baby orphan to Mother to nurse two children at the same time. The shopkeeper took care to provide my mother with cow's milk, sugar, plums, raisins, almonds and other goodies we had never seen before. My mother ate kasha and barley soup, and distributed the goodies to us children. We of course enjoyed it very much and loved the little orphan, and what's more, our baby brother -- the great provider.

When Shmuel Nissen was six years old my father took him under his supervision. "It's time, little boy, to become a Jew" he said, and pinched his cheek. He started teaching him to read and write Yiddish and Hebrew, Torah with the Rashi commentary, the rest of the Bible, and later Talmud as well. Shmuel had a good head, and caught on quickly. Our parents were pleased, and Father started talking about having a son who studied in Yeshiva, a scholar. Mother, however, argued that "a doctor is even better" But what did Shmuel Nissan himself do? Besides the Gemarah, he sneaked a look into the booklets brought by his older sisters from the "Sisters and Brothers".

I remember once on a Sabbath afternoon, Father and Shmuel were delving deeply into a particular Mishnah. Our grandfather Moshe enters the room. At first his face lit up with joy. Suddenly, however, his expression darkened when he noticed a booklet in his grandson's hand. He drew my father's attention to it. Father tried to take the unkosher booklet from Shmuel's hand, and accidentally tore a page. This created a stir, and amounted to a desecration of the Sabbath. Shmuel got a proper slap on his face, and a demand to know where he got this unkosher thing. Shmuel was ready for another beating, but didn't say a word.

There weren't any more beatings, however. Mother and Esther came from the other room. Mother embraced her youngest child and scolded the two men: "What do you want from the child? Why do you upset him?" Grandfather left angry, grumbling: "Wicked woman". Father also retreated, but never forgot the event.

The next day, Sunday morning, Father went to Avraham-Itshe the "Miracle Worker" (he got this nickname because of his weak bladder and therefore the need to recite the blessing after going to the bathroom that ends with the words "....and He does wondrously"). Avraham-Itshe also had a daughter who was a member of the "Sisters and Brothers". Both fathers reflected on what to do with their children who were leaving the righteous way, reading unkosher books, and desecrating the Sabbath. They came up with the idea to create a society, "Guardians of the Sabbath," to make sure that shops closed on time, and that the youth kept the Sabbath.

Shmuel Nissan didn't rest either. He went to his friend Monye Beises, a smart and energetic boy. Together they organized the "Little Bund". Telekhany thus got two new organizations from the older and younger generations. It didn't take long for their influence to be felt in Telekhany. The teenage boys and girls felt the watchful eyes of their parents, and the owners of the workshops noticed the activities of the 12-13 year-olds of the Little Bund who made announcements, and told workers not to be slaves. However, because people had no choice, the Little Bund even started breaking windows. People had to be at work on the eve of Jewish and Christian holidays, when the owners forced the workers to slave away for more than ten hours a day.

Shmuel gradually felt constrained in town and at home. After three years working for nothing, I also realized that earning 10 rubles a year wasn't enough for shoes and clothing. So we decided to follow our older brother to Warsaw. Our older sister, Chana, now Anna (Godiner) Garker, was already in America. In Warsaw, Shmuel became a steelworker and was proud of it. The free time he used to study and read. He taught himself Russian and German from books, and liked the big city. He was even happier later on when we managed to persuade our family to move to Warsaw.

Warsaw was overcoming the consequences of the unsuccessful 1905 revolution. The 16- year old Shmuel became confused. On the one hand were the disappointed intellectuals seeking God, while on the other, the libertine and trashy Yiddish theater and press. Shmuel got restless. He felt something had to be done. He began writing, sometimes until the early morning hours. He often talked to me, his older sister, about it, and once confided to me that he had written something he wanted to show to I.L.Peretz. He thus became apologetic, and said he wanted to ask Peretz why the great rabbinical leaders of our time were doing so little for Jewish youth.

A few weeks later Shmuel organized a cultural circle for boys and girls, to help I. L. Peretz in his effort to improve the quality of Yiddish theater and press. During a session at the Warsaw Philharmonic, Peretz excited the people with his call: "Don't watch the Yiddish theater, do not read the rubbish press."

Peretz inspired the youth greatly. Shmuel idolized him, and took to writing with even greater aplomb. He took his articles to Peretz and came home satisfied. "Peretz read it and told me to continue, but it's a pity that he considers me still a child," Shmuel said. Later I found out that after reading Shmuel's critique of Hillel Zeitlin's lecture on seeking G-d, Peretz told Shmuel: "You are still too young to write about such topics."

In 1913 my brother Shmuel wrote his sisters in America that a big world war is on its way, and in 1914 he was already in the trenches himself. He lived through everything suffered by a soldier in the Czarist army. Once he was deadly sick for days on the open field. He recovered and then later joined the Red Army. Miserable and in rags, they fought against the capitalist foreign intervention. In 1921 he came to Moscow. He was sent by the Soviet officials to get tuition-free higher education. He studied and wrote intensely –mostly about civil war and foreign intervention. He also painted pictures and hung them on the wall as if to say: "Look at this and be ashamed if you still have a conscience." His productive years began, and lasted for twenty years, until 1941. Besides his permanent job at the Moscow "Emes [Truth]", he wrote many books. Among them are "Jim Coopercop", "Figures on the Edge", "The Opposite Day" and others. His favorite was "The Man with the Gun".

Shmuel Nissen Godiner did a lot for the development of Birobidzhan. He was sent there twice a year to open Yiddish schools for children, libraries and in general to expand Yiddish culture. He did all this with great enthusiasm. He was proud of the Soviet system that restored national self-worth to the Jews. For this he was ready to work, create and die if necessary. In the summer 1941 Shmuel's literary work came to a stop. "There is no time for words" he said, no time for literature. The enemy will not understand it. The only thing the enemy understands is a spear or a bayonet.

In August, 1941, Shmuel Godiner wrote in his last letter to his sisters, Chana and Esther, in America: "I take my son Vatzlav -- he is with the Red Army, I with the partisans. "I hope that you will not just sit on the sidelines, but will become actively involved in the struggle against the bitter enemy. Remember my wife and two daughters!" The

48 year old Shmuel Godiner, shared the terrible conditions of the Russian partisans for a whole year. He believed in the victory of the Soviet Army.

In the summer of 1942 he came back to Moscow to see his wife and daughters. The government discouraged older men from going to the front, but Shmuel didn't want to stay in Moscow. He was determined to take part in the battle against the fascist invader, and couldn't just stay put. He returned to the partisans from where he never came back home.

There is nothing more to say ... Shmuel Godiner was a fine and productive person. He wasn't the only fine and productive person taken from us by fascism. "This is no time for words!" -- he said. Let us remember this, and let's also speed up our struggle against fascism here in the United States. Only by taking part in this battle will we be able to pay back the enormous debt we owe both our millions of martyrs and future generations.

[Page 71]
The Lives and work of the Telekhany Youth
Mina Baron
12 Av, 5719 [August 16, 1959], Haifa Israel

It's the 10th year that Jews from Telekhany in Israel are lighting a candle in memory of their sacred martyrs. The 10th candle is being lit in Tel Aviv on the 12th day of Av, in honor of their sacred memory. Seventeen years have passed, but the wounds are still fresh and open, and they will not heal as long as there is even one Nazi beast alive and free.

The town is overgrown by weeds, it is crying. Big cities have gradually recovered. Telekhany still bears the devastation they left in their wake – death and destruction.

Telekhany was a flourishing town with spirited dynamic young people; their characteristics were inherited from the first fighters from before World War I, the "Brothers and Sisters". At that time the "Brothers and Sisters" fought heroically against those who exploited them, and our youth followed in their footsteps after World War I.

When our parents returned to devastated Telekhany after World War I, we were still small children. They struggled hard to make a living, but spiritually they lived beautifully. Everyone found what he needed. Among them were Zionists, chasidim, non-chasidim, etc. The point is that nobody became demoralized under the yoke of everyday life. Everybody loved the printed word and everybody avidly read books. They kept Jewish traditions and observed Jewish holidays. Together with our parents, we children joyfully celebrated Passover, Shavuot, Simchat Torah and Chanukah. But this ideal didn't last for long. We children grew up, and each one chose his own path according to his own inclination.

The children grew into fine and happy young people. They aspired to work and to be industrious. They didn't want to become "Luftmenschen -- jack of all trades". Everyone learned a trade. In Telekhany the main professions were tailoring, carpentry, shoemaking, with a blacksmith here and there.

The young people were divided into different political parties. Sometimes they argued with each other, but they also participated in joint activities. But there was one place that united them all: the beautiful, flowering the little avenue where they enjoyed taking a stroll together and from where songs could be heard all over town until late into the night. Everybody in town, young and old alike, liked to meet the steamboat arriving from Pinsk each evening. If the boat was ever delayed, people would wait for it until midnight. They felt something missing if they didn't hear the sound of the boat's horn, or if they didn't see the water in the lock rising toward town and then later falling again. Next morning if somebody was yawning, you would know that the boat was late the day before.

Meeting the boat became a kind of ritual that lasted until the canal waters froze. But then again, the frozen canal brought fun as well. On Saturday mornings young people liked to take a stroll on the ice to Voulk Lake. The children skated, and the adults got a little winter sun, enjoying the children's happy laughter as the children ran and slipped on the ice.

Thus my little town enjoyed both winter and summer, and a happy life obviously made active young people. They loved life and strove to make it useful. They were focused on life's purpose, which was their main principle, and due to that principle each person sought to learn a trade, and excel in their work so they could always live normally. Everything they produced was filled with love. The Rightists used to say that if they were able to love working in the Diaspora, they would love working in Eretz Yisrael. The Leftists cited Lenin's words: "If you love your work here and now, you will like it under a proletariat system also." Thanks to these sacred goals, our young people lived active and happy, and their parents were proud of their sons and daughters.

Before I start writing about the political parties that divided our youth, I want to briefly immortalize my parents of blessed memory; our good neighbor Yisrael Mashiach and his wife; my friend Rifka Beinishes and my teacher Chaim Yeshayahu.

My Mother Malke Reuvens

This beautiful, tall person. Where are the words to describe her while my hands tremble and my heart pounds?

When the fatigue from her hard workday passed, her mild candid smile spread over her pretty face, and she was in a good mood, Mother would gather us children in the dining room, around the big table and told us beautiful children's stories. With her beautiful and rich language she enchanted us and excited our children's fantasy. When we grew older, she told us stories about wars, revolutions, and finished by singing the French national anthem, the Marseillaise. With this anthem she expressed her militant character, and with the stories she expressed her rich imagination. At the same time, however, she was a down-to-earth person. She ingrained in us the conviction that a person should not wander, because it destroys one's livelihood. Her slogan was: "Even a stone grows in one place." Oh, dear mother, who is able to express the horrendous pain? Death to your killers! For you, the eternal memory of your children and all freedom fighters.

My Father Reuven Gurstel

The working man, the enthusiastic chasid, the active Zionist who worked with such endless dedication and devotion for his ideal. His little son Motye asked him once: "Father, why do all people have lands of their own, except the Jews?" He cried bitterly in response to the question. Oh, how far I was then from your idea, Father! But when I stood years later with my little son Reuben in Israel, on a plaza and heard the proclamation of Israel's independence, saw our Jewish fluttering flag rising higher and higher, announcing our freedom, I saw our people standing there with bowed heads and tears of joy flowing from their eyes. Then, father, I fully understood your tears from years ago. And my heart ached for you father, who couldn't live to see the fulfillment of our age-old dream.

In building this land, we honor you father. Be your memory sacred and eternal.

Yisrael Mashiach and his wife Sarah Mashiach

Our best neighbors. Yisrael Schwarzenberg, the tall man with the friendly smiling eyes and skillful oven builder. He made his ovens as fast as a person can braid a challah for the Sabbath. Here he put up the base, and then before you know it, the chimney is already on the roof.

When he stood there looking satisfied at his work, you would think that he was working just for pure pleasure rather than for his livelihood.

Mashiach [Messiah] was his nickname. People in town liked to come to his house on long winter nights and sit at his table and pour glass after glass of hot tea from his samovar that stood in the middle of the table. They would enjoy drinking and telling stories from the past and of the future. His wife, Sarah, a tall and honest woman like her husband had warm kind eyes. She kindly offered her snacks and listened to their guests' conversation. The next day she would come over to Mother and discuss the issues. Their warm house is unforgettable. May their memory be engraved in our hearts!

The parents of my friend Rivka Beinishes.

They were a nice quiet family. They lived on the outskirts of town, on the road to Sventevolye. Her mother was a refined dear woman, and her father, a hard worker. When their five sons and three daughters passed the street, it seemed like the earth is trembling under their steps. They were the personification of health and beauty.

Rivka, my friend! The epitome of diligence. She worked nightshifts at the sawmill, and during the day she would help her mother in the house. She was in the fields in summer, and worked in weaving in the winter. She was always helping a friend or a little brother.

Rivka, Rivka! The memory of you will be sacred to me forever.

And last but not least ---

Chaim Yeshayahu Shneidman

My teacher who taught me the alphabet. I would like to dedicate a few words to my childhood, the poor childhood we all shared.

Coming back after World War I to the demolished town, Chaim Yeshayahu lived near the glass factory, and we lived in town, in Uncle Yankel's house. Since we studied into the late evenings, we had to bring a bottle of kerosene [probably meaning a kerosene lantern]. On our way home, the Landowner Filipowitch's dogs would attack us. Our cries would wake up the half sleeping town. At that time we also suffered from the terrible illness of malaria [trans.: should probably be typhus, since malaria is a tropical disease]. We often had to leave kheder and go home with chattering teeth. When we got home, our little bodies fell right into bed, suffering from chills and high fever. There was no doctor in town to help us.

In such a bitter childhood, Chaim Yeshayahu was our beacon. His small room was warm, and he radiated warmth and beauty, something which warmed and healed us children. I still remember him teaching us the song, Oifen pripetschuk brent a feirel [On the stove burns a fire], Yehudit stubbornly refused to sing along. So he patted her little braids in a fatherly manner and said: "Sing, sing, Yehudisel, why are you quiet?" The little girl then opened her mouth and sang. I can still see Chaim Yeshayahu's laughing eyes. I was sitting open mouthed after he finished the biblical story about Joseph being sold by his brothers. I expressed my astonishment over the misdeed carried out against Joseph. Chaim asked me, "Do you like the story?" "Yes, yes" I answered, "continue the story."

He used all his inborn pedagogic skills to enrich and sweeten our lives, cure our souls damaged by the recent war. He wanted to teach us not only the alphabet, but also how to laugh and have fun. His patriarchal look has never left me ever since I came here. He embodied the greatest virtues of the Jewish people. Praise and honor to his memory!

Now I can return to the youth of Telekhany, to whom I dedicate my article. As I mentioned earlier, the youth were active – they weren't reticent about seeking the truth. The main question was regarding which path to follow. Their slogan was "Know yourself first. You will then know what your life's purpose is, since knowledge is the basis for reaching the goal."

There were three political movements in Telekhany: the Chalutz [Pioneer], the Left Poalei Zion [Workers of Zion], and the Communists. Each person strove where his heart and will led him. There were also young people who were not affiliated politically – they were the children of the wealthy. However, their education wasn't better than ours. On the contrary, we never ceased to educate ourselves, while their main goal was material attainment. They also, however, loved reading books. Workers, craftsmen and simple poor unskilled shift workers all enjoyed reading, because they found intellectual satisfaction in reading as well as an opportunity to spend a couple of hours with the protagonists of the books.

It should be noted that a few years before I left (I departed in 1935) there was a modern Hebrew school in Telekhany, as well as a Polish school standing on a hill. The parents decided to bring in a woman teacher from Pinsk. One child after the other thereafter became attracted to a modern education.

There were political disputes among our youth, just like there are everywhere in the world. However, as I mentioned, there were activities that were undertaken together, and they were very successful, i.e. the cooperation in developing the library and other things. There was one place where in the beauty and mystery of nature the young people forgot about their disputes and arguments. It was the place where they were all united. In the evenings they would go out to stroll on the alleys and row on the canal. The beauty and stillness of nature brought hearts and minds together for the great thought of brotherhood and peace! They sang worker's songs, revolutionary songs and love songs.

I can still hear the words of one song that so strongly lamented the fate of the poor:

> People drink and have fun,
> And their pockets are always full,
> Yet I don't drink or have fun,
> And my pocket is always empty.
> (This song was in Russian and this was the introductory
> refrain).

The youth would walk along arm in arm until dawn because they all loved the stillness of the evening, and their souls longed to hear the sounds of nature, and lie and relax in its bosom. It was in the evening that nature revealed to us its entire splendor! Our feelings found themselves in a quiet tune, and we would just lie down, carefree, on the green grass and stroll along the fragrant paths and alleys. The water rumbled along freely, accompanying our singing.

The greatest expression of beauty was on Friday evenings. The young people would breathe quietly, listening to the sounds of the breeze, which they would then follow with revelry and song. Their parents were sleeping soundly on the Sabbath, and after midnight, when the leaves started rustling, the frogs croaking and the crickets chirping in the dark nooks and crannies. After midnight nature began its real symphony – the sound of the animals that were grazed by the shepherds in the hot daytime hours. This was the sign for us that it was time to go home.

We tiptoed home ever so quietly, and got into bed, making sure not to make the slightest sound to awake our parents, who were fast asleep at that time, and waiting impatiently for their pets. The next day, when daylight broke, we would hit ourselves, realizing that we were going to be late for work. However, the candlesticks on the table reminded us that it was the Sabbath, and we could relax as much as we wanted, and thanked G-d that he provided toiling people with a Sabbath.

Political Party Activities

I can't say much about the Halutz [Pioneer] movement, since I wasn't involved with their activities, but so I don't misrepresent anything, I am going to only record what I actually remember.

The members of the Halutz were extremely enthusiastic Zionists. Their slogan was to shake off the despondency of the Diaspora, and aspired to a complete redemption in the land of their fathers. Their activity focused on this idea, and they diligently studied the history of the Jewish People. In the summer they would organize seminars.

The Pinsk members would come to Telekhany and work in the sawmill. They would work diligently and with love, because they were dreaming about their homeland, for which it was worth sweating and toiling. In the evenings, they would go around with their koleikelach that would carry on boards and pilenas during the day; their joy and laughter used to cut through the air.

The Telekhany members would spend time in training in other places. They would stay there and work for a couple of years or longer. Some considered this training program a difficult activity, but they all believed they were working toward their goal of traveling to Palestine, building the Land and fertilize its earth. And did they ever fertilize it! They turned deserts into blooming gardens, and under the burning sun they added one brick to another, building their homes. They did this with the same devotion as they worked when they were in the Telekhany sawmill.

Now, on to the Left of the Poalei Zion [Workers of Zion]

The Left of the Poalei Zion believed that the redemption of the Jewish People could only occur in Palestine. They also believed in a socialist society in Palestine, and that there, in the center of the Jewish People, the proletariat would bring about their redemption and that of the entire Jewish People. They believed that Jewish class interests demanded a large area, which was possible only in their own territory.

There was a large library in town, and the readers elected the librarians. The readers eagerly devoured the best of world literature. The librarian would propose a book to a reader according to his knowledge and age. Everyone was careful not to ruin a young person with an inappropriate book. Since there was no movie theater in Telekhany, the minds of the young people remained as pure as crystal; there was no foreign influence to affect them, since Telekhany was far from larger centers, and each person shaped his own life without foreign influences.

Literature evenings were held from time to time. I can still remember the trial over Gladkov's book Cement, and how people concentrated on the defendant and plaintiff. They talked about the main protagonist, Dasha, and whether her ethical conduct as woman, wife and mother was correct. Each person offered his own opinion according to his own feelings about the issues involved, and was deeply concerned about the fact that the story took place in the opening stages of the Russian Revolution, when people were trying to figure out how to arrange his own life under the new circumstances. Most people justified their parents.

The Left Poalei Zion also had a drama club, and their performances were a great event in town. Young and old, and even the summer cottage residents would flock to the performances. The residents of Telekhany would welcome and escort the performers with stormy applause. They did it over and over again! This was the best occasion for the performers to be able to show their artistic talents, and since they would rehearse their parts, the result was very natural and beautiful. The Telekhany audience particularly liked tragedies, which would leave them with a strong impression. In fact, they actually liked seeing themselves on stage.

A couple of times we were visited by a theater group from Vilna, but not everyone could attend the performance due to the high price of the tickets. Once in a while a silent movie would also be shown in Telekhany. People were hungry for some intellectual stimulation. Sometimes a member of the Left Poalei Zion would come to town to give a lecture. When Zerubavel came to town, it was a major event, and everyone flocked to hear him. Younger people were a bit disappointed because they used to discuss the same issues day and night. Their parents especially enjoyed his stately presence and white beard, and they were highly impressed that a Jew with a beard could speak so freely about worldly issues, and then go off with the young people and sit on Yisrael Meltzer's bridge until midnight (Zerubavel used to stay at the hotel near Yisrael Meltzer).

Another pleasant and special evening for the young people was when Erem came as an emissary from Palestine. We surrounded him and devoured all of his stories. After he finished speaking, he would teach us Zionist songs and a shepherd's song that I can still remember. On that evening, I could imagine seeing a sheep prancing down from Mt. Gilboa.

An important part of our lives was when people took trips from the Pinsk area to Telekhany. Our town would come to life when the guests arrived. Pinsk school children would come on a field trip to the beautiful Polesia region, and members of political parties would come to visit their friends. The city folk used to love coming to visit us. We welcomed them warmly, and they loved to lie on the green grass when the town was fast asleep. The waves of the water in the canal moved softly, and the waterfall would break the silence with a pleasant faint sound, while a July breeze would caress their foreheads. When they would come home to sleep at their friends' houses, they would be surprised with fresh milk and tasty biscuits that mothers had prepared especially for their guests.

The Telekhany residents warmly greeted their friends. It was a way that only a small-town ordinary person could greet someone from the Big City, who even personified the great, rich and cultured outside world.

We were especially attached to our friend Topsha. I remember one Sabbath when we were all traveling on the steamboat to Vihonoshtz. It was a wonderful trip. Our friends from Pinsk treated us like their little brothers and sisters, and Topsha told us all stories about the big world out there, and we swallowed everything she said.

It was a time with a full and active life that taught us as much as the best schools or universities.

In the last pages of my article I would like to speak about the heroic boys and girls who kept their activities secret. Their lives were in danger merely for thinking about a better tomorrow.

They brought their ideas into every home. They were dedicated only as faithful honest idealists can be. They not only sought to change the regime, but also to change people so they would be mature to take on the great day that would bring about the new order that would liberate all the suffering, weak, oppressed and exploited masses, and thereby remove the clouds, allowing the sun to shine forever!

According to their beliefs was the range of their actions. They sought to bring the light of the new ideas to every dark corner. The story of their activities was as follows:

In my town of Telekhany there was a poor stooped woman, abandoned by G-d and Man, with the name of Meryankelicha, because of her husband, Meir Yankel. The only significant possession that she had was a son, Mordechai Zucker, who lived in Pinsk. One fine morning Mordechai appeared in Telekhany after being chased out of Pinsk for his communist activities.

The teenager was unafraid, and quickly found a new platform for conducting his work. He started thinking about spreading his ideas, and very quickly started attracting an audience to listen how to liberate mankind from his shackles.

The teenage boys of Telekhany, who were excluded from any form of productive work, joined the movement, seeing themselves as the vanguard of the struggle for freedom and justice. They enthusiastically spread light and knowledge in the far out corners of the Telekhany region. They were afraid of nothing, and never relented from their activities. During the dark summer nights they plodded through the deep sand, and in winter, through the deep snow and swamps. They filled their backpacks with proclamations and kept right on going. They lived the ideas that were in their hearts. Their activity had a strong effect, and attracted followers. The peasants in the area started to rebel against high taxes, and the Jewish community also respected these boys, who seemed never to tire or be afraid of their work. Whenever a member was in danger, a member of the Left Poalei Zion would help him out.

Their activities were so numerous that they gave no rest to the police. They were arrested, and then new publications and proclamations would come out again, like snow falling on the street. It went so far that the police in Telekhany were on alert day and night, and even their police superiors from Kosov would thunder into Telekhany like a gang of bandits, and strike people mercilessly all over the place.

A rumor circulated in Telekhany that everyone in town was a communist. Avramele the Scribe was involved in commerce, and he had to report where he came from. He was turned into the Grodno police. A teenager from Telekhany went to Slonim and got grabbed by the head, 'Where are you from? From Telekhany?' He then got flogged that night. There was a girl found a blouse made from red fabric and hanged it at the park. So then there was a roundup in town as the police searched for the person who hanged up the "red flag." I could recount many such stories.

I remember May 1, which fell on a Friday. Everything was green and in bloom, just like it's supposed to be in May. The fragrance of lilac was in the air; our house was surrounded by yellow sand, and the golden rays of the penetrating sun hit the yellow sand harmoniously. Everything was bathed in Sabbath calm. Suddenly, as if from underground, terrorists appeared, casting fear through everyone. Not only did people silently and painfully protest their arrival to disrupt the holy holiday and Sabbath calm, but even the barking of the dogs in the gardens sounded like a rejection of those who quite suddenly appeared in the quiet town, violating the Sabbath and the holiday. It didn't take long for the communists and those suspected of being communists to end up lying on the floor at the police headquarters and being kicked by the rubber soles of shoes and flogged on the shoulders.

I hated the Polish rulers from my earliest youth. I remember how when I was twelve years old I went with other children and women to gather berries and mushrooms. When we returned from the forest with our full baskets, the landowner, Filipovich, arrived with his assistants and two dogs. He stopped us and grabbed all the berries and mushrooms. He even took the new basket my mother bought for me. At first I was speechless. Then I screamed out, "Give me back my basket! Give me back my basket!"

He claimed that since we were out gathering in his private forest, he was missing something. The peasant women always brought him something of what grew in the forest.

I remembered the injustice, and many of us tried to figure out a way to get even with them. An opportunity arose only many years later.

We used to have a sea celebration with a large parade, and the Polish rulers believed that G-d only had them in mind when he created the beautiful natural environment of Telekhany. The police wanted to celebrate quietly, and arrested everyone for the celebration. They built a bridge across the middle of the Telekhany lake, and brought out an orchestra. The little walkway in the canal was all lit up, and everyone in town strolled around it. Three of us girls sat in a corner and planned to show them that they could never keep the forces of struggle behind bars. So we considered attaching little red flags to boards and sending them out with the current. We waited until more people arrived, and then we did our job, sending the little flags to their target, and they got there.

They went crazy, as Sarah Krupnick described it. She had the buffet out there on the bridge that night. She raised her hands to heaven and thanked G-d that there were others besides her brother Leibel, who was then sitting with his friend Mordechai Zucker in the birch kartuz.

They didn't only go after the teenage boys, but made their parents' lives bitter as well. The parents suffered in silence, but deep down they were proud of their heroic sons. The boys were the kind of people who had to run away from Telekhany in the middle of the night and leave Poland entirely. Others spent five or six years in prison under terrible conditions. Their mothers' eyes were soaked with tears over their sons! The fathers walked with their heads bowed. After several years the boys returned from prison, and the entire town went out to greet them. Their mothers washed away their tears, letting a soft smile cross their faces. Their fathers once again walked erect, and their sons resumed their activities.

The struggle in Telekhany continued for several decades uninterrupted until the arrival of the Nazis, who drowned everyone in blood.

I wrote these pages with the blood of my heart, and when I finished, it happened that I left the cemetery with an oath to remember and never forget the Amalek of every generation! May these lines serve as a brick for the monument that will be established for the martyrs by the freedom fighters.

———

[Page 83]

Shlomo Landman's Story
Transcribed by Sarah Rubenstein, January 30 – February 2, 1962
Edited by Esther Miller

Sol (Shlomo) Landman was among the few Jews of Telekhany (and nearby region) who survived the Nazi murderers in the Soviet Union. He now lives in Washington. He started his life all over again, opened a small business, married and came to Los Angeles with his wife for a visit.

The Telekhany Yizkor Book Committee met with him for two days. We had mixed feelings about it. On the one hand we were happy to be with a living fellow émigré from Telekhany, and on the other hand it was painful to hear him describe the horrible torture of our martyrs at the hands of the Nazis. He lived through awful inhuman experiences during the Nazi period. At the same time, he recounts, it seems that the wounds were starting to heal, and then something happened and they were opened again. He would be quiet as if he had been poked in the throat.

We looked at hunchbacked Sol as he was sitting there. He was unrecognizable. Only a few minutes earlier we had shaken hands, and he had been smiling; he was over six feet tall. He had broad shoulders and was middle-aged, with an open brown smiling face like that of a healthy villager. He had changed so much!

He rubbed his tall forehead with a rough hand down to the corners where his black hair was turning gray, and started speaking again.

"As you know, Telekhany was ruined in World War I, but Jews are very stubborn people. So Jews of Telekhany returned from various cities and towns where they had been deported, and built Telekhany all over again. There were no glass factories anymore. Only the sawmill was working. Children were off to work, and their fathers became small merchants and brokers. They opened small stores, became shoemakers, tailors, carpenters and bricklayers. They made a living off of each other and from their hard work. Others received help from the United States. Electricity came to town, and so did an electric bus. The train started running again. Making a living was hard because of the intense competition that arose among the merchants, and unemployment grew among the youth. However, Jews lived with the hope that G-d would help."

He paused for a couple of minutes, as if he were taking pains to say something.

"I was still a young boy, and I can remember how the Jews of Telekhany said that despite the difficult economic conditions they opened a Jewish school for the children, as well as a library, which Yosef Glick, the local rabbi, and the youth of Telekhany helped to set up. Various organizations were started: the Poalei Zion, the Socialists and the Communists.

"Anti-semitism and the reaction in Pilsudski's nationalist Poland became stronger under the leadership of Beck and other anti-semites. The activists among the youth were sent to the Kartuz-Bereza (a prison for political prisoners) with long prison terms. The hate, distrust and economic insecurity interfered with the rebuilding of Telekhany. Unemployment increased and children went hungry. Mothers cried, begging G-d for a 'little war' so their children could go into the army and have something to eat. This is how people lived during the decade 1931-1941."

Sol paused again, smoked his cigarette and continued to tell the story with bitterness:

"G-d of war noticed the motherly tears. World War II broke out, and even though people could feel it, things were still quiet in Telekhany. A few days later we heard that the Bolsheviks had entered Brisk and nationalized town property. Storekeepers and businessmen in Telekhany believed life would be better under the Germans. Rumors circulated that the Bolsheviks did nationalize property, but the Jews obtained work together with all the non-Jews, and the government sent the children to school to study. Young people went deeper into Russia. Then German spies organized bands from among the ignorant peasants. There was a rumor that the Bolsheviks were going to come and nationalize and seize things.

"The situation became more critical by the day. Nazi spies incited the peasants to hold pogroms against Jews. They pillaged, killed and beat Jews in the streets. Jews stood up against them with empty hands because the weapons held by the revolutionary young people were buried, and those revolutionaries were in prison.

"Our house was not spared either. The pogrom gangs broke in at 2 AM and stole everything. This went on for six weeks. I was not at home because I was off with the Bolsheviks. It was extremely difficult to go away. I left my wife and two children, parents, sister, brother - a large family. My father kept bothering me, asking what and with whom I would be doing whatever with the Borvesa (the term he used for the Bolsheviks). I asked him, 'Father, are you responsible for the results?' 'No, my son.....' he responded sadly. I left, and remained alive. Those who remained behind perished, and were annihilated. My friend Asher Gurstal and I are the living witnesses of the destruction and annihilation of Telekhany." He wiped the perspiration off his forehead and continued.

"When I left Telekhany with the Red Army, I met Jewish families in the wagons along the way. These were families fleeing Telekhany. I asked them why they hadn't taken along my wife and children. Their silence seem to say that my family were no longer among the living."

Sol looked at Gershon Gurstal. He spoke of his father, Alter the Carpenter, and how he had had the honor of dying a natural death. He did, however, get a taste of Nazism. They had torn out half his beard. We looked at each other with silent pain and fear for Gershon's weak heart.

"We the young people fought against the wild beast in human form. Before the Nazis arrived in town, Asher Gurstal, Ephraim Klitenick, his brother Leibel (now in Poland), Dov Landman, my cousin, Yisrael Kez (in Israel), a few non-Jewish young men from Voluka and I organized a self-defense unit. We got and hid weapons to face the enemy. However, a few of us left with the Red Army, others went to Palestine, and many of the leaders were put into prison. The weapons remained in where they were, and were never used.

"After the war I had an opportunity to remain in the Soviet Union to study and work there. However, since I knew myself that my entire family had perished at the hands of the Nazis in 1944, and the location of the remains of my parents, I felt an obligation to return to Telekhany and bury them properly.

"My friend Asher Gurstal (a little older and weaker than I) and I encountered many difficulties, suffering and misfortune on the way back to Telekhany from Russia. We traveled mostly by foot. Once in a while a peasant in a wagon would take us along. Silent discomfort separated us; we got off the wagon and continued walking. Though we knew that not all gentiles participated in the destruction of Jews, we were afflicted with suspicion.

"After several long and difficult weeks of suffering along the way, we arrived in Telekhany. The town was empty and dead. There were two long mass graves where there was once the glassworks street. With broken spirits and hearts we finally arrived in Viohonotshtch. Entering my house I found a familiar gentile family. We stood at the entrance and looked on in silence. We couldn't utter a word. A door to another room was open, and I could recognize our closet. Then I noticed some of our furniture. 'Shloma, how much? I'll pay you.' I glared back at him, and then sat down on a wooden chair, exhausted. With tears in his eyes the peasant described to me how the destruction occurred:

"'The Nazi army ordered the Jews of Telekhany to stand in rows of 25 people, and to dig two long trenches. When they had finished, the Storm Troopers gave the order to shoot. The Germans carried out the orders and shot them, and the Jews fell into the graves one after the other – men, women, children and the elderly.' The gentile crossed himself."

Sol's voice was choked with tears. His face turned gray-colored. He was reliving the experience. He collected himself and continued.

"The mayor of the town received an order from the Nazis to exterminate the rest of the Jews. Those were my parents, and none of the gentiles wanted to do it. They said they had nothing against the Jews and didn't want to kill them. The mayor himself went to our house, called out my parents into the yard and shot them. My father first, and then my mother."

He dropped his head as if he had no strength to hold it, and then after a brief pause started speaking.

"I am a strong person by nature. However, when I heard this from the gentile, I started to see my whole family before my eyes. The fact that the gentiles in our house were making excuses for themselves infuriated me. 'Let's go!' I said to my friend Asher. I wanted to get out of there as fast as I could. The peasant and his wife stopped us: 'Stay with us. We'll give you the biggest bedroom in the house,' they begged us. To show us how sincere they were, they again crossed themselves.

"We decided to perform the burial as quickly as possible and then leave. We obtained a permit from the rabbi and the Soviet authorities to bury my parents according to Jewish law. We couldn't obtain any linen to wrap the dead half-decomposed bodies. The peasants brought us long draw hard straw. I wrapped them and brought them to their eternal rest."

We, the committee of 10-12 people, remained seated with bowed heads and breathless. We felt like we were sitting shiva for the martyrs of our hometown. Someone broke the silence and asked a question: "Is it true that the Soviet authorities had given permission to turn the synagogue into a warehouse for grain, and had turned the cemetery into a gasoline station?"

"Yes, that's true," answered Sol. "We must always tell the truth," he added.

"How did the Jews live under the Soviet regime?" I asked.

"They confiscated the property of the rich, and sent them to work along with the poor. Write down everything I am telling you, and put it into the Yizkor Book. I am so busy in my business that I never have any time. No, I can't."

We understood that the real reason why he told us to write everything down was because he couldn't relive the agony a third time. We could see that on his face.

———

[Page 87]

Also from our Birthplace Telekhany
by Mashele Roseman

From our hometown we are fortunate there are
still a few men and women spread out all
over the place.
They all decided to record in a yizkor book
their murdered mother, their murdered father.
So that they should be remembered,
and so that future generations should know
that the German murderers annihilated the lives
of six million Jews.

———

[Page 88]

A Eulogy to Burned Down Telekhany
by Moshe Bernstein (Tel Aviv)

Along its streets that went up in flames,
my poor youth wandered around.
Above you and me, the same sky
that delighted in your bloody conflicts,
are now delighting in my teardrop

that fell onto your burned body.

I ramble, I look for some sense,
a support to hold my memory,
of how a town of Jews were sacrificed on the altar.

It's deserted, but the wind
quivers over a stray old page.
Only a few letters remain,
 recounting generations of life.

The scent of beards, candles and kiddush wine
waft through the air.
 I hear a mournful tune, and ramble and cry along;
My lips quietly blaspheme:
Why, why should only a stray page
be left to tell how Jews went up in flames?

I wander, and each step burns my memory,
each stone is a witness;
Trees rustle quietly, telling secrets.

I turn my ear; I want to hear
their secret, the essence of their lament.
Speak, trees, speak!
We were once friends,
and blossomed.

And perhaps in your shadow
is my never-ending dream;
at the very top of your branches
that kiss the heavens
flutters my old smile.
It's quiet, it's on an early morning.

The wind washes away the last sign
of my wandering steps through the ruins of my town.

———

[Page 89]

The Famous Date – Remembered Forever!

by Leizer Lutsky (Aharon Shmuel's grandson)

September 1, 1939 is a famous date – it is the date when World War II broke out, when Hitler's hordes attacked vulnerable Poland and took it over in 17 days. This date was the start of the great tragedy that resulted in the inhuman deaths of six million of our People.

The same date will always be recorded in my memory because it was when my lifelong dream of emigrating to Palestine was crushed. At that time I was already on my way to Palestine, and was waiting in Warsaw for notification about the second departure of the transport (because the first time, it returned from Romania. We had been a group of a thousand men involved in illegal immigration to Palestine). Instead, I found a German airplane starting to bomb Warsaw.

With great difficulty I was able to receive permission to leave Warsaw and return to Telekhany. The trip from Warsaw to Telekhany took ten days, and more than once the train was hit by a hail of bullets and bombs from German airplanes. On September 10 I arrived in Telekhany by foot from Sventevolia (because the small train had become paralyzed).

Telekhany was under the impact of the events of the previous ten days. No one knew what to do. It seemed a bad idea to wait for the arrival of the Germans, but on the other hand were the Soviets, and the question was whether they would open the border to people fleeing Poland so as not to fall into the hands of the Germans. A large group of young people, however, decided on the second choice – to go to the Soviet border and face whatever would happen. We figured no one would shoot at us.

Everyone prepared clothes, boots and food, especially dry crackers, and just waited and followed closely the radio reports about the battles in order to decide when to leave. On the evening of September 16 after a short meeting, we decided to start our departure for the Soviet border the next day.

We felt very bad. Most people had to say their goodbyes to their parents, who couldn't decide whether to leave on a trip that was mostly by foot. We wondered what the fate of those remaining behind would be, and were wondering even more about those walking to the Soviet border. Whatever the outcome, there was no other way out. The older people found it difficult to abandon everything they toiled for with blood and sweat – their houses and few possessions. They wished their children well and blessed them that G-d should lead them in the right way; they told the children that they would accept their fate, whatever it would be, in Telekhany.

The next morning, September 17, everybody in the world were impressed to hear the announcement from the Soviet regime that the Red Army was extending its "fraternal hand" to the people of west White Russia and west Ukraine to assist them. The situation ended with our unending joy since we could all remain at home, and instead of us having to go to the Soviet border, the Soviets were coming to us. A small part of the Jewish population, merchants, didn't hide their chagrin, worry and disappointment. They knew that private enterprise was abolished in the Soviet Union, and they worried about their businesses and future.

A few divisions of the broken Polish army started passing through Telekhany. One of the officers who were unable to bear the affront warned us not to be happy. They were going to gather forces and chase out the Bolsheviks and the Germans. As revenge, the Polish soldiers committed various offenses: they shot civilians (Aharon Landman, Yitzchak's youngest son, was wounded) and forcibly took away a few young men as far as the Krogelevitch villages and even further. The police in Telekhany ran around like drugged mice. Many young Jewish men who had been serving in the Polish army returned in half-civilian clothes.

As mentioned earlier, the Jewish population, which had suffered earlier, now started breathing easier, and had to begin taking care of their own defense and facing a short period of time without any local government. Jews realized the danger of anarchy. This period lasted for almost a week, until advance Red Army soldiers arrived, and people gathered at the police headquarters (near Avraham the Scribe's brick house). It was a warm day, and all day long smoke rose from the chimney on the police building – they were burning their papers and documents.

It was the evening of September 18. People were hanging around on the street in front of the police headquarters waiting for something, though not knowing what – they just felt something had to happen. On the balcony of the police headquarters stood the police commander and our representative, Rabbi Glick, brothers Leibel and Ephraim Klitenick, as well a few eminent members of the communist party in Telekhany. The commander briefly announced that they were leaving town. A few policemen were leaving their wives and children, and he assured the people that nothing wrong was going to happen to the people. In order to protect life and property, the commander gave out all the weapons at the building, except for revolvers, to the representatives of the Jewish community headed by Rabbi Glick. Rabbi Glick and the commander shook hands, and the rabbi announced to the assembly in Russian:

"From now on the government of Telekhany is in my hands. Whoever does not obey my orders will be punished very strictly. I am appointing Leibel Klitenick as the new commander in Telekhany."

Apparently Telekhany was the only case where there was such a procedure of the government being officially handed over by the Polish police. It was also the only case where a rabbi assumed power and appointed a commander. In addition to the tremendous impact it had on the crowd, this act was rare in the history of the revolutionary transfer of power from the government to the Bolsheviks.

The town went about preparing to meet the Red Army. A tower was built on Sventevolia Street, and was decorated with greenery, and people had to start sloganeering in Russian. I remember how I was asked to write the slogan (I could draw and paint pretty well). I didn't know any Russian, however. Someone came across an old moldy Russian book and showed me which letters to make. I followed him letter by letter and copied the letters over onto a large red piece of linen, without understanding what I was writing. Anyone at all who could help out with the preparations to meet the Red Army did so. Girls sewed red flags and decorated the People's Clubhouse.

Everyone was greatly disappointed when, instead of greeting an army, a jeep arrived in town carrying 3-4 officers and soldiers, who announced that soon Soviet rule would be established in town, and representatives would arrive to set up a socialist system.

The jeep left immediately, and we were again left without a governmental authority. The Jewish youth were then called to a meeting, and Leibel Klitenick handed out the guns. The group called themselves the Red Guard, and they intended to maintain law and order until the establishment of a local government. I remember that Beinish Mozrirer (Lieba Chaya's son) and I patrolled Sventevolia Street every night starting from the mill in Smolnia.

Everyone participated voluntarily and faithfully for several months without any compensation. When the Soviet government later paid each person fifty rubles for their work in the Red Guard, some complained that this meant they were serving in expectation of compensation. This showed how enthusiastic the young people were about the change in regime.

The arriving Bolsheviks started their propaganda, telling about life in the Soviet Union and painting it as paradise. The bragging of the new Soviets was rather curious. For example, when they were asked whether some kind of item was available in Russia, they always responded that they had huge factories, "what else do we need?" "Do you have lemons?" asked one Jew. "Oh sure, we have many factories that make them!" was the retort.

All of the arrivals from Russia were very poorly dressed, and when they noticed the difference in the way we were dressed, they responded that they had been mobilized directly from the factories and fields, which is why they arrived in work clothes. They also didn't want to reveal the lack of clothes and food in Russia. Then they bought as much as they could from the stores. Our prices were much lower than prices in Russia. For example, a pair of boots cost us 30 zlotys, while in Russia they cost 300-400 rubles. In terms of currency exchange, the boots cost the equivalent of 30 rubles.

Soon basic necessities became scarce. Even bread, sugar, biscuits and other food were available only after standing in line. However, a revival of community and cultural life wasn't concerned with that. There were many meetings at the Folks House, where the Soviet constitution, laws and practices were discussed. The various Soviet institutions were set up, and the young people started learning Russian. There were various courses on various subjects, such as bank employment and other specialized fields in the newly created offices. Due to the fact that the Jewish young people were more educated and dedicated to the new situation, they therefore filled all job positions. My younger sister Esther got a job as an employee with the government bank, and as far as I remember, for a brief time she excelled in her work by performing more bank operations than the norm.

The newly created conditions stimulated the young people to study. It should be remembered that studying in a gymanzia high school was very expensive, so very few people were able to send their children to study there. My parents tried to make it possible for me to attend high school, but after two years of study at Chechik's Pinsk high school, I had to quit in 1933 because the international economic crisis reached Telekhany as well. My father was unemployed because no one was building houses, and therefore there was no need for windows and doors. I started to work for my father in carpentry and continued to do so until the Bolsheviks came to town.

I knew that the same teachers were teaching at the high school that I had left 6 years earlier, so I departed for Pinsk. The teachers still remembered me and had been pleased with my work – I had been one of the better students. The winter of 1939-40 was a bitter one. The weather was very cold, wood was very expensive, and people had to wear their winter coats in the house. I had to spend two months preparing for the exams that I was going to take in the second half of the year in January 1940. I pored over my books day and night because in those six years I had forgotten a great deal. I also wanted to skip a class so I wouldn't have to study with children younger than me.

Our nourishment was tea and saccharine (because sugar was too difficult to obtain) with bread and bilberry jam that my mother made. Despite the difficulties of cold and hunger, I passed the exams. Classes in the first three months were taught in Yiddish, and at the end of the year, the last two months the school was run by a White Russian, and classes were held in Belarussian. How we disliked the coarse peasant language; we even had to study White Russian literature. However in the next school year (the last year of high school), the school went back to teaching in Russian, and everyone was very enthusiastic about going back to Russian.

Unfortunately, my hopes for completing the year and going on to study in a Soviet university were dashed. Two months after the start of the school year, a draft was imposed for all those who had not shown up to join the Polish army. (The Polish army took men at 21, while the Russian army drafted boys at 18). On Yom Kippur my parents, siblings, friends and acquaintances accompanied me and three other Jewish boys to the train station from where we were leaving, without even knowing our destination, for service in the Russian army. My parents shed a tear, but no one ever imagined that this would be the last time we would see each other.

I traveled together with Eliyahu Sender the tailor's son, Berl Ziskin the tailor's son, and Feivel, the son of Lemel Baum.

We traveled in closed troop transport train cars, and additional cars were added to ours along the way. On our train there was a group of boys from nearby towns and cities, including my cousin Aharon Shmuel, Rivka's son, who was eventually killed in the first days of the battle in Leningrad. There were cars that included Tajiks and Uzbeks in their national costumes, such as ladies' housedresses. They didn't know any Russian, and spent their time trying to figure out how to escape from the train, something that even our own group never thought of doing.

We passed through various train stations in the Russian areas. These were painful pictures that were engraved into our memories - barefoot and abandoned children surrounded the train crying to us, "Grandfather, throw us out a piece of bread." Since we didn't know where we were, I named the station where the train stopped Rivatskoya. Later I found out that it was on the way to Leningrad.

We arrived in an unpopulated area in the middle of nowhere not far from Murmansk, but we found concentration camps filled with arrested "settlers" and other criminals, kulaks and former wealthy Russians (who had been sent there after the 1918 revolution). When we arrived in October, the cold winter was already there, and it was dark almost the entire time, except for a few hours a day of a little light. Summer was the opposite, sunlight almost all the time; right after sunset, the sun started coming up again.

I didn't give up my hopes of studying, and for a short time I was accepted as a student at the Leningrad Institute of Technology. I had just sent off my first examination project when the war with Germany broke out, which made me forget about my studies. I marched off to the front, where I remained until December 30, 1945. I saw two of my friends from Telekhany killed before my eyes. They were the ones mentioned above, except for Eliyahu Sender, who remained alive, and who I met again after the war.

I would like to simply recount a typical event regarding the internal experiences and struggles that are worth mentioning and which took place one day. It was actually a calm day, with no bombing or shooting. We were lying inside the trenches, and there was something that was bothering me. I thought I was going crazy and my heart was going to stop. I couldn't figure out what was bothering me, so I decided that if I were fortunate enough to survive the war, I would try to find out what happened on that same day. I noted that it was August 4, 1941. Four years later I realized it was the day that the German murderers killed all the Jews in Telekhany, including my parents and family.

———

[Page 95]

Memories of Telekhany
by Golda Stolyar (Kefar Yehoshua, Israel)

My mother didn't say much about herself, but I knew that she had a difficult childhood. After my grandmother Slava had born him five children (four daughters and a son), and when the children were all still small, my grandfather Fishel divorced my grandmother, who out of embarrassment returned to her hometown, leaving all the children with our grandfather.

My mother Chana was the eldest daughter of my grandfather Fishel, and she was 9 years old when she was forced to assume the material and emotional responsibilities for her younger siblings.

She used to tell us that at the age of 9 she already knew how to make and bake bread, using a small stool to reach the oven. My grandfather didn't wait very long to remarry. Life goes on, and he married Gittel, the "speaker," and the children felt they had lost their father too. They didn't feel like they had much of a home.

After they grew up they went off around the world. Two sisters, Naomi and Beila, and brother Hershel, went to the United States. Our mother and her sister got married in Telekhany. The subsequent struggles with life's difficulties now began. Our father, a hard worker, a capable auctioneer and builder, worked from sunup to sundown, but didn't make much of a living. Our mother was a person naturally gifted with initiative, clear understanding and thriftiness. She opened a milk store, carried cans of milk from estates, sold butter and cheese, raised her children and sewed their clothes at night. Her hands were never idle, and because of her diligence the children never knew hunger.

In 1904, when the Russo-Japanese War broke out, our father was of military draft age. He didn't want to give his life for Russia, so he decided to go to the United States, where many others of his age had gone. He arrived in the United States after living through enormous danger and difficulties, depending on various agents. Mother remained alone with two children, Hillel and Feigel, and another on the way. These were difficult years for her until Father managed to get himself on his feet and learn a new trade, which took some time. In the meantime Mother was without a livelihood.

Grandmother Beilka loved my mother and would help her out when she was in need. Father was in the United States for four years. In 1909 he returned to Telekhany, though his luggage got lost along the way. He had saved some money, and our family's life was made easier.

I was born in 1910. We already had a nice home that was built together with Grandfather Fishel. Father usually worked outside of Telekhany in nearby areas, traveling with other carpenters in the summer months. The carpenters didn't work in winter because of the cold and snow.

I remember when Grandmother Beilka died. Father was at work out of town, and if I remember correctly, he was reached by telephone. Grandmother was a valiant woman. Grandfather Hillel Yaakov had been paralyzed while he was still a young man. It happened when he spent 9 months in jail for having signed as a witness to release Hillel Brombergs from the army.

Grandfather Hillel Yankel was a strong fellow, but sitting in prison with nothing to do affected his health. Shortly after leaving prison he became paralyzed, and at the age of thirty he became ill and then passed away. Grandmother Beilka was left behind with her 8 children, 5 sons and 3 daughters. Those remaining alive are two sons, Leiba and Froika. All the children were bright, honest, industrious and cheerful. They were known as good singers and were all married. They had children and raised them. Uncle Yehoshua Stolyar was especially known for being enterprising and intelligent. He would make the biggest podrads and put together the plans himself even without being a certified engineer. He had an outstanding sociable personality and a deeply human soul.

I loved him as much as I loved my own father, even when his economic situation was poor, he never lost his courage, and was happy with the little that he still had.

Five years after my father returned from the United States, the air once again began to smell of gunpowder. I was barely five years old when the first German airplanes appeared overhead. Everyone, young and old, were trembling from fear. The murder of the Archduke in Sarajevo was the excuse Germany needed to declare war.

My father had to be drafted, and we were extremely nervous about it. He didn't want to give his life for the "Papa Czar," and tried to extricate himself with money and was constantly worried. The war was in full force and the Germans were winning.

After a year of war the battles approached the Oginski Canal. An order was issued to evacuate the civilian population of Telekhany. The Russian aristocrats were raging and drinking the night before. The next morning, the soldiers received an order to bring out the first residents onto Sventevolia Street. Aunt Esther Leah's Feigel came running to our house in a panic, holding Donele (the child of her deceased sister, Rasha) by the hand. Aunt Esther Leah and Uncle Yaakov Aharon were in Kolonsk, where they managed a leased estate.

Feigel, Hala and Chantsha took off in the direction of Sventevolia Street, trying to save some household belongings from Uncle's house. Meanwhile, the Russian soldiers started plundering Jewish property. In the evening the decree spread throughout town, and the entire Jewish population locked their doors and windows together with everything they owned inside.

We gathered near the empty brick house in the open field under the open sky and spent our first night. The next day we saw how the fires had devoured the life-long work of our parents, and we acquired the new name of "homeless people."

We weren't allowed to remain outside very long. We were soon ordered to keep on moving. Some of the residents of Telekhany headed west, while others headed east, though without a specific destination. We continued our trek outdoors for six weeks, going right into the autumn.

We lived off of mushrooms in the forest and berries that grew in the woods. Here and there peasants had left potatoes in the ground, and we took whatever was available, thereby alleviating our hunger. We didn't see any bread the whole time we were wandering. There was one case when a soldier sold a loaf of bread, but it was as hard as a rock. Hungry fathers grabbed the bread, causing a chaotic situation where people were attacking and hitting each other over that hard bread as if it were a real prize.

Eventually the Germans pushed the Russians deeper into Russia. I remember clinging to my mother from fear as the dirigibles flew overhead. The frequent shooting scared us. We soon came to a Jewish community that was far away from a strategic location on the front. This was the town of Kletsk.

Uncle Yaakov Aryeh came from Kletsk, and he went to his relatives. We stuck close to him because of his wagon, which made it possible for us to transport our few belongings and small children. The adults, however, traveled all the way by foot.

Then new problems arose: getting an apartment and finding a way to make a living. In 1916 our family included 8 people. When Mother would ask about an apartment, everyone would ask how many children she had. Finally we found a room that had three army cots in it. We used them to sleep at night, and used them as tables and chairs by day. We were frequently prohibited from opening the door in order not to anger the landlady, so we used to go in and out through the window. Father was scared of moving around in open areas, so he didn't work. Mother baked bread for soldiers, earning us some money to buy food with.

The Russians were suffering defeats at the battlefront, and the government would make nighttime roundups. The difficult life we had caused my father to age as if he had just been discharged from the army. The rough health and economic situation that we found ourselves in at that time made people sick, especially with typhus. Mother was the first one to come down with typhus, and she was taken to a military hospital. We stayed alone, and then Hillel, Feigel and Sarahle got sick. After every occurrence of typhus, the local health commission would come around to disinfect us, which made the landlady very angry at the hapless refugees who were making her so worried. After a close call with death, Mother got well. The children got older: Hillel and Feigel started working – Feigel in gardening and Hillel in unskilled labor.

The war worked its way into a crucial turning point. Soldiers at the battlefront were getting tired and disappointed from the fighting. The Bolshevist party made use of the spirit of the peasants and working masses against the decaying ruling regime. The masses want peace! A new period in our lives began.

We stayed in Kletsk for seven years, and life began to normalize. Father got involved in construction, and the older children worked while the younger ones went to school.

We started to hear rumors originating from Telekhany that residents were returning there, and we started longing to return too. After Chantsha died from a lung ailment, Mother was unhappy in Kletsk. One morning we packed up our things.

We returned to Telekhany in 1923, and found that at the glassworks factory there were still barracks of the glasswork employees from the good old days. Those structures served as temporary homes for the returning residents. We received assistance and started building our new home.

It was hard to live in the barracks. Mother, who under the most difficult of circumstances never gave up, was very nervous. She wanted to make a future for her children. She sent me to a trade school in Pinsk, and she baked bread for office workers.

Little Telekhany had no real opportunities available for the youth. They started thinking about their future. Early on after our return to Telekhany we took advantage of the summer to gather berries, elderberries and mushrooms to prepare food for the winter. In the evening we would gather together at the little alley and enjoy the weather with joyful singing.

Later on, the more serious young people started organizing cultural and political groups. We opened a public library, and would make our very own theater productions.

These productions certainly didn't meet artistic standards. However, there was a desire to be creative. There were also self-study groups and political movements. I am sure that there will appear enough material regarding the political life and activity of the young people of Telekhany from among those who are more gifted than I, and who will devote more time and thought to the topic.

We made sure that there was enough room for our grandfather Fishel and Aunt Gittel in our home. We built a shed and brought in a young cow from Kletsk; we planted nasturtiums and crocuses around outside the house. We had a beautiful vegetable garden on the sandy ground. My mother's eye was on guard for everything, and we felt very much at home.

In 1927 we celebrated the wedding of our Feigel, and the occasion gave great pleasure to our parents. I learned how to sew by hand, after having spent many hours doing it by machine. We gave our parents a lot of worry with our political party activities.

The first arrest in Telekhany after the "Yossel Provocation" was when our Slava was arrested with the rest. The community and our parents suffered a great deal from the frequent police searches and records, arrests and provocations that we were subject to.

I remember when we, the Left Poalei Zion, organized a Borochov celebration at the home of Shimon Gurstel. The mass arrest was provoked when the police surrounded the house, and everybody there was arrested. By chance, all three of us sisters were among those arrested. The police took all of us near the Lubiesha synagogue, and my father was standing in prayer near the window – it was the onset of the Sabbath. He saw us escorted by police, and fainted on the spot. Nevertheless our parents expressed understanding for us in view of all the pressure and terrorism of the authorities.

New clouds started covering the sky, and the political situation in Poland became increasingly tense. The fascist Hitler party came to power in Germany, and was preparing its vengeful plans. The new anti-semitic law against Jewish ritual slaughter was the start of the first attack against the economic interests of the Jews in Poland. Anti-semitic speeches were made in the churches, and proclamations against Jews were announced. The first pogroms against Jews in Pshitek and Aptshna portended difficult times ahead.

The boycott against Jewish workers and Jewish businesses was a daily event. Jews were insulted and beaten. The dark forces among the Polish people were raising their heads. The young people increased their clarification among the peasants in the area, and some Jewish young people were forced to leave Telekhany for larger cities.

In 1936, I said goodbye to my parents, younger sister Saraleh and my friends and neighbors, all of whom were engraved into my heart. I said goodbye to my hometown of Telekhany, where I had lived during the best years of my youth; I said goodbye to my sister Slava, who at that time lived in Warsaw. I traveled to Palestine on the Polish ship, Polonia. Our Feigel and Michel and their three sons had arrived in Palestine a year earlier. Our parents and Sarahle remained together. I used to write home frequently, and frequently received letters from my parents and Sarahleh. They hoped for us to all be together.

In 1939 the fire erupted. World War II broke out, and we couldn't even have imagined the gruesome plan of annihilation that Hitler and his hangmen were preparing, and their whole life's work was one big war with few respites.

Everyone, young and old, tormented, emotionally broken, persecuted and defenseless were rounded up and killed on August 2, 1941. Without the slightest tremble the beasts in human form rampaged to satisfy their bloody lust for human blood.

The war in 1939 left us with shocking images of a tragic period. We lost our loved ones, and the purity of their humane lives will always remain engraved in our hearts, and serve as an example for the rest of our lives.

May their memories be honored!

[Page 101]

I Remember my Hometown
by Riva Chaim Reuvens

I remember my hometown when times were better and lovelier. Almost every young person strove to make something of himself. Whenever possible, people left to study in a larger city. Some went to gymnasia high school, while others went to technical schools. Later on there was a four grade high school in Telekhany, and the children pushed themselves to study. A library was opened containing Yiddish and Russian books. There were also reading groups, and people got together to read aloud in Russian and Yiddish. Also, people started to dress well and go for evening walks along the batshovnik, singing songs and going boatriding.

———

[Page 102]

The Power of Goodness
(In memory of Yisrael Rosenbaum)
by Chaim Finkelstein (Buenos Aires)

Superficially, it appears that goodness doesn't carry power. However, there are exceptions where a person's goodness converts into a kind of power that may even be stronger than any other type of power.

Yisraelik Rosenbaum was a living example of the power of goodness. When I met Yisraelik he was 10-11 years old. At that time he had just arrived in Brisk from a small town, Telekhany. He was an orphan and was brought up by his sister. We first met each other in the Tsisha [acronym] synagogue.

He was very handsome, slender and strong, with blond hair, and most important, with a friendly smile that never left his face. Whenever there was a problem, a challenge or a difficulty presented itself, Yisraelik stood out, ready to help anyone.

He had no anger or hatred in his heart. His nature was to be friendly to others, and whoever knew Yisraelik realized that he was as happy for another person's good fortune as he was for his own. He was this way as a child, and remained this way until we were separated from each other.

In 1946, after not seeing each other for twenty years, I met Yisraelik again, this time in Israel. Since then I have seen him very often, almost daily. I saw him at his home with his wife and child, and saw him at community activities, in the party and the Histadruth. He was the same old Yisraelik, filled with faith and optimism, devoted and loyal to friends, colleagues and everyone else.

Yisraelik's first years in Israel were very difficult. The country didn't greet him with plenty of milk and honey. Just like other immigrants in those days, in the early 1930s, Yisraelik lived through cold and warm situations until he developed roots in the country. He faced more than one disappointment and more than one challenge. The suffering and challenges didn't control his morale, but confirmed that he remained unaffected by the fiery tests of life because of his ethics. In general he understood Israel, knew the land, and accepted it joyfully. He knew that just as a person struggles in life, the country also struggles. Any person who loves the country should help it to attain its perfection.

He had already joined the Poalei Zion party in Brisk, when he was still a young teenager. In the youth organization he excelled in his devotion and limitless desire to do anything that was needed. He had the same attitude in the party and other community activities as he had had in the Poalei Zion.

I saw Yisraelik's activities in Israel close up. Usually it was after a hard day's work, but was not difficult for him. He loved the country, the party, the work, and therefore didn't notice the difficulties.

During the Knesset election campaign he wasn't in good health, and his illness had spread to his spinal cord. But Yisraelik didn't give in or talk about it so that he could continue total devotion to his work – something that was characteristic of him.

He felt that he was departing the world in the prime of his life, around the age of fifty. However, he never talked about it so as not to cause anyone pain. He never let a smile leave his face, and was never any different than he had been in his childhood.

Actually, he remained a big child his whole life, and more precisely, a person who kept the symbol of childhood: naiveté and authenticity, faith and love of his fellow man. If I had to characterize Yisraelik in one sentence, I would say that he had many talents, but his greatest talent was his rare goodness and love of others. This is where his strength, self and essence lay.

[Page 104]

The Oath
by Esther Miller

Tell me, O Telekhany, in your orphaned gloom
Do you still have any birds that can fly?
Or trees that can bloom?
Or stars that still sparkle in heaven?
Does the little water well in the forest
Still make noise and echo?
Does the river still flow mischievously?
And the pond, the alleys, that enticed my generation
With closed eyes, I can see you so clearly.

Suddenly I hear a voice, an awful voice, like from a wounded lion;
Everything is turned into dust and ashes;
How can birds fly and trees bloom?
How can stars in heaven shine?
A heaven that saw, and that was silent
When the Nazi beasts strangled Jewish children in cribs
And shot fathers, mothers, gray-haired old people in mass graves
The earth is ashamed, covered in blood.

In far away lands, across borders and seas,
O Telekhany, your roots and stems sprouted, and
We, the blood of your blood, bone of your bone, swear
On the holy names of our martyrs, yes we do swear,
Never to be still until the Nazi beasts are annihilated, destroyed.
We swear!

[Page 105]

A Letter from Telekhany
by Esther Miller
(about the visit in Telekhany of Ephraim Klitenick, a partisan in White Russia)

Through stormy days, and dark nights,
I returned to my little town of Telekhany,
That was once a place of natural beauty,
Here the children played and laughed in poor streets.

The houses I have known since a long time ago
Have locked windows and doors,
Fear grieves behind walls
The doorsteps lead to mass graves.

Death and devastation lie everywhere
In our birthplace, Telekhany.
Under a red setting sun, I walk and I walk
It is hard to walk across roads with overgrown weeds
Jewish hammers and saws stand silent.

I double over facing the graves of our martyrs;
And feel hot and cold,
My heart writhes in pain, and
The sun has hidden its face in shame.

   ****

On some early morning
Far into the future
New generations will come
And adorn the mass graves
With fragrant flowers.

[Page 106]

The Sacred Chain
by Dina Godiner-Klitenick

You smile, my town, with charm and with sadness
You call me, you tempt your fortune.
Your silence murmurs quietly around and saddens:
My child! You came home!
Back like before, with wounded glances,
You embrace the abandoned earth.

It wants to embrace and squeeze you.
You drew and lived here,
I walk once again over yellow sand,
With proud and sure steps.
Together with me, like a whole musical band,
Children make noise and transport me away.
They take me away to the forest and trenches,
And warn me to sit down,
And then sing for us a song about the Oginski Canal,
About green and sunny beaches,
About grass like velvet, bright skies
And the dark twilight.
Oh, take us away to the haunted house,
Filled with secrets and deep mysteries.
Grandmas used to tell us that ghosts
Rage there freely.
They tear doors off, and break windows off,
And then don't let them be rebuilt.
Someone carried over the bright red bricks,
and try to build a house.
But every child knows in an orphaned crib
How high is the price.
At night the ghosts will make merry,
And will never get tired.
Only frightened children will hold tight to each other,
And ask, "So sing your song!"

Somewhere near the Oginski Canal,
There is a town called Telekhany.
Boys over there dreamed about schools,
And girls dream about dowries.
But there are the grandfathers, the important grandfathers,
Sitting over the Talmud and studying.
And fathers would think that
The world was personified in the town,
And calmly the town would sink into sleep,
Lulled to sleep with prayer and calm.
Then something disturbed the village silence,
And someone called where....
Someone called the young colts,
Far away on the wide road.
Nearby the lake warmly wept and laughed today,
And those little village cabin doors
Quietly scraped and then closed,
Awakened children then disappeared
Far away, somewhere in the dark night.

A town of struggle! The gray of my youth is planted
On the unsettled canvas.
Even though I am far from you, from the haunted house.
Not dishonored, I have your sacred chain.

Chrysanthemums on the Mass Grave

My little daughter - a Song of Songs,
A butterfly, delicate and deft.
I kiss all her limbs.
How nice and sweet you are, my child!
Let her gently put down her brows
And with a grieving tone:
Say why there are black clouds
coming over the gray sky?
And why only us, only both of us?
Does my child shake like a leaf?
Oh, where is my grandmother, my grandfather?
Did I ever have them?
Oh, sing and tell me about your homeland,
Are there any Jews still alive there?
Your songs sound painful
And your glance squirts fire.

On the wings of my sadness
Let's fly, let's fly!
Even in a bright blue sky
black clouds are appearing, appearing
Chrysanthemums, dead flowers
I bring them to my friends, my intimates.
My child! They perished
Because of hordes of wild Hitler beasts!
Oh, hear: The dawn is weeping
And is afraid, calling ghosts.
Who draws water from those nearby wells?
Who looks at it through the window?
Maybe my sister? I am seized by a shudder,
and every bone in my body is trembling.
And maybe my father? I think he is calling me,
He calls me from the mass grave:
Come, my child! Come my child,
From far far away,
And sit down here!
With longing celebrate days gone by,
And bring your brothers back to life!
Oh, take them out of the mass graves,
The sisters, the mothers, the children.

And take them back to their own homes,
Your longing can do wonders.

No field in bloom,
No green meadows,
My heart is always green like a meadow.
Somewhere, among villages and towns
There is a town called Telekhany.
Brimming with magic and charm,
How the young people there struggle
For better days.
Here is a forest, there is a beach,
Deep sand on the road,
And a well sputters and flows

But can you be, then, well, as pleasing as before,
I should be able to greet you warmly
When you looked on indifferently and saw how
My friends were being led away to be shot?
How should I warmly greet the forest?
The forest was then a guard
That muffled the screams, the painful violence
And the trees looked on indifferently.

Oh, well, I want to convert your water into poison.
My hate could poison your water.
I want to go light a fire in the forest
And exterminate the anger down to the tree trunks!

And in the meantime, a reminder,
A yahrzeit of death
Only holy names remained;
Mass graves with flowers planted
With snow-white chrysanthemums.

[Page 110]

The Tormented Community of Telekhany
by Yehoshua Sklar (Tel Aviv)

It is with pain and deep chagrin that we recall our dear community of Telekhany. The word *Telekhany* , which always conjured up joyful and warm memories and the happiness of our youth, now conjures up mourning and sadness. We stand with bowed heads as we remember the catastrophe we all encountered.

Our hearts are filled with endless pain, suffering and anger whenever we recall what our hometown of Telekhany once was. Our dear and unforgettable parents and siblings perished in a murderous and savage manner. There is no longer any signs or memories of them; not even any gravestones of those who died before the War. In its place the Soviet regime built an oil storage facility.

The rich and colorful Jewish life of a toiling community was cruelly and tragically destroyed, lost forever. Jewish Telekhany, just like all other large communities, had a brief history. After World War I, Jews returned to town, and without noticing the ruins they encountered, they started rebuilding a brand new life, and despite the young age of the town, it began blooming with cultural and community activities.

The little town of Telekhany had a Jewish school, beginning with the study of the alphabet with the unforgettable and beloved teacher, R. Chaim Yeshayahu Shneidman, to the establishment of the higher grades with our dear teacher, Hershel Rudkovsky. Although it wasn't in the form of a gymnasia high school, we enjoyed studying there. There was also a Polish school, a library and a reading room. There was a free loan fund, a hospice for the poor and a Jewish bank, which assisted artisans and small businessmen. This is the way toiling Telekhany lived and worked.

Jews formed a small part of town, but their creative life was felt throughout the region. There were merchants, craftsmen and wagon-drivers – there was everything in Telekhany. The Oginsky Canal, which had tree-lined streets (the so-called alleys) on both sides, was always filled with young people. A hundred meters beyond the Canal stood the empty brick house that had a long history of stories of demons and other fairy tales.

That bubbly Jewish life was extinguished and destroyed forever. Jewish Telekhany ceased to exist. We speak of our destroyed hometown with great awe, and want to memorialize the martyrs of Telekhany, who are engraved in our hearts forever. With our Yizkor Book we want to memorialize in history the rich cultural activity and tragic end of the Jewish community of Telekhany. May the Yizkor Book serve as a gravestone for the unmarked mass graved of our dear community of Telekhany.

———————

[Page 111]

Telekhany

The secluded town of Telekhany is located many miles away from the nearest large Jewish community and is near the Oginsky Canal, which served as the most important link among the towns of White Russia, in the heart of the Pripet Marshlands and surrounded by dense forests.

Telekhany made its meager living from surrounding villages, the Belarusian villages built on the poor Polesian earth, which couldn't sufficiently sustain the peasants, even when the sweating peasants toiled heavily from sunrise to sunset. Therefore, the peasants were forced to look for work beyond their fields, chopping wood in the forest, fishing in the local lake, and producing wood and clay vessels. In order to save money, the family members of the peasant had to produce most of the household items themselves – clothes, shoes and dishes.

They would bring a portion of the goods they produced to Telekhany for sale or barter, and would get what they needed – some food, tools for work, some fabric for clothes, etc. This type of interaction made up the pinnacle of economic life in Telekhany.

The poverty of Telekhany depended on the poverty of the villages. Whenever the peasants were impoverished, so was the town. Telekhany was a town that was similar to many other such Jewish communities that were spread out across the marshes of Polesia. Only the "scenic" walk along the Canal, the "ditch" along the edge of the forest, and the area of the forests surrounding Telekhany offered the town a special charm.

2

The men of Telekhany were laborers, craftsmen, shopkeepers who cherished and were helpful to each other, and who were connected to each other through family ties. The shopkeeper didn't abandon the peasant in bad times, and offered him credit. His measures were proper, and his scales truthful. The artisan knew his customers, their families and problems. He participated in their worries, helped them in hard times and shared their joys.

At the beginning of the twentieth century, new winds blew into the sleepy town. The younger generation noticed the poverty in town, and was dissatisfied with an impoverished existence. The youth aspired to change, and looked for a different way. Some sought their aspirations through emigration overseas; others organized political movements that sought extensive social change.

In the meantime, World War I broke out, and Telekhany experienced the horrors of war. Eventually Telekhany was at the battlefront, and most of the homes in town were consumed by fire as the residents fled.

3

The war finally ended, and some residents returned home. Others remained in the places of refuge during the war. Many left the country and moved to other countries in the New World. Those who returned to Telekhany rebuilt the ruins, built small wood houses and returned to their former way of life.

There was no change in the region, and Telekhany sank into poverty just like before. New technology didn't reach the cut-off region, and never found its way to town. There were no cars, no paved roads, no agricultural machinery, and of course no electricity. The peasants and their families made do with their primitive methods of working their small piece of land from sunup to sunset, and the earth responded meagerly to their toiling.

The artisans toiled together with their young apprentices for twelve hours a day. Income was meager, and could barely support the artisans' families. The older people lived with these oppressive conditions, but not the young people. Many of them decided to join youth movements. A few joined the Socialist-Zionist movement with others joining the other leftwing ones.

Many sought training as pioneers for emigration to Palestine. However, what united all the movements was the desire to change society, which didn't allow for a possibility of getting out from under the mournful conditions of poverty in Telekhany.

Striving for a finer, better and safer World

Revolutionary expressions began to develop. The youth in Telekhany stood at the head of the revolutionary movement that was struggling against the oppressive yoke of the Polish regime. Many who aspired to education who were turned away from schools pursued self-study and culture societies. They read extensively and broadened their horizons. In general, Telekhany developed a lively cultural movement, with lectures about political issues, readings and discussions about literary subjects, and drama groups that put on productions on social and national topics. Telekhany became famous for its enlightened youth and rich political and cultural activities.

The Polish authorities didn't approve of these activities. The members of the Communist Party were mercilessly persecuted, and were imprisoned and sent away to the Kartuz-Bereza camps that were unfortunately near Telekhany.

All elements and movements within the local Jewish population were proud of those comrades, and viewed them as an example of dedicated fighters willing to sacrifice themselves for their precious goals. Many of the Zionist-Socialist youth movements joined the pioneer training camps, and upon completion departed for Palestine.

Approximately eighty families from Telekhany are in Israel. Many of them arrived before World War II, and have settled all over the country, both in towns and cities. They participated together with the rest of the Jews in the struggle for the right of independence. They fought in the War of Liberation and secured the arrival of others from home who survived who were warmly welcomed by the Telekhany families.

Survivors of Telekhany maintain strong ties. They share celebrations and sorrows, and retain the customs of their parents, as well as their ordinary traditions, in love and work, with sincerity. Former residents of Telekhany are still proud of their hometown, and hold an annual memorial for the martyrs who perished during World War II. Our Telekhany was worthy of its name, and it should be memorialized in a book. Let us exalt the images of our people of Telekhany and our dear families with love and respect.

May the book be a sacred memorial to a typical Jewish town in its struggle to exist, and in its observance of the eternal traditions of the Jewish People, and that was destroyed together with other Jewish towns under the accursed Nazis.

When we read chapters of the book to our children, the source of their origin shouldn't seem strange to them, and the memory of our parents should be retained from generation to generation.

[Page 114]

The Mordechai Gurstal Family

The Zionist movement started to penetrate Telekhany in 1904-5, and was especially attractive to middle class young people, though adults also joined it. One example was the family of Mordechai Gurstal, who was also known as Motel the shipper. He was already a mature adult, but his children joined the Zionist movement, and today we find that all of his grandchildren live in Israel, and many of them participated in the building of the country and occupy responsible positions in economic and political life.

Mordechai Gurstal's son was the late Yaakov Gurstal. His daughter and her husband Zelig Zelikovitch lived in Israel. Zelig was a military officer during the War of Liberation. Likewise, the children of the late Reuven Gurstal also live in Israel. They also participated in developing the country, and the children of the late Shimon Peretz Gurstal were also accomplished individuals. They all arrived in Palestine, and finally he too arrived in Palestine with his wife in 1925.

Until the present the entire family is concentrated in Israel: the parents, three sons and two daughters. Shimon Peretz and his wife Sarah died in 1952 in the Geva kevutsa [agricultural group]. Two sons, Yosef and Shlomo, and the eldest daughter Chana are also in the Geva kevutsa . One son, Yaakov, is in the Geva kevutsa named after the martyrs of Pinsk. The second daughter, Yehudit, lives in Haifa.

The children of Nissel Gurstal, who was also known as Nissel the Shipper, also live in Israel. One son, Asher and his son Binyamin, as well as Mendel, the son of Reuven Gurstal, are in Israel as well. The son of Shimon Peretz Gurstal changed his name to Gurion, and everyone else in the family, according to the branches, also took the name Gurion.

This gives some idea of the town of Telekhany that contributed much to the honor of its residents, especially the image of the late Yosef Gurion, who contributed significantly to the development of Israel. After his premature death, his Geva kevutsa published a book called Yosef Gurion, His Life, Words and Accomplishments.

Yosef Gurion was born in Pinsk in 1898. He studied in the local school in town and joined a Zionist youth group. In February, 1914 at the age of 16, he traveled with a group from Pinsk to Palestine to study at the Petach Tikvah Agricultural School. When World War I broke out, he was forced to go to work. He and his friends leased some land in a settlement and began cultivating vegetables. After he finished his agricultural course, he decided to join the Be'er Tuviah kevutsa, which was one of the first kevutsas in Palestine.

Gurion joined the first Jewish Legion, and when the Legion was dissolved, he returned to the kevutsa and became one of the most active entrepreneurs in the kevutsa and the moshav. For various reasons, the Be'er Tuvia kevutsa didn't work out, and broke up. In the meantime, Yosef got married and joined the Geva kevutsa in the Jezreel Valley. In 1924 he and his wife were admitted as members, and he remained there until his death.

Over the years, Yosef was involved in a variety of activities and community undertakings. He was always a member of the agricultural workers' council, a member of the Regional Cooperative Bank, and a founding board member of the milk company Tnuva .

In 1942-43, Yosef ran the Haifa branch of Tnuva, and thereafter of the Jerusalem branch. He served as a member of the board of the company *Nir* ,as well as on the Kupat Holim Health Fund.

In 1936-37 he traveled to the United States on behalf of the Histadruth Labor Federation, and in 1938-39 he managed *Kofer Hayishuv*. In 1944-47 he served as a representative of the Jewish Agency department concerned with settling soldiers, and visited a brigade and other Jewish military units in Egypt and Italy. Yosef was a leading member of the organization that resettled people liberated in the war. He was also a leading member of *Otsar Hachayal [Soldier Fund]*.

At the end of the War of Liberation he was hired by the Ministry of Defense to administer the department for the rehabilitation of soldiers and the wounded. He devoted all his energies for that work. Shortly thereafter he served in the Development Authority of the State of Israel.

When he finished his work for the government he went back to work at *kevutsa* Geva. However, he wasn't allowed to stay long, and was soon asked to become the secretary of the Federation of Kevutsot and Kibbutzim. When he returned home after completing his work in poor health, he was then asked to run a sugar factory in Afula.

He worked very strenuously, and after he completed his work for the period for which he was hired, he returned home ill and weak. He worked around home for a few moths, and then passed away on 19 Shvat 5717 [corresponds to English date January 21, 1957, not 1955] suddenly for a heart attack.

May he be remembered for a blessing.

———

[Page 117]

Memories of Telekhany
Akiva Ilivitsky (Tel Aviv, Israel)

Our friend Michael Ziss, who was a community leader in his hometown of Telekhany, tells us how dear Telekhany and other nearby towns and villages looked before and after World War One.

Telekhany was situated among forests, fields, rivers and lakes, and among the famous ten locks of the large Oginsky Canal. Therefore, its location in such an area, its beautiful natural environment with its alleys for strolling, and its empty brick house made Telekhany popular.

Many people would stroll in the forest to the glassworks and the Hutner Forest; it was very popular because of the fact that hundreds of families would earn their living from it, and because their husbands, wives and children worked in the large glass factory that was called the glassworks.

There were hundreds of people who would come to stay in cottages in the Hutner Forest to relax in the good climate and dry weather. In the turpentine area people would extract the sap from the pine trees and make turpentine out of it. Spending time around the pine trees would make weak and weary people feel better after spending 10-14 hours a day at work.

There were 300-350 Jewish families in Telekhany, in addition to the non-Jewish residents. The Jewish population lived in a chassidic environment, especially on the Sabbath and holy days. Suffering and joys were forgotten, and the melodies and songs of the Chassidim would fill the streets and alleys of town. The beautiful Chassidic melodies provided charm and a feeling of brotherhood and warmth: always be joyful; forget your problems, and live with hope that everything will pass and things will turn out all right; forget your worries and troubles.

Not far from us there was a Jewish community – a settlement in a small town named Sventa Volya. The people there were different from us. Whenever they spoke, they sang. It was a different way of speaking, a different dialect. However, we lived together with them, raised our children with them, and conducted a community life together with them. This was the case also with the Jewish community in the town of Lohishen. All the residents in the nearby towns shared a Jewish life together. At times they got together at election time and to improve our economic situation and cultural needs.

Most of the people were killed, and many of them emigrated to various countries, including Israel, where many currently live. We remember those who died every year – they were our dear and beloved parents and siblings who perished so tragically.

The Red Army in Telekhany in 1939–1953

Mr. Michael Kruptzik of Telekhany, who recently came here from Russia explains:

When the Soviets were arriving in Telekhany, the residents were impatiently awaiting them. At that time, the Poles, who had been in control of the government fled, leaving us without a local government, and without any assistance or protection.

The peasants of the nearby villages were ready to rob the community. The government was taken over by communists Leibel and Ephraim Ber Klitenick and a few Christians. There was also Leibel Minkes, Yisraelik Bernstein and others. Though the Poles had left town, they were in the forests, and would occasionally come back to town. On one occasion when they left, they took with them fifteen young boys. I believe that their screaming reached the heavens until the decree was revoked and we were able to save them.

The courageous among us, almost the majority of the community, decided to go over to the Red Army and ask them to come into Telekhany as soon and as fast as possible. The army was then located in the town of Hontsevich.

When the Jewish community was attending synagogue at noon on Yom Kippur, the first soldiers arrived, accompanied by an airplane. Everybody went outside and thought it was a *nalosh*, and we were now overjoyed. None of us was afraid any longer, and everyone relaxed. We all now suddenly fell asleep, since the community had not slept out of worry of an order to kill us.

A "revolutionary committee" was immediately set up, and Leibel Klitenick was appointed "commander." The situation now settled down, became calm and normalized. The local talented and important members of the Communist Party took over the government and the revolutionary committee until Russia sent in other officials. The local communists eventually started filling various positions and work in town:

1. The communist Ephraim Klitenick worked as an accountant in the regional organization (Raysoyuz);
2. Leibel Klitenick worked in the financial institutions and organizations;
3. Yisrael Bernstein was elected as an official in the combine of industrial plants (Raykombinat);
4. Yudel Landman was appointed director of the regional agricultural department (Rayzemotdyel); a few of the local communists went away to study and complete their education in programs in Pinsk so they could work as accountants in the bank.

I was appointed secretary of the village council (Syelsoviet) in Hartal, and later was transferred to Telekhany to serve in the same position. My work was difficult because I had to work on administrative office statistics. I had to prepare various residents lists, and lists of artisans, tradesmen, houses, stables, trees and an inventory of livestock: cows, horses, goats, hens, geese, ducks, pigs and dogs. Everything was recorded in the books of the village council.

The situation was worse when the village council had to provide lists of young boys of 16–17 years of age who were sent to study in trade schools. The children and their parents would curse me mercilessly because of my being involved with them. The mothers didn't appreciate the idea and the decree that we had to prepare the younger generation so they would study and thereby be saved from death. I believe that had they known this, they would have acted differently and supported the decree and the work we were doing.

My sister Yehudit was appointed as secretary of the regional agricultural department, and Zadok, the son of Chaytsha Chana Pesha, was also elected secretary of the Krolevitch village council. Almost all the Jews got positions in various places. The shoemaker and tailor moved to the workshops, and the police were housed at first in Avramel's brick house. All the positions were located at the estate, and at one point the police moved to the building of the former municipality.

When the Soviet army arrived, of course, they organized courses for learning Russian. At Yoshchemka's house, beyond the river, a hospital was set up. I requested that my younger brother Yisrael and my cousin Molya, the son of Chaytsha Chana Pesha, not go to trade school. Unfortunately, they were killed by the Germans in the hospital.

The economic situation was poor; people suffered, and many of them were in constant hunger. It was awful just to be able to obtain a loaf of bread every day because there were very long lines to get into the stores, shops and businesses, but unfortunately the stores and businesses were empty. If any products arrived in town to fill up the stores, the wives of the recently arrived commissars would take it. Eventually the storekeepers Isaac Shalom Yudel's son, whose shop was in Asher Nissel's house; my uncle Moshe Chaim Ziss worked in the store's warehouse to make sure that no one stole anything in the store.

The bakery was in the house of Nachman the baker. Nachman was arrested and expelled to Brisk. After serving 7-8 months in Brest-Litovsk he was released. The Soviet army and communist activists reformed our socialist foundations, creating an active cultural life so that our children and youth would study. Temporarily, during war and breaks in fighting, our lives slowly got back to normal, we lived under such circumstances from 1939 to June 22, 1941, when the Germans, the Nazis and their savage army attacked Russian territory.

At that time I was hired to mobilize people into the Soviet Red Army. I would devote almost 24 hours to this task without any rest, and increase manpower for the Red Army so we could defend ourselves in case we were attacked, and so that if the Red Army ordered us to engage in war, we would be ready to attack and assault the hatred.

My mother was in Motele, the hometown of Dr. Professor Chaim Weizman, staying with my sister who had gotten married in 1939. On the night of June 23-24 the civilian population and the Red Army were shuddering when the weapons warehouses in the large city of Pinsk were dynamited, and we could even see the flames in Telekhany. Of course, this created panic and chaos, and the mobilized soldiers of the Russian Soviet Army ran to Pinsk, but unfortunately, didn't get there. All the residents of the town had fled, and each person looked for somewhere to hide for a while until things calmed down. Everyone looked for help and ways to protect themselves. The panic worsened when the authorities in town fled. Of course, without any governmental authorities there was panic and anarchy. It was terrible to see how people plundered and pillaged, robbing the stores and warehouses. The bakeries were attacked, and people stole hot bread, getting in there through the bars over the windows. All the women were wailing and crying, and the young just fled the town.

That evening my mother returned. In the morning hours I can home from the village council, and when I saw my own mother, I was surprised and overjoyed to know that she was still in Telekhany and among the living. Her instinct was correct when she told me to leave town, and I survived because I listened to her. It was hard for me to have to leave all my loved ones, including my own mother.

A Christian named Khmielevska approached me on the street, and asked why I wasn't leaving. She knew what I was involved in, and started gushing forth, "You never did anything bad to anyone, but simply felt your human obligation and task; if the Germans get here, they'll hang you up on the first tree. Get going!" This is how the Christian woman spoke to me. When I started on my way, and got to Asher Nissel's house, I saw Shamshel Alter Bashes who said that he wasn't going anywhere since things wouldn't be worse for him under Hitler than they were under Stalin.

I decided to flee, and called Sima Asher Nissels Gurstal, but she didn't want to leave her mother Chana alone. I made the suggestion to Sarah Chana Stolyar as well as to Dina Gittelman, the daughter of Nachman the packer. They decided not to go with me, and refused my proposal. When I left I took along my only sister Yehudit, as well as Zadok Chaitsha Chana Peshas. We went alone because everyone else had already left earlier. When we approached Vihonoshetz we met Shlomka of Bobrovitch, the husband of Machlia Zadok. When he recognized us, he turned to Zadok and said, "Where are you going? Come back! If you've already decided to go, then take along the horse in the stall." When Zadok heard this, he went back with him. I never saw him again. My sister Yehudit was tired and had large calluses on her feet. She couldn't walk any further.

Not far from Hontsevitch I met a large group of Jews from Telekhany, including Motel Meidelov and his wife, Isaac Zavel's children and many others. My sister decided to go back together with this group, even though it pained and disappointed her to do so. However, in such circumstances it is very difficult to tell someone what to do. I went on a long journey deep into Russia all alone, without being helped or part of any group of wanderers. When I got past Vihonoshetz, I met many young people from Telekhany who had been employed there: the judge, police official, NKVD official and others. They were going further and stopped to tell us that it was incorrect and a lie that the Germans were approaching. They asked us to go to Vihonoshetz and tell the gentiles to come with wagons, meaning they should harness up the horses and take the Jews back to Telekhany. I understood that they wanted to get away from us. I was against it, while others believed them and went to Vihonoshetz.

Seeing that the young Jews listened to them and left, the gentiles departed in the direction of Russia. Watching the Christians, I left with them, stayed at a distance from them, and didn't join them in the refugee camp. I never saw or heard about the young people who left for Vihonoshetz again. I don't know whether they got to Vihonoshetz or were killed by the gentiles there. Berl Meltzer, the young son of Moshe the barber, left his things with me and asked me to watch them until he returned from Vihonoshetz, but I never saw him again.

Along the way we found out that the Russian border guards wouldn't let anyone from the new regions ("westerners") across the border. We continued on our way, and through a large marshland, until we got to the town of Hontsevich. There were no longer any border guards when we crossed over the border. Their barracks were empty, and the first town on the other side of the border crossing was Krasnaya Sloboda, not far from Bobruisk. I met there many people from Telekhany: Moshka Roshchintzer and the children of Feibel Chasha Leah; Gittel Izuk and her husband Yeshayahu and their children; Chaya Leah of Kolonsk and her brother Yankel; Yisrael David Kagan (Gershons) and many others such as Yehudit and Chaitsha Chana Peshas.

When the latter recognized me, she started to cry and told me that she fled in the morning with Feivel's children, but now they were being chased away because they had nothing to eat. I had a few buns that I had exchanged for some possessions that Berl Moshe the son of the barber had left behind before going to Vihonoshetz. I was thinking that if I survived, I would have to make an accounting and pay for it.

I took along my cousin Yehudit, and told her that we both would live and eat the same thing. As we went further away from town, we met Gittel Yuzuk [sic], who started crying and demanding that we return home. She told Yehudit that wherever she goes, she could return home. After this sermonizing and explanation, she suddenly started saying that she wanted to go home. I didn't know what to advise her under the circumstances, but I didn't let her go, but she insisted on returning home. I didn't want to convince her otherwise, since I didn't want her to blame me in case anything happened on our journey.

She returned home with an entire group of refugees, however I don't know whether they ever got there, and I proceeded on my own all alone. In Krasnaya Slaboda I met Chaytsha Lutsky (Freidels) and the children, as well as Feigel Minkes. They told me that they couldn't go any further because Chaytsha was on the verge of giving birth, and their husbands, Hershel and Yisrael Bernstein had gone on ahead. So Chaytsha Lutsky, Feigel Minkes and their children were killed in Krasnaya Slaboda.

I continued on my journey – the journey of a hapless Jew walking with his walking stick and people he didn't know. Behind the town of Starobin in the forest, I met Gronya the wife of Chaim the bathhouse attendant, who had swollen feet, as well as the Telekhany teacher Melech Asher and his wife. Gronya began to say that her husband Chaim and their child, as well as Ephraim Ber Klitenick, Bracha Dinhan and Asher Godiner had gone on ahead, and she stayed behind because she couldn't continue. We remained together for a few hours, but the German armored troops soon arrived in Starobin. They were the first soldiers who came to inspect the area as a strategic location.

Hunger soon prevailed, and it was difficult just to buy bread. I left immediately, leaving everyone who had been with me behind. I went by foot in an unknown direction. The road I was on was unknown to me because it was my first time there.

In 1941 I ended up in Kazakhstan, and being among the living, I found out that among those people were the following people from Telekhany: Asher and Naomi Gurstal, Leibel Eisenberg, Minkes, Feivel Rubacha's children, Moshele Kamadiyeev (Avraham Chaim'o), Shlomo Landman and Gronya.

In 1943 in the city of Swerdlovsk I happened to meet Ephraim Ber Klitenick, who informed me that his wife Bracha Dina, Asher Godiner, Mashka Roshchnitzer and a few other Telekhany Jews were still alive. Sometimes I would write letters to Palestine to my cousin Michael Ziss (Chana Peshas) who now lives in Kefar Yehoshua not far from Nahalal in the Jezreel Valley on the way to Haifa. I found out from his letters about other people from Telekhany who would write letters to friends and relatives in Palestine.

Several times I have mentioned the Red Army, which was approaching our area. When I found out about it, I immediately started writing letters to my relatives in Telekhany. Even now it's hard to believe that the Germans killed everyone.

I wrote to my mother and aunt Chana Pesha, Henoch Stolyar and others. I also wrote to my sister in Motele. Unfortunately, all my letters were returned, with the statement that the Germans had killed all the Jews. I wrote to the Telekhany village council and received a response saying that all the Jews had been killed by the Germans on August 6–7, 1941. I received the same answer from the Motele village council. My sister and her husband and child lived there for ten months.

In August 1946 I arrived in Telekhany to visit my hometown and those who remained alive after the great catastrophe and the Great War. When I got off the airplane at the Telekhany airfield and went to the estate near the river, I found a terrible situation. The river had dried up and was filled with weeds. The locks were gone, and only the empty brick house and the well remained. I went to the place where our house had been built, and it pained me to see what happened and what remained. Only the lilac bush that my father had planted for the bar mitzvah of my brother Alter remained. The trees and the bush had become overgrown, and there were pieces of paper between the branches. I thought I might find something written on those papers from my relatives, and with their handwriting. I went further among the trees and bushes and picked up various pieces of paper, but unfortunately they were pieces strewn around by the wind.

When I stood there deep in thought, and looked at what happened, looking among the branches, I suddenly noticed a figure of a woman, a Christian, who started to cry profusely. While I was staying with our neighbor, Voit Kovolevsky, I started to feel frightened, and my heart hurt from everything that occurred. I wouldn't go out onto the street – it was really frightening, like a solitary person who finds himself in a large forest among wild animals. I was frightened to look through the window; it seemed as if I could see Henoch and Chana through the window.

The Stolin and Lubisher synagogues of the Chassidim were burned down and destroyed. The alley where my aunt Chana Pesha lived was destroyed and erased from the face of the earth; only the earth and the houses remained where Berel Tchernomertzes, Bashes, and our family had lived. Everything was destroyed, even the fences. There were only the fields and a few lonely houses. Where you used to see Jewish faces, all you saw now were the faces of old gentile women of the villages of Babrovitch and Viada who had moved to Telekhany due to the fact that the Germans had burned down the houses and villages. After the murder of the Jews, the Germans brought in people from deep inside Russia, from the Smolensk region.

Our large glassworks factory, where hundreds of men and women worked, was destroyed. It had provided sustenance for the community and its development, and attracted new residents. At one time to come to the factory was a long trip, and now it was faster to get there. I had then met Yossel Grushko, the wagon driver.

We went together to the mass graves, where our loved ones were buried – people who were torn away from us too early. The graves are located at Salomka's fields, not far from Vasilev's forests. There are three large graves of men, women and children in those fields. My heart turned to stone as I stood there, since I couldn't cry. The description of the massacre is awful. They were shot in their underwear, and with a burst of machine-gun fire, they fell over into the large open graves. Many were buried alive, including Reuven Rubinstein's wife from Babrovitch. They repeatedly shot Feigel, the wife of the gravedigger (Avraham David), but the bullet didn't work. They wanted to take away her child, but she refused, so they shot her and the child, a newborn. I was told that my aunt Chana Pesha was shot while lying in bed because she wouldn't go. Her grandchild, Zadok Chaytsha's, hid out for a while. After the massacre, he was lost and ended up not far from Kraglevitch. A gentile woman who he knew gave him food. The gentile police of Kraglevitch caught him, brought him to the commander who shot him at the estate of the Pole Koszciol, where he was buried.

In 1946, while I was in Telekhany, we told the gentiles that I had wanted to transfer him to the Jewish cemetery, but no one knew where he was buried. The local priest, who knew, had left for Poland. The bodies of the people were never reburied in a Jewish cemetery, but remained around in fields and forests. This included all my friends, my mother and younger brother in Telekhany, my sister Rachel and her husband in Motele, my sister Yehudit along the way between Telekhany and Hantsevitch.

The local Jews suffered greatly from the gentiles and neighboring villages. When the Red Army left, and the Germans had not yet arrived in Telekhany, the local gentiles would surround the town after sundown every day with horses and wagons, and break tires, rob and beat all the Jews. They would have pogroms like in the time of Khmelnitski and Petlura.

Jews would hide wherever they could. My mother and brother looked for protection, as did Henoch, Chana and Sarah Stolyar, with our neighbor Kovalyevsky. Yudel Nissels and his family, and Chana Asher's Gurstal and her children would seek refuge in the loft in Radek's stable, where he stored hay and straw. Each person in town looked for somewhere to hide.

As soon as the Germans arrived, they prohibited the gentiles from rampaging. This didn't last long, and shortly thereafter all the Jews were killed. They were taken to the glassworks, and on the road stood Krutchenka, the sister of the priest. She saw how my mother was being led away for the last time, and she said, "Be well, who knows whether we'll see each other again." Soon people heard shooting. The screaming and crying could be heard far away until there was silence again.

There was the case where they captured Yenta Potrebnick (a grandchild of Avraham David). She told the German not to shoot her because she was so beautiful. The German didn't shoot her; instead a gentile policeman shot her on the spot.

I left the mass graves and went to the cemetery, where my father and older brother Alter are buried. Unfortunately, I couldn't find their graves, and only a few complete gravestones remained. The rest were erased. There were also Christian graves with crosses.

At the end of 1946 I left Kazakhstan for Pinsk. There are no Jews today in Telekhany, nor in the neighboring towns. I visited Telekhany a few times; when I went there the Christians would tell me how they had helped to save Jews.

I once went to Telekhany with Aharon Natan Matuskis and Motya Reuven Gurstels, and we entered their home. There is today a store in Reuven's house. The walls dividing the rooms were removed. When we arrived in Telekhany, all the non-Jews surrounded us because they all knew me. They asked about Motya, and whether he was also from Telekhany. We answered no, because Motya was registered under the name of a family outside of town.

I couldn't watch Motya's pain as I relived with him the pain of the situation we were in, and what happened to us after we lost our best and most devoted. In Malka Reuven's the storekeeper's store, we saw an old gentile woman from a village selling produce. I visited Telekhany more often, and looked at everything and the orphaned houses, how the gentiles turned windows into doors and doors into windows. Everything was renovated. The cemetery was totally destroyed, and in its place they built a warehouse for kcroscnc.

The non-chassidic synagogue was now used to store rye and wheat, and turned into a huge granary. Asher Nissel's house was turned into a dairy, and Yitzchak Landman's house was turned into a court. Sklyar's house became the prosecutor's office, and Isaac's Zavel's house an army, police and NKVD headquarters, and Avrahamel's brick house, the bank. Alter Crystal's house became the village council, and Aharon Landman's house the financial administration. The barracks were turned into the regional executive offices.

Telekhany Jews who remained in Russia, and whom I know about, are: Moshel Komodyov in Leningrad; Berl Feivel Rubacha's and Moshka Roshtsintser in Kiev; Aharon Feivels in Tashkent; Hershel Bernstein and Gedaliah Kortshmer in Russia.

In Pinsk there remained Hershele Tuvias Terepolsky; in the town of Summi, Shimon Bresky, the grandson of David the bathhouse attendant; Malchiel Itskovitch left Pinsk via Poland and went to Palestine. The following families went to Poland: Aharon Begun Natans, Leibel Klitenick and Gronya, Ephraim Ber Klitenick and Bracha Dina.

[Page 128]

A Chapter from "From Telekhany to America"
by Esther Miller
The Glass Factory

One mild summer morning a sharp whistle suddenly cut through the air, notifying Telekhany that the glass factory was open and people should come to work. Doors flew open. People spilled out of their houses to see and hear the factory's first signal. They didn't see a thing, but heard a shrill whistle coming from the town's outskirts far behind the woods.

The wide road leading to the glass factory was crowded with people. Old and young walked in the direction of the horn. The contractor and builder of the factory, Shia Beilkes, a Jew in his late thirties, tall, bony, quick, with sharp facial features, happy gray eyes and a short trimmed beard walked proudly forward. He was the only carpenter in Telekhany who could read blueprints. People said that he could understand construction blueprints as well as the engineer Krutchenko, who created the entire glass factory construction plan. Under Shia Beilkes supervision several hundred tradesmen worked, a fact that filled him with enormous joy and pride on his way to the completed factory.

The glass factory promised the town prosperity, and when construction started there was no shortage of tradesmen; most of the tradesmen were brought in from the nearby communities. Even before the factory started production, Jews in town earned a living from its construction, and shopkeepers earned their living from the tradesmen and peasants who were employed in the construction.

The truth is that the factory didn't open all of a sudden, but gradually, involving one group of tradesmen and then another, section by section. However, on that morning the first signal coming from the factory was heard all over town, calling those who had already been hired to come to work. Many peasants came from the villages with their wives and children. They arrived in horse-drawn wagons and on foot. Old overworked peasants with brown faces like the brown wrinkled bark of old trees, and broad-shouldered young people from villages, full of strength in their limbs. Many of the peasants crossed themselves and expressed amazement at the new wood houses and the new roads at the huge new glass factory, which were spread out on a huge piece of land, covered since time immemorial with wild trees and tall swamp grasses.

More than anyone, Jewish mothers and their young children were pleased with the factory. All the women whose husbands were religious teachers and tradesmen took their young daughters to the factory to apply for jobs with the Jewish businessmen, the Tchernichov brothers. Shmuel Tchernichov was the younger brother, and was in charge of hiring workers. Rumor had it that the Tchernichovs only hired tall and healthy-looking girls. The younger and weaker children were sent home to "eat porridge." The mothers of such children found a way around this obstacle. They dressed the children in their older sisters' dresses and high heels and went to try their luck. Maybe they would succeed, and many did. There was almost no household in town without at least one child employed or promised employment there.

On that morning, Fradel took Bailka by the hand and Chaim, dressed in a Spencer, by the other. She knew that her children were still too small to work in the factory, but she just wanted to share the big event with everyone else and revel in the new source of prosperity, in the revival that the factory was bringing to town. With tears of joy in her eyes she thought it would now be unnecessary to send children away to work as housemaids or to factories in the big cities. Pearl would come home from Pinsk where she worked in a match factory, and get a job here. Even today she would ask the Yanover wagon driver to bring her home for G-d's sake. Looking at the people around her coming along to Tchernichov's office to look for a job for themselves or their children, she felt that everything up till now was just a run up to the great event that the factory was now bringing into the life of the town.

Long before the factory opened, the town sizzled. Wherever a person stood or went, in every home, everyone was talking about the great prosperity coming to Telekhany. Boats would travel the rivers, and people would send crates of glass products to big cities, and they would even go abroad by the hundreds, and even thousands, of crates. From there they would bring back merchandise never seen before in Telekhany! Everybody would live like a king.

Even before they started working, children dreamed at night about what they would do with the money they earned. Hodel, the daughter of Avremel the bricklayer, who was just about to leave town and take a job as a maid in a big city also got a job at the glass factory. She was so overjoyed that she had to share her joy with someone. She confided to her mother that she had spent a few days thinking about what she would do with her first earnings. Her mother Zelda advised her to save it for a wardrobe. Avremel the bricklayer said that she was still too young, and that there would be plenty of time to save money for featherbeds and cushions. In the meantime, he said, they should fix the straw roof, or even remove the straw and replace it with shingles so that the Christian priest wouldn't be able to pull the straw from it for not paying him his interest on time.

After haggling for a long time, her parents arrived at a compromise, i.e. when Hodel brought home her earnings, they would then decide what to do with it. When Hodel came home with her first three rubles and placed them on the table, the family rejoiced, and her little brothers and sisters attacked the table and looked at the shiny silver rubles with yearning eyes, not daring to touch them. Avremel also approached the table. Zelda, his wife, followed him. Her small gray eyes gray eyes looked at the coins, and her wrinkled face, surrounded by a white kerchief, shone. She too was scared to touch the coins. Avremel picked up one silver ruble, examined it carefully and bit it with his strong yellow teeth. He did the same with the other two coins. He bit them all around and suddenly dropped them on the table. When he heard the fine sharp sound they made, he smiled, and was now convinced that they weren't counterfeit, but real silver rubles. Then he raised his eyes to the ceiling and started counting as if he were deliberating with someone. "Three rubles, fourteen hours a day, for six days, how much does it come to for one hour?" He wrinkled his forehead and scarcely moved his lips. It was obvious that his mind was working hard. After a few minutes of calculating, he said: "It comes to about 3-4 kopeks an hour."

Avremel the bricklayer was a tall wide-shouldered Jew with a hard diffuse beard, the color of mature dry straw. He was very poor and burdened with many children. He calculated figures on paper, but he was excellent in his head. Whoever had some calculation problem in town came to Avremel the bricklayer. He would raise his eyes to the ceiling, rub his straw beard and start thinking. When he found the right result, his clay-spattered face gave a smile. He clapped his calloused hands and said: "That's it." He was always exact to the cent. Now, as always, he was satisfied with his result. He played a little with the three silver rubles, then handed them to Zelda and said, "Here, put it away so she can make herself a new dress for the holidays." Selde took the coins, went to the dresser, opened a drawer, found a white handkerchief, wrapped the rubles in it and hid it in a drawer under the white holiday tablecloth. She said: "With good health, it will come in handy." Hodel took note of where her mother hid the money.

The next day after work, she ran to Arieh Leib the moneylender, gave him the three rubles and got back her mother's pawned candlesticks. The next Friday night Zelda kindled the Sabbath candles in her brass candlesticks, not in the scooped turnips.

When the factory opened, life in town started moving faster. Every morning children hurried to work. They returned home late and exhausted. Many girls complained of aches and pains in arms, necks and spines. The mothers didn't make a fuss of it, the children rested, forgot about their pain and continued working. Life for mothers became easier. Debts were paid off, pawned pillows, blankets or small pieces of jewelry pawned off to the moneylender since people were married were bought back. Barefooted girls got stockings, shoes and new dresses. Fathers and mothers were happy and thanked God for the income provided by the glass factory. Everything was going fine, girls saved for dowries, started wardrobes, and began to dream of marriage.

It shouldn't be said that everyone was pleased with the glass factory. Jews of the old generation complaining, "What a stir, what a commotion! Children working, becoming breadwinners! Giving advice! Girls coming in contact with boys and getting spoiled. Young people going to work in a glass factory. The yeshiva in Vilna will become empty." This is how Moshe's brother-in-law, Aharon Shia, talked. He had a long gray beard all the way down to his belt.

Beilka's grandfather Moshe was the most pious Jew in town. He never spoke on the Sabbath, and if he ever had to, he did so with just a few words and in Hebrew. On weekdays he said: "Well, what a world! Such strange habits people have!" He and made a gesture as if he wanted to give up on the whole world. Later, when he heard that the Tchernichovs declared bankruptcy, he fumed and raved, and shook his head saying "Nothing good can come from such behavior."

The 20th Century came in raging and stormy, disturbing the peace of the great people. The factory workers became restless as well. They weren't just awed children any more the way they were when the factory opened, but grown adults with rheumatism. The work was hard on the girls, and all the factory workers complained about their pains, about long hours and low pay.

The owners felt the oncoming crisis among the workers. In addition there was the issues of large competition from other glass manufacturers, and poor business management. One autumn day the office ordered work stopped and the furnaces put out. A note on the doors announced that the owners had declared bankruptcy. Worry about earning a living again affected the town. Workers were unemployed and had no means of support. The town lived through a long hard winter.

One spring day, when the snow just began to melt, a wagon brought a chubby, handsome, Jew with a trimmed beard to town. A coachman was driving a reddish brown horse, and soon the good news spread around that Leib Turek was taking over the glass factory. He also contracted to build locks over the river and a steam mill to make flour.

Joy returned to town, and when the factory horn sounded again, people all over town went around with smiling faces since most people were workers, and they felt secure again, like people who knew where they were going and what they wanted. There were now young Polish glass blowers, specialists, molders and mechanics. Peasant workers returned from the villages, and the town came back to life. Not only was the factory working, but now there were sounds of carpenters' hammers building the mill and locks on the Oginsky Canal. Mothers again took their daughters to apply for jobs, and again children complained of aches and pains, and of long hours and low wages. And again the unrest among the workers began to increase.

———

[Page 133]

My Flowers on the Mass Grave and also on our Annihilated City of Telekhany

by Laibel Eisenberg

It was long before the idea of publishing a Yizkor book for the city of Telekhany was born that I had wanted to write down and perpetuate on paper certain thoughts and memories about our city Telekhany that is engraved in the hearts of us all. However, every time I began this task so many images, event and experiences from our town come to mind, that I don't even know where to begin. Should I begin with different personalities, tradesmen, storekeepers and ordinary people? Or with the Oginsky Canal and its ten locks that links Pinsk with Telekhany by steam ship? Or with the well known alley where people strolled and romanced for generations, starting with our grandparents, parents and siblings; or with the empty brick house with the imagined demons we would pass on the Sabbath during our strolls in the forest. Or possibly with the Rabbis and religious schools where I spent eight years of my life studying until the outbreak of World War I in 1914. Starting with the teacher Chaim Yeshayahu, then on to Hershel the secular studies teacher, and ending with the modern worldly Jewish teacher who we had in Telekhany, Shia Leizer.

I cannot accurately remember how old I was when I, like other children, began going to *kheder*; it must have been at about four or five years of age. I just remember, however, that in the year prior to the outbreak of the first World War, my father Jacob, who was very concerned that children should study worldly subjects, hired Sonja Boaz's to teach me, the youngest child, and the oldest of my brothers, Joshua, Russian and mathematics in the evening after we came home from *kheder*. All of these and dozens of other childhood memories, already virtually obscured in my memory, used to fill my thoughts and how they would lead from one to the other to be perpetuated in my memory.

I have to admit that I myself used to push aside all of these thoughts because I feared touching them lest, God forbid, because of my poor ability to describe lives and events, I minimize and obscure their brightness. However, all the following events served as an impetus, and forced me to record and describe some of my memories about our town of Telekhany: the aforementioned letter from the memorial committee; my last visit as a delegate from the Brazilian

Jewish delegation to the International Congress for Disarmament and Peace in Moscow in July, 1962, where I had a chance to meet my cousin's brothers Motel, Aharon and Shlomo Shlachman, as well as with the old politician Yossel Mashiach's, who currently serves in the important position of director of a textile factory near Moscow; my visit in Warsaw, Poland, with the brothers Ephraim and Leibel Davids Klitenick, two friends in work and battle; my subsequent visit to Israel when I participated in a memorial meeting held by the Committee on August 13, 1962 in Tel Aviv. The last encouraging letter I received from Esther Miller, a member of the Yizkor Book Committee, with whom I met in Telekhany in 1933 when I returned after spending four years in prison. All of this impelled, demanded and insisted that I record and take note of some of my recollections about our town of Telekhany.

I bring to this task my entire being and power of imagination to produce before my eyes the image of our Telekhany. I can now start to see the town's wood houses lined up together, creating a fire hazard; Telekhany's streets and wooden sidewalks, bringing its residents back to life just as I had left them the last time in 1936, when I was being persecuted for political reasons and had to leave for Brazil. I recall the economic and political situation of those days when the young people set off into the big world. Many became pioneers in Palestine. I remember the unemployment and the political and economic slavery. Fascism had already dominated Germany, and was poisoning and encouraging the growth of Polish fascism.

During my brief revolutionary activity in Telekhany in those days, from 1925-1936, I had undergone all of the torturous experiences of the Polish defense movement, including spending four hard years in prison, working on renewing the first concentration camp in Poland, Kartuz-Bereza.

Telekhany, that little town in Polesia in western White Russia had already distinguished itself with quite a few "political criminals" listed in the police archives. These were young people who had lost the fear of police torture, imprisonment and Kartuz-Bereza. The Mordechai Mariankellers, the Shammes Landmans, Yisrael David Kagan, Yisrael Feigel Bernstein, Ephraim and Leibel Klitenick, the Minas, Grunyas, Ethels and Devorah Dinas are recorded with dignity and pride in the revolutionary history of our destroyed town of Telekhany. With their courage and faith, battle and endurance, they showed that they remained faithful heirs of the fearless rebels and fighters, the Sisters and Brothers of 1905, who put our town of Telekhany on the map of revolutionary history in those days.

And our mothers? What honest, illustrious figures they were! They followed their children's involvement in "unkosher things" with tremendous devotion and motherly concern. They remained silent and consented to it, knowing how much mortal danger this involved. These mothers suffered tremendous pain and human dignity whenever a child was imprisoned or confined to a camp for his revolutionary activity. Many of them maintained intermittent illegal contacts after their sons were captured, and with their straight and pure thinking they understood that this was their child's life, and that his future and freedom was inexorably linked to it.

Many a year my dear, warm mother Rachel spent with the police's constant night searches with their electric lamps! She was white as chalk, shaking from fear as if she had a fever. My mother would ask me nervously, "My son, you thief, do you have any of your papers with you? Give them to me and I'll hide them." My poor devoted mother! She could not imagine that her son would soon be sent away after being proven not to have any papers.

It makes you shiver and shudder when you think about how all the gruesome and awful experiences were a mere trifle compared to what the Nazi beasts were thinking about how to murder and slaughter our loved ones. Is there a way to measure the deep pain and suffering of those who were murdered, raped and shot at the gravesite? Is there a comparable punishment that these murderers and rapists should pay for everything that was dear, holy and beloved to us? Is there any consolation for the few survivors who remained outside the mass graves?

If we who were not there were unable to help save their lives from the gruesome death, at least now we should feel our obligation and promise not to ever allow the memory of our heroes and martyrs to be forgotten. Material should be collected, and memories should be eternalized in a yizkor book about our town of Telekhany, both about those who lived long ago and about the bloody pages of history of our town. This should be a symbol of our resolve to do everything possible so that the world and the Jewish People never again know about ghettos and genocide. May our pain never disappear until we use our collective strength to do everything to liberate mankind from the horrible danger of war that in the Atomic Age is a mortal threat for all mankind, including the Jewish People.

———

[Page 136]

A Free Loan Society
and Food Bank for the Poor in
Telekhany
by Golda Bookman-Landman

As in every other city and town where there were various associations to assist the poor and needy such as free loan societies, hospices, wedding funds, clothing funds, etc., we in Telekhany also set up a free loan society and a food bank for the poor. These two organizations were created with money received from former Telekhany residents living in the United States who had organized a Telekhany association.

For many years, my grandfather, Nisan Gurstel, was treasurer of the free loan society, and worked in it joyfully and devotedly for many years. By providing interest free loans to poor artisans and shopkeepers repayable in small amounts, many poor people were assisted and helped back on their feet. My grandfather was so devoted to his work and to those receiving loans that he would go around collecting the weekly repayments so that the recipients didn't lose time bringing the money to the committee.

I was very familiar with the work, and knew about the situations people who received the loans were in since my grandfather made me his secretary and bookkeeper for both funds – the free loans society and the food bank. I remember when Gershon Gurstal came to Telekhany, and we, the free loan staff, welcomed him as a great guest, and prepared a special meeting in his honor.

When I was preparing to leave Telekhany, the administration together with our Rabbi Glick made a banquet for me to thank me for my devoted work. I was also assured that my work would also be appreciated in the United States. They kept their word. They wrote the Telekhany émigrés in the United States that I was coming, enumerated my services, and told them that I would bring greetings from Telekhany. Before I arrived, a meeting where I was to speak was already announced.

My report to the Telekhany émigrés did a lot to broaden the assistance provided by the American émigrés. Even those people who were not that interested and who did not send much money decided to start becoming involved with people in Telekhany following my report.

I told them not only about the needs in town, but also how the organizations function; I told them about the help that we received from the Telekhany association and the Joint Distribution Committee; I told them that we went to a conference that the Joint Committee in Warsaw had organized for the representatives of the towns that received assistance from the Warsaw committee. The president of the Free Loan Society, Michael Ziss, and I traveled as delegates from Telekhany to the conference. We had to take along our books to be able to provide a full report about the money we received.

My report made an impression, and this initiated significant assistance. I was also pleased by the fact that I could also be helpful here in the United States to my brethren in need. I was very proud of my work and the assistance that I was able to provide to our poor brethren and follow in the footsteps of my parents and grandparents whose primary concern was to help those in need. My grandfather and grandmother and my parents always had an open home, and were always inviting guests. There was nowhere to sleep, so people would sleep on the oven, or on doors that were removed and placed on chairs. I was also pleased to meet members of my family. They were extremely helpful to our hometown, and they also sent funds to Palestine.

[Page 137]

What I Remember from my Childhood in Telekhany
by Chana Godiner

It is over half a century since I left my hometown of Telekhany, but the tiny houses, streets, the people from my little town are engraved into my memory. This is especially true concerning the poverty and the everyday struggle for a piece of stale bread.

My father, Israel David, was a teacher. His pupils were the poorest of children in town. Of course, people did not have the money to pay him, so his income was not enough to feed our family a piece of bread. Our mother became the breadwinner, and between the two of them, we scarcely had enough to get by.

Among my father's pupils was his youngest child, Shmulik, who was just ten years old. Shmulik was very talented and whatever father taught him, he learned by heart. His oldest sister Chana, who worked for fifty hours a week at the glass factory, used to send him the "Self Teacher" from Pinsk, which inspired Shmulik even more to learn and write.

When our family moved to Warsaw, Shmuel was just fourteen years old, and went off to work in a steel factory. He would study in the evening, and aspired to become a writer. His writing skills soon became recognized, and he came to be considered one of the outstanding writers in Jewish literature. When Hitler invaded the Soviet Union, Shmuel joined other Jewish writers in the forest as partisans to fight the Nazi barbarians, who wanted to dominate the world, and who killed six million Jews, including the Jews of our dear town of Telekhany. Shmuel was killed as a partisan in battle in 1942.

We, his two sisters Esther and Chana, established a reading club in his memory here in Los Angeles. It is called the Shmuel Godiner Reading Circle. Let this be another page in the Telekhany memorial book.

———

[Page 138]

A Letter to the Yizkor Book Committee
by Mendel and Keyle Bernstein, Edmonton Canada

Dear friends committee of the Telekhany Yizkor Book!

We apologize for the delay in responding to you. It was hard for us to write given our feelings and knowledge about what happened to our dear and beloved town of Telekhany – its beautiful river, the bridges, the alley, and more than anything else, the dear people who were killed by the Nazi-German murderers. We should never forget it, and it is our obligation to immortalize their memory in a Yizkor Book.

We will of course make also a monetary contribution to help finance it, but we don't have any photos.

Since we left Telekhany so long ago, it is difficult to return to the days of our youth and remember the significant episodes of a life that was so mercilessly destroyed. However after thinking about it for a long time, various events and images from the distant past return to mind.

We remember when the peasants could no longer tolerate the oppression of the landlords, and rose up and burned the landlord's buildings. It happened that my uncle Mendel Nissen the butcher was searching for a lost cow, holding a lantern in his hand. The police accused him for having burned the buildings, arrested him and sent him to Siberia. Despite extensive lawsuits in court, it was not possible to get him released. There was a distinguished Jew in town, a Chasid and a scholar, Shmuel Chaim Segalovich, who had an influential friend in high society in Moscow. My uncle went to his friend, and after some petitions and payoffs to the Czar, my uncle was finally freed on the condition he change his name from Eisenberg to Bronstein. I,

Mendel, still remember how on high holidays the fine Jews in their chassidic fur hats called "streimels" would gather in the synagogues on the holidays, make a *Lechaim* [toast], and sing three times in Russian: "Abraham, why aren't you pleading God for us?" Our mothers at home would say the following rhyme on the Sabbath night in the dark: "When the Messiah arrives on horseback, there will be good years ahead, if he arrives on a wagon, there will be good times."

Now let me begin discussing the time when the movement began. I was then working in Pinsk. When the first strike at the match factory took place, my friend Hershel Zvodner and I got assigned to find out which of the strikers and leaders the police were about to arrest. We spent a long time investigating this until both Hershel and I were arrested ourselves. We got our first taste of jail and beatings during the week we were incarcerated. We came home for Passover.

We brought home new songs like: "You plough and you sow," "New Times", etc. We also brought back from Pinsk a book by Mendele Moikher Sforim called "The Jade". We met together in our house and read it. My mother liked it very much. She then hid it with the songs in the attic under the straw roof.

We could perhaps remember many other episodes from our teenage years, episodes that were serious and mischievous, happy and sad, since no matter how hard life was, we became accustomed to it. We also had acceptable moments when we got together – parents in their style, and we in ours. This is how life was until the German destroyer, Hitler, may his named be erased, and his wild German cannibals destroyed our life.

May this be our modest contribution to the Yizkor Book, and may our people and the whole world never more experience such a catastrophe.

———

[Page 139]

We had "Sarah-Do-Good" in Town
by Riva Rosenbaum

We had a "grandmother" named Sheina Sarah. She was a tiny, skinny lady with one eye (a hen had pecked out her other eye). She always went around with a cane, and wore an apron with deep pockets. She always had something in those pockets. She collected a challah, a piece of fish or a small chicken and other things for poor families. In addition to helping women give birth, she also took care of dowries for brides, medicine for the ill and shrouds for the dead.

Grandmother Sheina Sarah had women assistants who would collect contributions from the wealthy to give to the poor. When Chaim Reuven had his fifth child, a fifth girl, Grandma went out of the room and said to Chaim, "Well, Chaim Reuven, a baby girl is just like carrot pudding [*tsimmis*] which costs money." At the same time there were Treina Aharon Mushkas and Tsifra Bezes, and Grandma winked at them for them to remain. She realized that she would get what she needed faster with women than men, and what she needed was a burial shroud for Chaim Yossel and a dowry for Beilka Shmerls.

She had a nice life and was always thinking of how to help the needy. She carried all of the problems in town in the pockets of her apron, but never needed anything for herself. She only cared about others. Everyone in town loved her and respected her.

When she died she was over hundred years old, and when her many Telekhany children and grandchildren would ask her, "Granny, how old are you?" she would answer, "What difference does it make to you? A hundred and one is all the same." When she died all the storekeepers closed their businesses, and even children went along to the cemetery. The gown she was wearing when she passed away was cut up by elderly ladies and distributed among themselves as a good omen for a long life.

———

[Page 140]

A Report from Gershon Gurstel
(Gershon Alter, son of the carpenter)

Throughout our years in the United States my wife and I always missed our dear town of Telekhany, and hoped to have the opportunity to visit there one more time, until finally in 1936, we took a trip there. It was summertime, and everything was in bloom, and the nights were bright. The hens still cackled as they had years before, but the poverty had become much worse. Most Jews were unemployed, and all of the shops were in the names of the wives of the storekeepers. When I asked why the businesses were registered in the names of the women, I was told that the taxes of the Pilsudski regime were so insufferable that the men had to declare bankruptcy and sign over the businesses in the names of their wives. When I asked what would happen if their wives also had to declare bankruptcy, I was told that they would register their businesses in their children's names.

Since they lived on money sent from the United States, each person asked for the addresses of relatives. There were no bakers in Telekhany because they had to pay high taxes, and there were no customers for bread either. The people had no money to buy baked goods.

We were in Telekhany for four weeks, but didn't enjoy it too much. There was the poverty, the struggles and insecurity about what tomorrow would bring. For the Sabbath they would slaughter a single calf for the entire town. The few new houses and the Lubesh synagogue were built with money from the United States. The power of the American dollar was very great. There was once an auction for *aliyahs [being called to make a blessing on the Torah reading],* and I bought all of the *aliyahs* with my American dollars. Before leaving Telekhany, I arranged that all of the *aliyah* honors should be distributed among my relatives.

We departed Telekhany broken-hearted as we watched young people feeling abysmally lost and in a state of hopelessness. They weren't allowed into the United States, and no other country was willing to accept them. Some were confined in Kartuz-Bereza, and the only other hope and aspiration was to go to Palestine and work on the kibbutzim and in other trades. Indeed, a large number of young people ended up in Palestine, and they were very useful in the country. They would work the fields, haul water and dig wells with a gun in their hand.

We saw their accomplishments with our own eyes when we traveled to Israel in 1959. They were proud Jews, and had achieved what Jews had dreamed about for two thousand years!

May Israel live in peace together with all other peoples!

———

[Page 142]

Azriel the Son of the Mute Tragic Death and the Fate of his Family

One day in 1915, Ezriel the son of the mute and his brother Chaim left their houses together with their wives, Minka and Ahava (Lieba). They were on their way to visit their parents. During the night, Telekhany was flooded with a large group of Russian soldiers who were madly fleeing in retreat of the strong German army. The sky shone with holiday light onto the unsettled ground. The beautiful round sun provided warmth, and revealed nothing of what was hiding in the air as far as Ezriel, his brother Chaim and their families were concerned.

The two brothers found their parents well when they got to their home. At the same time a peasant entered the store to buy something and asked for change of 10 rubles, but this request was merely a provocation. In those days the anti-semites were planting horrible libels against the Jews, and one of them was that the Jews had shipped off their money, gold and silver to the Germans. The peasant asked for change of 10 rubles, and their father said that he had no change. This then supposedly confirmed that the Jews had sent all their gold and silver to the Germans, and the peasant began hitting their father with a cane, screaming that the Jews had shipped their money to the Germans. Their father told the peasant he could have the bit of merchandise for free, but even this didn't help. Finally their mother Elka managed to appease the peasant by giving him a few other items for free.

The brothers were standing on the street wondering what was going on, and heard the drunken singing of some Russian officers in Rimmer's orchard across the street. The drunken officers soon came out onto the street and started chasing Jewish women. One officer noticed Ezriel and Chaim and their wives, and started harassing Ezriel's wife, Minka. He also slapped Ezriel across the face, and Ezriel fell to the ground. Ezriel stood up and started hitting the officer. His brother Chaim and the women tried to stop Ezriel, but then other officers ran over and arrested Ezriel and Chaim, and took them over to their parents' home, where they tied the two men up by their feet and hands as the officers decided what to do with them. Soldiers armed with swords were standing in and around the house, and wouldn't allow anyone enter or leave.

In the meantime the German army was approaching Telekhany, and the Russians had to escape as quickly as possible. However, they didn't forget to take the two brothers along. As they were fleeing, the wild officers gave Ezriel fifteen lashes, and Chaim ten lashes. Ezriel lost consciousness from the lashes, and soon died. Chaim tolerated them and survived. He and his wife Ahava now have a beautiful family and live in Hadera, Israel.

The fate of the Eisenberg family in Israel during the construction of Israel and the War of Liberation was very difficult. This is what the family reported: The first victim was Yaakov, the son of Chaim and Lieba Eisenberg. Details about his struggle and death can be found in a separate article in Hebrew in the Yizkor Book.

Hershel, the son of Ezriel the son of the mute and his wife Minka, was killed after falling from a broken veranda while he was working on a building. Chaim's eight year-old daughter Chayaleh, who had brought him some food at the same moment, was wounded and became an invalid.

A second son, Mordechai Yitzchak, a heroic young fellow, joined the Haganah when he was fourteen years old, and four years later, when he was 18, he joined the Jewish army as an experienced soldier. He was assigned to search for landmines that had been placed by the Arabs on the roads where Jews traveled. One year later he was sent to the Negev. Upon his return he was riding in a tank with other soldiers when the tank overturned. Two soldiers were killed and Mordechai Yitzchak was wounded in the head, causing him to now be an invalid.

Chaim's son Moshe left the Haganah in 1941 and joined the Jewish brigade under the British. He suffered for being a Jew, and the brigade was sent to the Italian front. Moshe was wounded, and when the war ended, he returned to Palestine and was sent directly to Yesod Hamaleh to fight the Arabs.

Motka, the third of Chaim's sons, and a young man of 17, joined the British army. In 1944 he was sent on a patrol on the Italian front. He was wounded there and spent six months in the hospital. In 1946 he returned, and was sent to the Sea of Galilee to organize a local defense brigade. He met his wife, married her and now lives as an official in the State of Israel.

Ezriel's wife Minka arrived in Palestine with two sons, Mordechai Yitzchak and Hershel, but left behind her daughter Zippora together with Zippora's husband and two children in Telekhany. They were all killed by Hitler's Germans, may their names be obliterated. Minka also left behind a son, Leibel, who fled from the Nazi murderers, and made his way through the forests of Russia, until he got to Tashkent. He worked very hard there, and even spent time in prison because of an informant who reported falsely that he had spoken against the Soviet regime. Along the way he met up with fine Jewish family, and married their daughter Golda. After the war they returned to Poland and from there they headed for Israel, stopping off along the way in Germany.

One week before they were supposed to go to Israel there was a football game that Leibel and many others went to watch. Along the way their truck overturned, and Leibel was killed. His wife, Golda, and their small daughter Zippora, were left alone to travel on to Israel, where Leibel's family and his mother Minka lived.

———

[Page 144]

Pictures and Images of Life in Telekhany

by Gershon Gurshtel

The Eve of Yom Kippur in Telekhany

The entire town would be wrapped in a G-d-fearing mood. Young and old performed the custom of atonement through the turning a chicken around their heads on the eve of Yom Kippur. Men used chickens, women used hens, and whoever had no chickens simply used a coin instead. The coin was distributed among the poor afterwards, and we children envied other children who used coins for the atonement ceremony because although they could give out the coins to the poor, they would use some coin to buy a snack after Yom Kippur.

My grandfather was the treasurer of the *Chevra Kadisha [Burial Society]*, and my grandmother Beilka would bake cookies. Grandfather would prepare small glasses of vodka to give out at the cemetery to the Jews who came to visit the graves of their ancestors. My grandfather would take me along to the cemetery, and I would love to watch people walk around the graves reciting verses and then go inside the small structures over the graves and drink some vodka.

These scenes made me wonder about certain things. I wondered whether when the Messiah came, the dead would roll underground to the Holy Land. Wouldn't it be better to travel alive to the Holy Land and when the Messiah comes, be resurrected and enjoy eating everything with the Leviathan?

Coming home from the cemetery we would prepare for the pre-fast dinner. After dinner, grandfather put on his white robe and we, his grandchildren, would gather around him for his blessing. He put his hands on each of our heads and blessed us individually.

After the blessing, I felt assured that I and all other Jews would have a good year.

Sabbath Bereishit in Telekhany
(the First Sabbath After Simchat Torah)

The Sabbath when we start reading from the beginning of the Torah, known as Sabbath Bereishit, follows Simchat Torah. The Chasidim enjoyed themselves during the entire nine days of Sukkot. They would get together in the evenings in the Lyubesh synagogue to dance and sing and drink a little vodka. When Simchat Torah arrived, there was no limit to the rejoicing and dancing. They wanted to forget the approaching autumn with its rain and cold. They had to have boots for themselves and the children. Firewood had to be stocked up for the cold winter. The roof was leaking and there wasn't any money to fix it. They wanted to forget all their problems, and hoped that G-d would help somehow. It was very hard to plunge back into the rough reality of every day life after the holidays.

But there is a great G-d in the world, so he prepared a Sabbath Bereishit for his children, the Jewish People. It's no big deal for him! We now started to read from the beginning of the Torah again, and we again have a new holiday of Simchat Torah. People got together again on Friday night in the Lyubesh synagogue to dance and to sing the Rebbe's melodies. The principal singers were Yossel the ritual slaughterer and Alter the carpenter, who didn't read from music sheets. As soon as they heard a tune, they started singing along.

What did they do after the singing and dancing? The chassidim had their own custom of going from house to house and sneak out kugels from the ovens. The women were already prepared, and had already cooked two kugels for Sabbath Bereishit. The question was how to sneak into a house on the Sabbath. Alter the carpenter knew how to open a door or a window, or through the attic. Yossel the blacksmith would have to go along because he was needed to open the hot oven since he had hardened, heat resistant hands. They knew that a hot oven shouldn't be opened too early, but a fresh kugel, dripping with oil and there for the taking, plus a noodle kugel, were worth the risk.

They once wanted to enter a house that was locked shut, and they couldn't manage to get in, and wondered what kind of chassidim these people were here. So Alter the carpenter became a "ladder," and Yosef the blacksmith climbed up on him and crawled in through the attic. He climbed down into the house using a ladder and was about to get the kugel. However, Yosef Abba the blacksmith was groping around in the dark, tripped and fell as he tried to go down the ladder. Yosef Abba didn't get confused. He managed to get into the house anyway, opened the oven and grabbed both kugels to get back at the owners of the house. When he returned back, his friends laughed at his find – the two kugels – and at Yosef's appearance.

How Alter the Carpenter Became a Doctor in Telekhany

Our town was blessed by G-d to have many Jews who suffered from hernias. Once it happened that Alter the carpenter was in Yechiel the painter's house when Yechiel started suffering from the symptoms of this illness. The doctor was called at once, and during the doctor's procedures, Alter watched him attentively, and became an expert in treating hernias himself.

Shortly thereafter, my grandfather Meir Yankel suffered from a hernia just like Yechiel the painter. The doctor was out of town, as was the country surgeon. Alter soon heard about the problem and came at once while other chassidim were running to synagogue to recite psalms. He performed the entire procedure that the doctor had done to Yechiel the painter, and helped my grandfather. The town found out about what Alter the carpenter had done for my grandfather, and from then on, he did the same thing for other Jews. They started calling Alter the carpenter instead of the doctor.

Once on a Sabbath morning, during the prayer service in the Lyubesh synagogue, the congregants were in the middle of the Torah reading when a peasant entered the synagogue asking for Alter the carpenter. The congregation was startled to find a gentile suddenly coming to the synagogue on the Sabbath to look for Alter the carpenter. Alter asked the peasant what he wanted. The peasant responded, "Dear doctor, a man in our village of Klitenyu got sick and the doctor and country surgeon are nowhere to be found. However we heard about you. Please come and save the man's life."

Alter got scared. After all, it was the Sabbath in the middle of services during the Torah reading. What should he do? He went straight to the rabbi for guidance. The Rabbi said: "Go home, Alter, eat your Sabbath meal and go with the man, a human's life is more important than the Sabbath." The congregation then watched Alter the carpenter get on a wagon on the Sabbath to save a peasant on the Sabbath. From then on he was known as "doctor."

The Synagogues of Telekhany

Our town had four different synagogues: three chassidic ones and one non-chassidic one. The synagogues were run in accordance with the economic condition of the chassidim. The Lyubesh synagogue was named for the Rebbe of Lyubesh, and was the synagogue of the Lyubesh chassidim who were considered "year long" Jews who were not poor, meaning that it was a synagogue of the happy beggars, Jews who were not considered as full-time beggars. When the rebbe would come to town, people were happy all week, and they would go to visit him. Some asked him to advise them about financial problems, others about marriage proposals for a daughter, and others who wanted to have children.

The Stolin synagogue followed the customs of the Rebbe of Stolin, who had illustrious ancestry. He was a rebbe of businessmen, and rarely came to Telekhany. Whenever he did come to visit, it was only for a couple of days. The businessmen would consult him about their businesses and rewarded him well. The rebbe himself conducted himself in a royal manner. He would travel with a train of horses. He would always change the horses for better ones. He loved horses.

When he came to the synagogue on Friday night for the prayer services, the chassidim would have to wait until the end to receive wishes for a good Sabbath from the rebbe. However, he would converse with the wagon drivers until he came to synagogue; he loved talking with them about horses.

The Yanova synagogue. Since the Yanova Rebbe was a rebbe of the poor Jewish masses, the synagogue was not for the wealthy. In fact, a tailor named Hillel the Tailor had provided the funds to build the synagogue. Nevertheless, the chassidim greatly respected their rebbe.

The non-chassidic synagogue. The wealthiest Jews in town belonged to the non-chassidic synagogue. It was a beautiful synagogue, and the wealthiest man in town, who happened to be a Lyubesh chassid, attended the non-chassidic synagogue as well. We children would often sneak into the synagogue to warm up because it was the only synagogue in town that had a coal oven. However, we didn't like the Jews of the non-chassidic synagogue. We used to call them "dry Jews." The chassidim were a happier and friendlier group.

[Page 148]

Yosef Tchernichov Danieli, of Blessed Memory

Among all other martyrs who perished in the great catastrophe, we want to pay respect to our "almost" landsman, the prominent cultural and public figure, renowned and great attorney, Yosef Tchernichov Danieli.

The record of the family Tchernichov goes all the way back to at least the 18th century. It was a family of great businessmen and scholars. The family always lived in the town of Kosovo, Polesia. The head of the family, Yeshayahu Moshe Tchernichov, owned a tobacco processing factory in Kosovo. He had three sons: Aba, Shmuel and Leima. Shmuel moved to Slonim and was also in the tobacco processing business, and had four children: two sons, Yosef and Binyamin, and two daughters, Reisa and Mina.

Our story is about Yosef Tchernichov who was killed during Hitler's destruction of the Jews. Yosef was born in 1882. Until his Bar Mitzvah, he studied Jewish subjects. After his 13th birthday in 1895, all three brothers, Yosef's father Shmuel, Abba and Leima, opened a glass factory in Telekhany, and Shmuel and his family moved there. From this point Yosef was considered a native of Telekhany. Although he had also studied in the large cities, he would return for vacations and thereby came to be considered as a native son of Telekhany.

While he was still a teenager, Yosef joined the Zionist movement, and later, under the influence of the Socialist movement, he joined the Socialist Zionist party in which he was known as an important theoretician and orator of the movement. He was arrested and released several times, and after the failure of the 1905 revolution he returned to his law studies at Kharkov university, where he excelled in his studies. He married, moved to Vilna and practiced law. At the same time he became active in the city's Jewish cultural life, and became a great supporter of the Yiddish language.

During World War I, when Jews within the boundaries of Polesia and Poland suffered from Czarist persecution, Yosef moved to St. Petersburg to organize a defense committee. During the first months of the revolution, he got an important job in the Kerensky government. After the October revolution he moved to Kiev and devoted himself to political and cultural activities.

In 1921 Yosef received a visa to return to Lithuania, and stayed briefly in Kovno, where he got involved in important cultural work. He represented HIAS and edited a newspaper. However, this work left him dissatisfied, and he missed his law practice. He returned to Vilna and resumed his law practice; he soon became renowned as one of the greatest attorneys in Poland, and specialized in defending clients in criminal and political cases. Although he opposed communism, he nevertheless strenuously defended those persecuted as communists by the Polish government. During his legal cases Yosef excelled as a former resident of Telekhany.

In Telekhany and neighboring areas, a group of thirty young people, both Jews and gentiles, was arrested and accused of actions against the Polish government. They faced severe punishment. Prior to the trial, Tchernichov was approached to take up their defense. He didn't ask for any money, and threw himself totally into defending them. The trial received great publicity throughout Poland. He worked very hard in their defense, and many of the accused were acquitted; some of the rest received light sentences. When asked later to state his fee, he responded, "Whatever you can afford." Some of the released young people now live in the United States.

Even with his busy law practice, Yosef found time for community service and cultural activities. He didn't have much faith in the Zionist solution to the "Jewish Question," however, he did join the "territorial movement" and looked for a territorial solution. Together with Y. N. Steinberg and others, Tchernichov founded the "Free Land League." He was one of the founders of the Jewish Scientific Institute in Vilna, and attended the founding of the ICOF [?] in Paris.

Tchernichov was a great humanist, a man of high culture. He wrote a lot about important Jewish national and cultural problems. His writings were printed in numerous magazines and newspapers. He also published many pamphlets on Jewish historiography and other polemical pamphlets. As a great loyal son of his people, he didn't ignore their awful fate, and together with many other great Jews and the six million, he perished in the terrible Flood, though not directly at the hands of the Nazis.

When World War II broke out, the Nazi hordes stormed eastward, and the Soviets occupied parts of Lithuania and Polesia. They arrested many people of distinction in Vilna who were suspected of being disloyal to the Soviet regime. Among these outstanding individuals, both Jews and non-Jews, was Yosef Tchernichov. He was accused for having written his brochure, "Revtribunal" and for having committed many other such "sins". The investigation dragged on until the Nazis attacked the USSR in June 1941. When people were fleeing the Nazis, the arrested suspects were also driven deeper into Russia. Tchernichov was already weakened by his long incarceration, was unable to keep walking, and fell down. The soldiers had orders from their superiors not to leave anyone alive, so apparently one of the soldiers shot him.

Thus, this is how yet another of the dear sons of our Jewish People was added to the list of martyrs. Honor to his memory. Yosef's son Michael was arrested together with his father, and was sent far away to work at hard labor. He managed to live through it and survive.

[Page 150]

A Sacred Memorial to my Dear Mother, Chaya-Esther

(Buried in Telekhany)
by Mashele Roseman

I lost you when you were only 44 years old,
When I, the child born in your mature years, was only a year old,
I was so very young,
I still remember what I saw at your funeral, especially how
They placed a small bag of earth from the Land of Israel under your head,
When you were laid to your eternal rest.

That small bag of earth and the prayer "To Jerusalem your City..." that I recited
Three times a day enabled me to get through the bitter Exile.
Then when the *Poalei Zion* movement appeared in Jewish communities,
It was easy for me, deeply rooted in Judaism, to find my life in it.
And when during the First World War President Wilson proclaimed
That if the Allies helped oppressed peoples, their independence would be restored,
And then a Jewish legion was therefore organized,
I joined the fight under its banner.
(Frank Lieberman of Telekhany also did the same thing).

Unfortunately, our independence was not realized because of Britain's treachery,
But thanks to our bitter struggle against England, she had to give up the Mandate in Palestine,
As soon as England left Palestine, the Arabs attacked us from all sides,
And a great miracle occurred in that situation, just like in ancient times,
That is: "giving the mighty into the hands of the weak...." and because of that,
After an Exile of two thousand years, the State of Israel was established in Palestine.

Since I know what a loyal Jewish woman you were your entire life,

It is only right that I give you the good news about the State of Israel.
That's it for worldly news, and now let me report to you about your children.
Unfortunately, the report is a sad one, because except for me, no one is alive today.
Your eldest, Monya, died in Shanghai as result of World War I,
He was lonely and sick when he gave up his soul.
Leah, who looked exactly like you,
Was laid to rest in the United States.
Aharon died in a typhus epidemic, and the Germans killed Chana and Chava and their families when the Germans invaded Poland.
Dear Mother, you only lived 44 years, and it's already been another 72 years,
However, my love for you has not diminished the slightest,
Rest, Mama, in your eternal peace.
Advocate on our behalf for mercy and salvation for all oppressed and persecuted Jews.

[Page 152]

Telekhany Burial Society, Hillel the Custodian and the Pot of Carrot Pudding
by Gershon Telechaner

Like many other cities and towns, Telekhany had a burial society. Hillel the tailor was the official custodian of the Telekhany Burial Society. Although tailoring was the way he earned his meager living, the entire town knew him best by the nickname "Hillel the Custodian". He was a tall man with a black beard and always wore a long black coat. The burial society was his entire purpose in life. He never missed supervising a funeral, and knew where the grave of every person – man, woman and child – was located.

According to a Telekhany community regulation, he could have advanced to the position of treasurer of the Burial Society because the regulation stated that anyone serving two years as a custodian could become treasurer. Hillel, however, declined the honor. He felt that he was indispensable in the role of custodian. He was expert in all aspects of religious law relating to Jewish burial, washing of the deceased, putting the shrouds on the deceased, digging the grave, cutting the boards for the grave, and all other laws and customs.

Once each year new members joined the burial society. The event was accompanied by a dinner, and what a banquet it was!

There was a very wealthy and respectable man named Leib Turok in Telekhany who wanted to become a member of the society. At the same time someone else, Alter the carpenter, also wanted to join. A dilemma now arose. Hillel was more than willing to bring in Alter the carpenter, and Hillel knew that Alter could be of great assistance. However, what were they to do about Leib Turok? The burial society in Telekhany was run in a democratic fashion. Anyone who wanted to join the society had to serve first as a custodian for two years. Everyone knew that Alter the carpenter would agree to fulfill the requirements, but Leib Turok? Could he be refused membership? Who would dare turn down this wealthy man?

After extensive deliberation, it was decided to accept both candidates as members. On the spot, Hillel the Custodian figured out a way for Leib Turok not to have to serve the two-year training period as a custodian in the Burial Society. Since both Leib and Alter were Libash chassidim, Alter the carpenter would serve as a custodian for himself and for Leib Turok. So whenever someone found out about a death in town, Hillel would quickly call Alter the carpenter to assist him in the burial preparations. At each burial, the custodians would drink a little alcohol, which understandably enabled them to be able to tolerate the weeping of the family of the deceased.

Hillel the Custodian was occupied with his work as custodian, and dealt with suffering the whole year round. However, when it came to the holiday of Simchat Torah, he did not rejoice with all the other chassidim, but instead celebrated it on his own. He wanted to be able to forget about the dead and the graves just once a year. However, he would walk down the streets. In one hand he carried a pot of carrot pudding prepared especially for him by the butchers, and in the other he carried a bottle of alcohol. He would sing and dance, shouting, "Holy Flock!" We children would follow him and respond, "Mah, mah, mah!"

This was how life was in Telekhany, with its holy Jews, Hillel the Custodian and others, until the arrival of the Hitler-murderers who destroyed everything.

———

[Page 153]

Moshe Vichnes and his Family from Telekhany

(Picture on page 163)

Moshe Vichnes, as he was known in Telekhany, was a goodhearted person. He was known to be hospitable with his home and charitable with his money. His doors were always open to the needy, and he saw to it that no one left his house hungry or empty handed.

His children in America uphold the ways and traditions of their father. His son Khuna Lev is a philanthropist who generously helps friends and fellow émigrés, and spends a great deal of money on Israel. Moshe's son, like his father before him, excels in the trait of giving money anonymously. He dislikes people talking about his help and open hand. His sister Vichna Kaplan from Chicago writes that her brother Khuna Lev does not know that she is writing about his great character traits for the Yizkor book.

[Page 155]

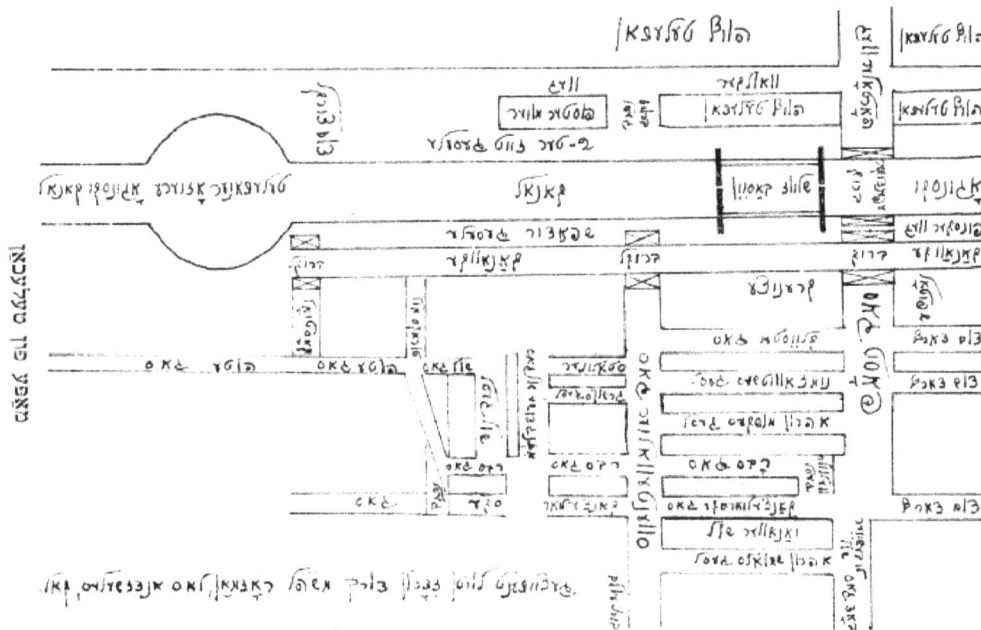

Map of Telechan

[Page 156]

מאפע פון פּאָלעסיע

Map of Polozia

[Page 157]

Telechan in Pictures

The Mitnagdim (non-chassidic) synagogue

The Lyubisher synagogue

[Page 158]

The Stoliner Rebbe and Rabbi Yosef Glick leaving the Stoliner synagogue

Telekhany Jews reciting *Tashlich*
The first man with the beard on the left is Alter the carpenter

[Page 159]

A class from the Jewish religious school.
The religious Hebrew school "Horeb"

A class from the Polish Public School.
46 of the students are Jews. Three survived and live in Israel.

[Page 160]

The Telekhaner Drama Club.
In a performance of *The Brothers Luria*

The last photo of Telekhany Jews.
The community attending a performance of the Jewish drama club on a Sabbath
evening in 1939.

[Page 161]

Telekhany youth, members of *Poalei Zion*.
With Moshe Grub, a representative of the Central Committee

***Hechalutz* movement in Telekhany (1930)**
[in photo:] The Telekhany Hechalutz Association, 8/10/1930.

[Page 162]

The Yiddish Public School in Telekhany [Volksschule] (1936).
Two of the children survived and are in Israel,
1) Motty Reuven Gurstel; 2) Yaakov Meltzer, son of Moshe the tailor.

A group of Chalutzim from Telekhany (1930)

[Page 163]

The Free Loan Society Committee in Telekhany

Moshe Vichnes' family
(a description of Moshe Vichnes in on page 147)

[Page 164]

The parents and family of Jenny Bloomberg.
They all perished except for Golda Buchman (indicated with an arrow).

She lives in Chicago.

Moshe Landman
[Moshe Landman helped
his family move to Israel.]

Shlomo Landman

**Shmuel Godiner; a famous Jewish-Soviet writer.
Killed fighting the Nazis in World War II**

[Page 166]

"Telekhaner klezmer group"
1908.

[Right to left:] Hershel Melnick, Nissel
Melnick, Feivel Arkes Kagan. Feivel
Kagan now lives in Hollywood and is a
distinguished member of the music
world.

[Page 167]

Yisrael Moshiach with his wife Sarah and neighbors, all perished

Chaim Reuven and his wife Reizel and son Eliezer. All perished.

Chaim Yeshayahu Schneidman

Gershon Meir Yankels

[Page 168]

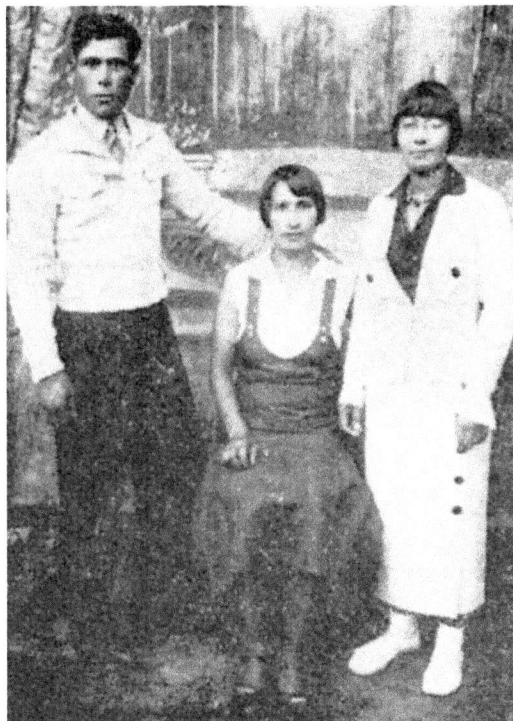

Family of Ezriel the Mute
In the middle:

Minka, Ezriel's wife.
Right: Daughter Feigel.

Left: Son Leibel

Ezriel the Mute (Ezriel Eisenberg)
Photographed in 1904

Leibel Eisenberg
(when he served in the Polish army)

Zvi Eisenberg
Son of Ezriel and Minka
Died in a work accident

[Page 169]

Family of Shmuel Chaim and Liba Eisenberg (No photo of Liba exists)

Daughter Chaya

Shmuel Chaim Eisenberg

Son, Motka, (Mordechai)
Now an official in Israel

Son, Zvika
Badly wounded in the War
of Independence

Son, Yaakov
Died in Israel
War of Independence

[Page 170]

**Everyone in the photo
perished**
Except for Leibel Eisenberg from
Brazil, indicated with an arrow.
He visited them in 1934

**A group of neighbors who
perished**
Except for the partisan Dina
Godiner, indicated with an
arrow. She lives in Lodz.

**Malka Kupa
(Aharon
Moshka's
mother)
[A member of
the Yizkor Book
committee. She
died in Los
Angeles]**

**Herschel
Eisenberg
[Hershel
Eisenberg edited
the original
manuscript of
the history of
Telekhany].**

**Khatsha
Bernstein
Mendel's
mother**

[Page 173]

Introduction

Near the Oginsky Canal, which serves as an important transportation artery among the lines linking cities in White Russia, in the middle of the Pripet swamps and surrounded by thick forests, is located the isolated town of Telekhany, far from any other Jewish community.

Telekhany ekes out a living from the nearby villages. Belarusian villages are located on the meager land of Polesia that is insufficient for the livelihood of the peasants dwelling there, even as they work tirelessly from sunup to sundown. The farmer is forced to acquire additional livelihood in other areas, such as wood cutting in the forests, fishing in the village lake, and making wood and clay vessels. In order to reduce expenses, the farmer's family had to make most of its own household vessels, clothing and shoes.

Part of the village output was brought to the Jews in town, and in exchange the farmer would buy what he needed from the Jews in town – some food products, work tools, fabric and haberdashery. The Jewish craftsman would make clothes and shoes for the peasant, the blacksmith would repair his plow, and the carpenter would install the doors to his home.

A reciprocal relationship set the economic level of the town, and the poverty of the village environment determined the poverty level in Telekhany. The poverty of the Belarusian farmer determined the poverty of the Jew in town. Thus, it was a town like any other Jewish town, one town among many spread throughout the Polesia marshlands. Anyone strolling along the canal, the trough in the hinterland of the forest, the dark scenery of the forests surrounding the town provided Telekhany with a special charm.

2.

The artisans in Telekhany, the small shopkeepers were honest and dedicated to each other, and maintained strong family connections. The shopkeeper would not abandon the village customer, he would extend credit in hard times, and he was honest and fair. The craftsman knew his customer and his family, joined him in his times of trouble, was available in difficulty and shared his joys.

3.

At the beginning of the twentieth century, new winds started blowing through the sleepy town. The young generation saw the poverty in Telekhany insightfully. The young people did not make peace with poverty, and aspired and sought another path. They found their way abroad, organized political groups that aspired to far-reaching social changes. In the meantime World War I broke out, and Telekhany experienced the events of war, and was constantly surrounded at the battlefront. Most of its homes went up in flames and its residents fled.

4.

At the end of the war some of the residents returned to Telekhany, while others remained in the places to which they had fled during the war. Many left the old country and emigrated to the New World. Those who returned rebuilt the ruins, and rebuilt their wood houses, continuing their old way of life. The village environment did not change either. The town groaned under its poverty just as before. The dark village was mired in its ignorance as it always had. New technology never got to this area, and no automobile, paved road, agricultural machinery, and especially electricity made its way there. The farmer continued to work his wretched plot under his primitive conditions from daybreak to sunset, and he and his family only managed to barely eke out a living.

The Jewish artisan and the farmer (the source of his livelihood) worked for some twelve hours a day, and income was meager and hardly enough to support the family. Parents accepted this depressing situation, but the youth, many belonged to the Socialist Zionist and left wing revolutionary youth groups. Many sought pioneer training for emigration to Palestine. Their common bond was the desire to change values, and to reject the sad current life of the miserable town residents.

Aspiring to a finer, better and wealthier world!

There was revolutionary ferment. Town residents headed the revolutionary movements struggling against the oppressive regime of the Polish government. Many thirsted for education, but there were no appropriate schools, so the youth studied on their own. They established cultural institutions, read avidly, and expanded their horizons. In general there was cultural ferment in town. There were lectures on political subjects, evenings for readings and debates about literary subjects. There was a drama club that put on performances about social and nationalist issues. Telekhany became famous for its enlightened youth and its rich political and social activities.

These activities were looked down upon by the Polish authorities, and the Communist Party was persecuted mercilessly. Their members were imprisoned in jails and in the infamous Kartuz-Bereza concentration camp near Telekhany. All the residents of Telekhany, despite their differing loyalties and worldviews, took pride in their friends, finding in them an example as valiant fighters struggling for their worthwhile goals. Many of the young people were members of the Socialist Zionist movements who embarked on pioneer training for preparation for emigration to Palestine. Emigrés to Palestine from Telekhany established approximately 80 families. Many of them arrived before World War I, and settled in towns and villages. They participated with the rest of the Jewish community in Palestine in the struggle for rights and independence. They were involved in the War of Independence, anticipated the arrival of other survivors from Telekhany, who were welcomed warmly by the people in Palestine.

Emigrés from Telekhany maintain strong connections. They share joys and sorrows, and continue on the path of their ancestors with love of work, honesty and respectability. Until today, they are still proud of Telekhany. They mention it every year at the memorial for the martyrs who were killed in the Holocaust during World War II. Our town of Telekhany deserves to be immortalized in this book, so let us present the images of our townspeople and loved ones with love and admiration. May this book serve as a testimony to a Jewish community of a typical town that struggled to exist, and that preserved with self-sacrifice the eternal values of the Jewish People, and which went up in flames together with other Jewish communities at the hands of the Nazi persecutor.

Let us read sections of this book to our children so that their origins are not alien to them, and so that they preserve the memories of their ancestors from generation to generation.

Dov Landman (Tel Aviv, Israel)
(Edited by Moshe Bagan)

————

[Page 175]

The Home of Rabbi Yosef Hakohen Glick
in Telekhany
by Meir Goldschmidt

It was in the period prior to Passover, 1928, when the snow was melting and springtime signaled the approach of summer. The sun stood high in the sky, and its rays were pushing off the cold of the winter, and expelling the winter from wherever the spring had conquered. The windows of the houses started to have their winter coverings removed – straw and cotton that warmed the houses during the cold season – and they were opening to receive the important and warm guest whom they were looking forward to seeing.

At this time the town of Telekhany was astir after having been partially rebuilt from the ruins brought on by World War I, and its economic situation was improving. Workers toiled for their bread, and merchants engaged in trade; the youth of the town started establishing and organizing their own cultural institutions, and some of them started to join the pioneer movement to be trained to move to Palestine. There was also an awakening among the entire population in town, and they decided to appoint a rabbi and spiritual leader.

Since the time that the esteemed rabbi Eliezer Yeshayahu Alovitsky served the community, the position of rabbi in Telekhany remained unoccupied, and the two ritual slaughterers in town, R. Yosef, an enthusiastic elderly chassid from Lyubshov, and R. Aharon, a Stolin chassid, who was an honest and righteous person, filled the role of the rabbi when it came to halachic matters and questions of permitted and forbidden issues.

As was customary in Jewish communities under these circumstances, there were differences of opinion, and three parties developed, pulling in different directions. One group claimed that they should hire a rabbi who was an outstanding scholar, and whose primary role in Telekhany would be study, as had been the custom with the previous rabbi; the second group argued that times had changed, and a rabbi should also be a person who could teach Jewish law, be in touch with the people, and be able to represent the town with the government authorities. The third group wanted to leave the existing state of affairs the way it was, and to make do with the two ritual slaughterers who were devoted and loyal religious Jews. News of this situation reached the yeshiva located in the town of Pinsk, about 60 kilometers from Telekhany. This yeshiva was called Beit Yosef [House of Yosef] in Pinsk, and was part of the Stolin chassidic synagogue that had been transferred to the yeshiva from the Luria family, and was known as Chayale Luria's kloiz [chassidic synagogue]. Most of the students at the yeshiva were refugees from White Russia and Ukraine who had escaped persecution from the Bolsheviks and found refuge in Poland after the border between Poland and Russia was established. Pinsk also opened its doors to host the yeshiva, which had approximately 200 young men in addition to the rabbis and teachers.

The head of the yeshiva in Pinsk was my brother, Rabbi Shmuel Weintraub, who was later appointed rabbi of Karlin, where the esteemed rabbi R. Yudel Karliner had previously served as rabbi. One of the loyal assistants of the head of the yeshiva, and someone who had joined our family when he married our sister Miriam was Rabbi Yosef Glick, who had been renowned in Russia and then in Poland for his enthusiastic preaching and profound scholarship. The name of Rabbi Glick reached Telekhany, and the second group wanted to bestow this great spiritual leader upon the residents of Telekhany.

After family consultations, the head of the yeshiva decided to send me, one of the yeshiva's students, to take a look at Telekhany in the same way that Moses had sent the spies to take a look at the Holy Land before the Israelites went there. I decided to go to Telekhany by foot, and it's worth explaining why I did this.

In that year I was drafted into the army, and the day of my call-up fell on the Sunday after Passover. As was customary among Jews in Europe, and especially among yeshiva students, I started to go on a diet for several weeks to lose weight. Several friends and I stayed up all night for several nights. We drank black coffee after a meal of salt fish and ate sunflower seeds night and day. I had the good fortune to make the trip of 60 kilometers by foot, and had the opportunity of taking someone else along with me on the arduous journey. We left early in the morning. It should be noted that there was no other way of getting to Telekhany without going on a circuitous trip via Pinsk, Yanov, Kobrin, Brisk, Kossov and Ivetsvitz, and from there with a small train to Telekhany.

It was virtually impossible to get there by wagon because of the melting snow that created huge and deep puddles that interfered with travel and destroyed the bridges. The lively link between Telekhany and Pinsk was broken at those times, even though it was around Passover time, as I will explain further on. I did, however, meet some wagon drivers from Telekhany along the way. They struggled exhaustively to get through the roads. Even the Pina River that flowed through Pinsk and emptied into the large Dnieper River had not yet melted, and the boat traveling from Pinsk to Telekhany in the summer through the Oginsky Canal, which had been dug during World War I and linked up with the Pina, had not yet begun operating.

With a staff in hand and a prayer on my lips, we left Pinsk through Lachishin Street in the direction of the village of Lachishin, which is located between Pinsk and Telekhany. For morning prayer services we made our way to the village of Ivnick, around 6 kilometers from Pinsk. This village was populated by Jewish agricultural workers, who fulfilled the biblical verse of "Through the sweat of your brow shall you eat bread."

We got to Lachishin during the afternoon hours, and we were greeted by a surprise. My fellow traveler felt ill and could not continue on. I was forced to leave him in the merciful hands of good and merciful Jews, who promised to take care of him and send him back to Pinsk. Treating him took several hours, and I was forced to stay in Lachishin overnight, and continued on my way the next morning. Between Lachishin and Telekhany I met two wagon drivers from Telekhany: R. Yosef Gurstel and R. Avraham David Eisenberg, who despite the dangerous road situation filled their wagons to capacity with merchandise and were on their way. Conditions of earning a living prior to Passover forced them to fight against nature and proceed on their way in the dark and in the mud. More than once they were forced to stop and recite psalms.

Exhausted, worn out, dirty and covered with mud and clay, I arrived in Telekhany in the early evening. I went to the home of Mr. Michel Chernomoritz, a member of the committee choosing the rabbi. Although he received me cordially, he was dry and tense. Later I discovered that I almost got into trouble because Mr. Michel was a member of the first group that was concentrating on the public synagogue of the non-chassidim, and who were engaged in a bitter struggle with the third group who were the congregants of the Lyubash and Stolin synagogue, and who had already secretly delivered their invitation to Rabbi Mordechai Rogov Lipnishick of the Vilna area, and who was renowned as a scrupulously honest person and great Torah scholar.

After I explained my mission to him and delivered the sealed letter from the head of the yeshiva in Pinsk, I also discussed the reason for my trip to Telekhany from Pinsk in person. I requested that he direct me to a quiet hotel, and explained my desire to meet the rest of the members of the committee that very evening or the next morning. He asked me to wait for him in his house, and he would go to meet the members of the committee. He proposed that I enjoy a nice meal and rest from my journey.

I waited for him for a long time, and when he returned, he took the very diplomatic step of offering to let me spend the night in his home, and to then return to the topic the next morning. I fell into bed dead tired and awoke the next afternoon. Mr. Michel Chernomoritz did not even allow me to attend prayer services in the synagogue of the Lyubshov or Stolin chassidim, claiming that it was already late. He also said that there was no purpose in meeting with the other members of the committee because he had already met with them, and they already had a detailed plan to invite Rabbi Glick to preach on the Sabbath before Passover. He advised me to leave Telekhany as soon as possible because my appearance in Telekhany would only worsen the dispute among the groups without any benefit deriving therefrom.

I was not very experienced in these matters. I listened to him, however, and believed him. He was holding me prisoner without letting me see the town or its residents. In the afternoon, I snuck out to the train station and left Telekhany on a small train through many cities and villages with Jewish populations. Luckily I got through from Ivtsevitz to Pinsk via Kossov, Brisk, Kobrin and Yanov.

Things developed rapidly thereafter. The committee members who were part of the group of businessmen found out about my visit to Telekhany, and a number of them then went to speak to the head of the yeshiva in Pinsk. The entire committee agreed to invite Rabbi Glick to visit Telekhany. During the week of Passover Rabbi Glick made his maiden speech at the synagogue of the Lyubshov chassidim, where all the people in town were congregated, some of them standing outside. Rabbi Glick's speech made a tremendous impression on the town and the region, and it was decided to offer him the position of rabbi of Telekhany.

On Lag Ba'Omer Rabbi Glick married our sister in the large yard of the head of the yeshiva in Pinsk in the company of many heads of yeshivas and their students, as well as community rabbis and residents from all over Poland. This festive occasion was the time when he was officially handed the offer to be rabbi of Telekhany, and was attended by an esteemed delegation of all three synagogues in Telekhany: Avraham Chaim Komdyov, Ephraim Garbuz, Mordechai Shlichman, Mordechai Eisenberg, Isser Beckelman, Shammai Krupchik, Yudel Gurstel, David Lozen, Shkalir, Yonah Kravitz and Asher Gurstel [the last three being alive at the time the Yizkor book was written].

Telekhany got busy preparing to welcome the rabbi. The house of Berla Sotenz-Alfred, which was almost completed and which included three new [word missing] and a large hall, was rented as the residence of the rabbi, and on Friday after the holiday of Shavuot, Rabbi and Mrs. Glick were welcomed at the gates of Telekhany, accompanied by his brother-in-law, the head of the yeshiva in Pinsk, Mrs. Glick's mother, many friends and acquaintance, my brother, younger brother-in-law and I. My brother-in-law began activities in the underground, and is now outside of Telekhany living happily.

That Sabbath after Shavuot will never be erased from my memory. Those from that generation who are still alive, and the younger generation who were able to get to Israel and live with us here, will always remember that festive Sabbath. Telekhany was dressed in a special holiday atmosphere. The Lyubshov synagogue, where the rabbi and his entourage prayed, attracted most of the congregants from the other two synagogues in Telekhany, Stolin chassidim and the non-chassidim. The reading of the Torah on the Sabbath was broken up into many verses to accommodate calling all the visitors to pronounce the blessings, and the prayer service lasted until the afternoon. The kiddush held in the home of the rabbi was attended by a large crowd, wine was poured like water, and the potato kugels were taken out of the Sabbath ovens in wave after wave and consumed by the guests. Special fish were delivered for the Sabbath by Mr. Aharon Landman from the village of Viginoshetz.

The residents of the town hardly managed to complete their afternoon meal and take a nap, and then attended the Third Sabbath Meal that after the evening prayer service on Saturday night merged into the post-Sabbath meal [Melaveh Malka – Accompanying the Sabbath Queen]. These meals were spiced with talks on Torah, Halacha, Aggadah [Talmudic stories], and chassidic and folk songs punctured the air with dances that lasted until the next morning.

Then life began to return to normal. The guests returned to their homes, and the home of the rabbi took its place among the other residences of Telekhany. The livelihood of the rabbi was assured by providing him with the monopoly on the sale of yeast for the Sabbath, and the other income pertaining to rabbis, cantors and slaughterers. Each Thursday housewives streamed to the rabbi's house to buy yeast from Mrs. Glick.

The rabbi initiated the development of spiritual assets. He established study groups to learn Mishnah and Talmudic stories from the *Ein Yaakov* anthology, and a Talmud class was also set up. The participants often recounted the pre-Sabbath strolls of the rabbi, who wore his top hat and Sabbath clothes. Shops closed early because of respect for the rabbi, and the Sabbath spread its wings to shelter the residents of Telekhany in rest and peace.

Rabbi Glick held a prominent place in rabbinical families among the ultra-Orthodox and traditional Jews of Poland, and was known as an outstanding community leader. His public speeches made waves and produced fruit. Rabbi Glick took many trips around Poland and even went abroad to Scandinavia, France and England on behalf of the yeshiva in Pinsk and institutions in Telekhany. He was beloved by the residents of the town because of his sharp halachic rulings and ability to compromise and bring peace among people. The house of the rabbi was open to everyone every evening. He even had an impact on the younger generation. Many of them decided to study Torah and follow tradition, and sent their children to study in yeshivas.

In the final years prior to the outbreak of World War II, the rabbi was primarily devoted to establishing a school where teaching would be in Yiddish. Hebrew also attained an important place instead of the public school, "Pwszechny" which taught its classes in Polish. At the

initiative and intercession of the rabbi, the regional governor agreed to
expand the network of Jewish education to Telekhany, and granted a
permit to establish a Jewish public school. Rabbi Glick devoted all his
energies to this school. A public committee and parents' committee
was established, and a large building was built to house all the
school's services. A graduate of the teacher's seminary was appointed
principal, and veteran teachers and Hebrew teachers were transferred
there: R. Chaim Yeshayahu Schneidman and R. Hershel Rotkovitsky.
The educational program included Judaism, general and Polish
history, Polish, etc.

In addition to the school, Rabbi Glick devoted himself to building a
modern public bathhouse with all accoutrements for the residents of
Telekhany instead of the small and primitive one that did not in any
way meet the needs of the residents from a health point of view. Just a
few days before the outbreak of the war, the town celebrated the
dedication of the rabbi's private large home that was built on a large
lot purchased at the initiative of the rabbi with the assistance of the
town residents. It included a large meeting room for a public
rabbinical court in addition to living quarters.

The brutal and total war and the large hand of the persecutor that
arose in our day reached Telekhany and put an end to all the work
and efforts that had been invested. During the Bolshevik conquest, the
rabbi fled even without taking along his family. Mrs. Glick and two of
their children, Moshele and Chanale, remained in Telekhany even
after the German conquest, and they were killed with the other
residents by the murderous and bloodthirsty Nazis in the nearby
forest on the 10 th of Av [Sunday, August 3], 1941. May G-d avenge
their blood!

Were it not for the extermination of the Jews of Poland, there would
be many more generations to tell about the history of Telekhany,
which saw the flowering of the best of the Jewish People, chassidim
and non-chassidim, craftsmen and businessmen, youth seeking
freedom and liberty, and a large and rooted pioneer youth and Zionist
movement whose finest sons and daughters undertook training and
emigrated to Palestine to establish themselves in their labor and
development.

The Telekhany Book should serve as an eternal light to the glory of
a community that was wiped off the face of the earth, and to pure
souls who devoted themselves to sanctifying G-d's name.

**May their souls be bound up with the living and in the building
of Israel.**

[Page 180]

The Gurstel-Gurion Family
and the Zionist Movement in Telekhany

As we noted, Zionism began to penetrate Telekhany in 1904-1905, middle-class youth were particularly attracted to it, though older people were also attracted to it. As an example, let me discuss the family of Mordechai Gurstel, or as we referred to him, Mordechai the ship hand (or Mottel the ship hand in Yiddish). Mottel the ship hand was already on in years, but his sons joined the Zionist movement. Today we are witnesses to the fact that all of his grandchildren are in Israel, and many of them took part in building the country and occupied responsible positions both in its development and in politics.

Mordechai's son was Yaakov Gurstel. His daughter and her husband Zelig Zelikovitz, who served as a military governor, were in Israel. Today Reuven Gurstel's children are in Israel. They too were involved in building Israel. However, the children of Shimon Peretz Gurstel accomplished the most. They all moved to Palestine, and Shimon and his wife joined them in 1925. Thus, until today the family in Israel included the parents, three sons and two daughters. Shimon Peretz and his wife died in 1952 at Kvutzat Geva. Two sons, Yosef and Shlomo, and the eldest daughter Chana also live at Kvutzat Geva. One son, Yaakov, lives at Kvutzat Gavat named for the martyrs of Pinsk, and the second daughter Yehudit lives in Haifa.

The family of Nissel (Nissan) Gurstel, or as he was known, "Nissel the Deck Hand," son Asher Mattityahu and his son Binyamin are in Israel, as are Mendel, the son of Reuven Gurstel. The son of Shimon Peretz Gurstel changed his name from Gurstel to Gurion, and all the members of his extended family use this name.

It is worth describing the town of Telekhany, which contributed greatly to raising the images of some of its residents, especially the respected and outstanding personality of Yosef Gurion, who contributed greatly to building Israel, and in whose honor Kvutzat Geva posthumously published the book, "Yosef Gurion, his life, words and work." Yosef Gurion was born in 1895 in Pinsk, studied in the town school, and was educated in the Zionist youth movement. In February 1914, at age 16, he and some friends in town moved to Palestine to study at the agricultural school in Petach Tikvah. When World War I broke out, he was forced to earn a living, and he and several friends leased a plot of land in and near the settlement, and started growing vegetables. After he completed his studies, he joined a group of friends and moved to Kvutzat Be'er Tuvia, one of the first kvutza [group collective settlements] in the country.

At the end of the war he was drafted into the First Hebrew Brigade, and when the Brigade was disbanded, he returned to Be'er Tuvia and became one of its activists both in the kvutza and in the settlement. For a number of reasons the kvutza did not survive, and was disbanded. Yosef, who had married in the meantime, went straight to Kvutzat Geva in the Jezreel Valley, and from 1924 he and his wife were accepted as members. He remained there until his death.

For a number of years Yosef participated in numerous public activities. He was a life-long member of the Council of Agricultural Workers; a member of the board of the Central Bank for Cooperative Institutions; a founding member of the management board of the Tnuva milk company, and from 1942-43 he was the director of Tnuva in Haifa, and later in Jerusalem. He was a member of the board of the company Nir, and of the supervisory committee of the Health Fund [Kupat Holim].

In 1936-37 Yosef traveled as a representative of the Histadrut Labor Federation to the United States, and in 1937-38 managed the Settlement Fund. In 1944-47 he was the director of the Jewish Agency department responsible for settling soldiers, and visited the brigade and other Jewish military units in Egypt, Libya and Italy on behalf of the department. He was a member of the governing board of the institutions settling discharged soldiers and of the Soldier Fund.

At the end of the War of Independence he was appointed to head the department for rehabilitation of soldiers and war wounded on behalf of the Department of Defense, and dedicated all his energies to this task. He served for a long time as the director of the Israel Development Authority. When he completed his work for the government, he returned to Kvutzat Geva, but even here did not rest on his laurels. He was asked to serve as secretary of the Association of Kvutzot and Kibbutzim. When he returned home after completing this job, he was in poor health, but went to work for the sugar factory in Afula during its most difficult early period. After he finished working there for his committed amount of time, he returned home in ill health. He worked at home for several months, and then died suddenly from a heart attack on January 18, 1957.

[Page 181]

Jacob Eisenberg, son of Liba and Shmuel Chaim Eisenberg

He was born upon their arrival in the land in the year 1923 in February. He grew up and was educated in a house of workers and at an early age went out to work to help his father who had a family of seven people to support. Jacob loved his work and every day he happily went out to work in the orchards. He lived for his work. As time went by, he transferred to construction work, learned the subject and specialized in it to the point where few people could compete with him.

Jacob was educated in the pioneer movement. When the time came for him to go to the kibbutz he was already engaged to be married and wanted to set up his home and family. Therefore he did not go to the kibbutz but remained in the city and set up his house in 1945.

Slowly Jacob began to build his own house. He bought a parcel of land and with the help of his father and brothers he began building. In the meantime he had a daughter whose name was Yael.

But fate was cruel and didn't allow him to continue his life quietly. In 1948 the war of independence broke out and everyone was called to serve in the army to protect Israel. Jacob, like everyone else, left his family and home to serve in the defense forces. While he was in the army, it was suggested that he take a course in explosives. He agreed to this, and it was impossible thereafter for him to return to his home frequently.

He successfully completed the course and excelled in placing mines. There is an old saying that a demolitionist who makes one mistake in life never gets to make a second mistake.

He served in this fashion until three days after Rosh Hashanah in 1948, when the army went out to chase the enemy from its three borders and to free the central part of the country. Jacob's unit had the task of freeing the settlements around 'Pardes Chana' and 'Yakov Zichron'.

His unit completed its task successfully; however, Jacob and his group went to search out the way the enemy infiltrated the country. Jacob was wounded while he was laying mines and died. His friends were unable to save him. They could only bring his body home for burial.

So came to an end the life of Jacob who was unable to enjoy his days and didn't finish building either his family and his house. A heaviness fell upon his family and friends. However, with the establishment of the State there was consolation for the loss.

May his soul be bound up among the living.

Shmuel Chaim Eisenberg, Chadera, Israel.

——————

[Page 182]

Biography of Laibel Eisenberg, the son of Azriel and Minka

He lived with his mother in the city of Telekhany, and he remained with his mother, and married and had children. However, the bitter war separated them. He escaped to Russia, but his wife and two children remained at home and were killed by the Nazis. After a short while he remarried in Russia and had a daughter who he named Tzipora, after his sister.

However, they could not remain there, as they were not Russian citizens. They traveled to Germany in order to reach Israel. However, fate was bitter, and when they traveled to another city to watch the games, there were 35 people with them. The bus overturned, they were all injured or killed. Laibel was among the injured and lived for a few days. He was 40 years old when he died. May his soul be bound with the soul of the living.

[Page 182]

Biography of Tzipora Eisenberg, the Daughter of Minka and Azriel

She lived with her mother, Minka, in the city of her birth, Telekhany, and married Israel in the year 5715 (1934). Her mother traveled to Israel. Tzipora remained alone with her husband and children. The tragic war broke out and her husband was taken captive by the Germans. She remained with her children in Telekhany where they were killed with all the people of the city and buried in the common grave of the city.

Thus, they died. May their souls be bound with the souls of the living, never to be forgotten.

[Page 182]

Biography of Zvi Eisenberg, the son of Israel

He came to Israel in 1934 and went to live with Chaim Eisenberg. It was some period of time before he found a job. He worked in the foundry and was injured by a piece of metal hitting his eye. He was in the hospital in Haifa until he recovered. He returned home and did not work for a few weeks, until he found work as a carpenter. Even in carpentry he wasn't lucky. He was working on a machine and injured his arm. He lived for several months with an injured arm. Obviously, from the date he came to Israel he had no luck. This is it in a nutshell. His hand recovered and he returned to work in the same carpentry shop and they sent him to build a roof for a building that was outside the settlement. That morning he was confused, told Liba that he did not want to go to work. Liba told him go and I will send your lunch with my daughter Chaya. Chaya was then ten years old, and went to bring him his lunch. There was no place there to hide from the sun. On this building there was a covering under the door. Chaya sat under the covering. Zvi came down from the roof to eat. He climbed on the covering and the covering overturned, split his head and he died. Chaya who was sitting below was choked by the roof and she stretched out her hand and her hand was completely crushed. At that time there were no good doctors and they had to amputate her hand. Until this day she suffers from the hand and also one foot that wasn't properly healed.

———

[Page 183]

In sacred everlasting Memory of our Martyrs

Eisenberg, Aharon
Eisenberg, Avraham
Eisenberg, Itsche Meir
Eisenberg, Mordechai
Eisenberg, Motye
Eisenberg, Nissel
Eisenberg, Rachel
Eisenberg, Feigel

Abramovitz, Aaron
Abramovitz, Gershon

Alper, Ze'ev

Itskovitz Family

Begun, Efraim Meir
Begun, Natan
Begun, Berl
Begun, Chaikel
Begun, Yakov
Begun, Avraham
Begun, Efraim Moshe
Begun, Ziskind

Bresky, Moshe
Bresky, Shiye [Yehoshua] Yosef

Bronstein, Todres
Bronstein, Khlavne

Bagelman, Isser
Bagelman, Gershon

Bromberg, Mereh
Bromberg, Michael
Bromberg, Mordechai
Bromberg, Chaim

Bregman, Zemach

Bobrov, Menashe

Bernstein, Shlomo

Burstein, Yosef (Yosel the Butcher)

Bontchick, Abraham

Garbuz, Efrim

Gluck, Musia the rabbi's wife

Gottlieb, Moshe Meir
Gottlieb, Todres
Gottlieb, Moshe

Goldberg, Sima Rachel

Grushka, Leiba

Gittelman, Nochman

Godiner, Yisrael
Godiner, Aaron

Gurstel, Shimon
Gurstel, Nissan
Gurstel, Yosef
Gurstel, Alter
Gurstel, Avigdor
Gurstel, Yisrael
Gurstel, Yitschak Shlomo
Gurstel, Sender
Gurstel, Aharon Yehoshua
Gurstel, Shlomo
Gurstel, Michael
Gurstel, Natan
Gurstel, Reuven

Gurstel, Itshe
Gurstel, Avraham Ber
Gurstel, Velvel
Gurstel, Yudel
Gurstel, Moshe (Bobrovich)
Gurstel, Chana (Asher's wife)

Gurstel, Golda

Gloiberman, Yaakov

Danzig, Makhe
Danzig, Mordechai

Drison, Lipman
Drison, Yaakov

Hegelman, Alter

Wasserman, Avraham

Wiedman, Herschel

Wiener, Yeshayahu

Weinstein, Leib
Weinstein, Moshe

Winnik, Yossel

Khaikin, Moshe Michel

Terespolsky, Tuviah

Treibush, Alter

Tshizsh, Arke
Tshizsh, Moshe Chaim
Tshizsh, (Motele's Family)

Chernomoretz, Michael
Chernomoretz, Berl (son of Leizer)
Chernomoretz, Leiser
Chernomoretz, Aharon Yehoshua
Chernomoretz, David
Chernomoretz, Berl (Aharon's son)

Yuzuck, Yehoshua
Yuzuck, Yonah
Yuzuck, Yaakov
Yuzuck, Moshe
Yuzuck, Chaim

Yoshpe, Avraham

Yosef (Cherna's son-in-law)

Cohen, Herschel (Asher's son)
Cohen, Herschel (Zadok's son)

Cohen, David
Cohen, Shimon
Cohen, Khana [male]

Kagan, Chaikel
Kagan, Gershon
Kagan, Shmuel Avigdor

Lutsky, Moshe
Lutsky, Avraham Leib
Lutsky, Freidel
Lutsky, Chaitshe
Lutsky, Brakha

Lev, Meir
Lev, Isaac
Lev, Sarah

Landman, Yerachmiel
Landman, Yitzchak
Landman, Aaron
Landman, Mendel
Landman, Frume (Shlomo's wife) and two daughters

Levin, Abraham
Levin, Itsel

Liss, Yisrael

Leifer, Michal
Leifer, Rachel daughter of Leifer

Mazrier, Khananiah
Mazrier, Leibe

Mudrik, Moshe
Mudrik, Shmuel
Mudrik, Zipporah

Meltzer, Herschel
Meltzer, Moshe (Yaakov's son)
Meltzer, Moshe (Avraham Ber's son)
Meltzer, Shlomo
Meltzer, Shalom Yudel
Meltzer, Isaac
Meltzer, Yisrael
Meltzer, Yoshke
Meltzer, Rachel

Stoliar, Henikh

Epstein, Yeshyahu
Epstein, Eliahu

Feldstein, Beinish

Feinschmid, Chaya (Danzig)

Freiman, Yeshayahu

Perlov, Rivka

Perlstein, Elke
Perlstein, Avraham Eliyahu
Perlstein, Shmuel Chaim
Perlstein, Shlomo

Pickman, Moshe

Potrebnik, Yerakhmiel
Potrebnik, Yaakov

Piontek, Noach

Pindrus, Eliyahu Moshe

Tsinovitz, Reuven

Klitenik, Israel
Klitenik, Gershon
Klitenik, Yaakov
Klitenik, Zelig
Klitenik, Zavel
Klitenik, David
Klitenik, Shamshel [Samson/Shimshon]

Klitenik, Bashke
Klitenik, Malka
Klitenik, Beila Rivka
Klitenik, Charna
Klitenik, Rachel (Isaac's wife)

Kaplan, Moshe

Kruptchik, Esther

Kobrik, Aharon (the butcher)

Kupetz, Yosef

Kasovsky, Shlomo
Kasovsky, Yossel
Kasovsky, Michael

Korolitsky, Sheina

Kartschmer, Zachariah
Kartschmer, Rachke [Rachel]

Kamadiev, Avraham Chaim
Kamadiev, Eliezer

Kristal, Alter

Kolodny, Yosef

Kleingeviks, Yitschak

Kostrinsky, Motye Ber
Kostrinsky, Avraham

Kat, Yisrael
Kat, Velvel

Kaz, Malke

Rosenberg, Aharon

Rubenstein, Moshe
Rubenstein, Yitzchak

Rutkovitsky, Hershel

Roshtchintzer, Gavriel

Rubacha, Feivel

Schneidman, Chaim Yeshayahu

Shalachman, Chishe

Schwarzberg, Yisrael

Strauss, Abraham

Shklyar, Isaac
Shklyar, Motel

Our respected landsman Dov Ber Landman, who now lives in Tel Aviv has sent us this list of the victims of Telechan. In his accompanying letter he states: Unfortunately we don't remember all the names of each family, so we have to make do with the names of the heads of household.

———

Telechaners who perished in other places

Chaim Reuben Eisenberg, wife Reisel, son Motel and daughter

Atshe with her children	Pinsk
Yehoshua Stoliar, wife Peshe and children	Pinsk
Sarah Bassevich and children	Pinsk
Mendel Stoliar with wife and daughter	Lida
Yisrael Eisenstadt	Riga
Itshe Eisenstadt's daughter, Rachel	Riga
Itshe Eisenstadt's daughter Reizel	Pohost
Yosef Roseman's daughter, Chava Garbuz	Pinsk
Yosef Roseman's daughter, Chana Krainyuk	Warsaw
Leibe Turok's daughter, Gittel Hellberg	Pinsk
Leibe Turok's son, Meir Turok	Pinsk

We express our deepest sorrow for the untimely passing of our respected fellow émigrés:

Morris Lutsky	New York
Morris Stone	Denver, Colorado
Aharon Bronstein	Delano, Calif.
Leah Mader	Hartford, Conn.
Netty Siegel	Binghamton, NY
Malka Kupa	Los Angeles, Cal.

What a pity on losses that cannot be recovered!

Table of Contents In the Original Yizkor Book

3　On the Trail of the Telekhany Tragedy　　*Boris Ustinov*

6　A Great Loss for the World　　*Esther Miller*

10　How it all began

13　The Tragic Death of Azriel the Mute

5　Introduction

6　Foreword　　*Mashele Roseman*

9　The Story of how Telekhany was Destroyed　　*Asher Gursthtel*

28　The world became poorer　　*Esther Miller*

43　The Munich Conference　　*Aaron Klitenick*

47　My brother is alive!　　*Dina Godiner*

52　Telekhany and World War One

62　September 21, 1939

66　My brother Shmuel　　*Esther Godiner Miller*

71　The Lives and work of the Telekhany Youth　　*Mina Baron*

83　Shlomo Landman's Story

87　Also from our birthplace Telekhany　　*Mashele Roseman*

88　A Eulogy to burned down Telekhany　　*Moshe Bernstein*

89　The Famous Date - Remembered Forever!　　*Lazer Lutsky*

95   Memories of Telekhany   *Golda Stolyar*

101   I Remember my   *Riva Chaim Reuvens*
      Hometown

102   The Power of Goodness   *Chaim Finkelstein*

104   The Oath   *Esther Miller*

105   A letter from Telekhany   *Esther Miller*

106   The Sacred Chain   *Dina Godiner-Klitenick*

110   The Tormented   *Yehusha Sklar*
      Community of
      Telekhany

111   Telekhany

114   The family of Mordechai
      Gurstal

117   Memories of Telekhany   *Akiva Alevitsky*

128   A Chapter from "From   *Esther Miller*
      Telekhany to America"

133   My Flowers on the Mass   *Laibel Eisenberg*
      Grave

136   A Free Loan Society and   *Golda Bookman-Landman*
      Food Bank for the Poor
      in Telekhany

137   What I remember from   *Chana Godiner*
      my young days in
      Telechan

138   A letter to the Yizkor   *Mendel & Kaleh Bernstein*
      book committee

139   We had "Sarah-Do-   *Riva Rosenberg*
      Good" in Town

140   A Report from Gershon
      Gurstel

142   Azriel the mute's tragic
      death

144   Pictures and Images of   *Gershon Gurstel*
      Life in Telekhany

148   Yosef Tchernichov
      Danieli, of Blessed
      Memory

150   A Sacred Memorial to   *Mashele Roseman*
      my Dear Mother, Chaya-
      Esther

152   Telekhany Burial   *Gershon Telechaner*
      Society

153   Moshe Vichnes and his
      Family from Telekhany

155   Map of Telechan

156   Map of Polozia

157   The Mitnagdim (non-chassidic) synagogue

157   The Lyubisher synagogue

158   The Stoliner Rebbe and Rabbi Yosef Glick leaving the Stoliner synagogue

158   Telekhany Jews reciting *Tashlich.* The first man with the beard on the left is Alter
      the carpenter

159   A class from the Jewish religious school. The religious Hebrew school "Horeb"

159   A class from the Polish Public School. 46 of the students are Jews. Three survived
      and live in Israel.

160   The Telekhaner Drama Club. In a performance of *The Brothers Luria*

160   The last photo of Telekhany Jews. The community attending a performance of the
      Jewish drama club on a Sabbath evening in 1939.

161   Telekhany youth, members of *Poalei Zion.* With Moshe Grub, a representative of
      the Central Committee

161   *Hechalutz* movement in Telekhany (1930) [in photo:] The Telekhany Hechalutz
      Association, 8/10/1930.

162   The Yiddish Public School in Telekhany [Volksschule] (1936). Two of the children
      survived and are in Israel, 1) Motty Reuven Gurstel; 2) Yaakov Meltzer, son of
      Moshe the tailor.

162   A group of Chalutzim from Telekhany (1930)

163   The Free Loan Society Committee in Telekhany

163   Moshe Vichnes' family (a description of Moshe Vichnes in on p. 153)

164   The parents and family of Jenny Bloomberg. They all perished except for Golda
       Buchman (indicated with an arrow). She lives in Chicago.

164   (bottom left) Shlomo Landman

164   (bottom right) Moshe Landman [Moshe Landman helped his family move to Israel.]

165   Shmuel Godiner; a famous Jewish-Soviet writer. Killed fighting the Nazis in World
       War II

166   [in photo:] "Telekhaner klezmer group" 1908. [Right to left:] [Right to left:] Hershel
       Melnick, Nissel Melnick, Feivel Arkes Kagan. Feivel Kagan now lives in
       Hollywood and is a distinguished member of the music world.

167   Yisrael Moshiach with his wife Sarah and neighbors. All perished.

167   Chaim Reuven and his wife Reizel and son Eliezer. All perished.

167   (Bottom left) Chaim Yeshayahu Schneidman

167   (Bottom right) Gershon Meir Yankels

168   (Top left) Family of Ezriel the Mute

168   (Top right) Ezriel the Mute (Ezriel Eisenberg), photographed in 1904.

168   (Bottom left) Leibel Eisenberg (when he served in the Polish army).

168   (Bottom right) Zvi Eisenberg, son of Ezriel and Minka. Died in a work accident in
       Israel.

169   (Upper left) Daughter Chaya

169   (Upper right) Shmuel Chaim Eisenberg

169   (Lower left) Son, Motka, (Mordechai). Now an official in Israel.

169   (Lower middle) Son, Zvika, badly wounded in War of Independence

169   (Lower right) Son, Yaakov, died in Israel War of Independence

170   (Upper left) Everyone in the photo perished except for Leibel Eisenberg from Brazil,
       indicated with an arrow. He visited them in 1934.

170   (Upper right) A group of neighbors who perished, except for the partisan Dina
       Godiner, indicated with an arrow. She lives in Lodz.

170   (Lower left) Malka Kupa (Aharon Moshka's mother) [A member of the Yizkor Book
       committee. She died in Los Angeles]

170   (Lower middle) Herschel Eisenberg [Hershel Eisenberg edited the original manuscript of the history of Telekhany].

170   (Lower right) Khatsha Bernstein Mendel's mother

173   Introduction

175   The Home of Rabbi Yosef Hakohen Glick in   *Mayer Goldsmith*
       Telekhany

180   The Gurstel-Gurion Family and the Zionist
       Movement in Telekhany

181   Jacob Eisenberg, son of Liba and Shmuel
       Chaim Eisenberg

182   Biography of Laibel Eisenberg, the son of
       Azriel and Minka

182   Biography of Tzipora Eisenberg, the
       Daughter of Minka and Azriel

182   Biography of Zvi Eisenberg, the son of Israel

183   In sacred everlasting memory of our martyrs

INDEX

A

Aaron Shmuel (Riva's son), 7
Aaron Shmuel (Rivka's son, 37
Abramovich, 60, 61
Abramovich (Gotshnitsa), 56
Abramovich (Nochnitsa), 58
Abramovitz, 180
Aharon Shmuel, Rivka's son, 92
Aharon the Slaughterer (Nachum Perlstein's son-in-law), 59
Aleichem, 3
Alovitsky, 169
Alper, 180
Alter the carpenter, 58, 138, 139, 146, 150
Alterke, Chaim, the bathkeeper's grandson, 49
Arieh Leib the moneylender, 124
Atshe, 187
Avraham-Itshe the "Miracle Worker", 69
Avramele the Scribe, 80
Avremke, 36
Azriel the Mute, 12

B

Backelman, 56
Bagan, 168
Bagelman, 180
Baron, 71
Bashes, 115, 118
Bassevich, 187
Baum, 92
Beck, 46, 83
Beckelman, 172
Begin, 62
Begun, 121, 180
Beilka's grandfather Moshe, 124
Beilkes, 121
Beinishes, 73, 74
Beinus, 4
Beises, 69
Ber, 62, 121
Bernstein, 42, 48, 50, 51, 61, 62, 63, 86, 112, 113, 117, 121, 127, 131, 165, 181
Bezes, 133
Bloomberg, 156
Blumberg, 16, 27
Boaz, 126
Bobrov, 181
Bobrow, 62

Bolodovitch, 48
Bontchick, 181
Bregman, 180
Bresky, 121, 180
Brestski, 4
Bromberg, 61, 62, 180
Brombergs, 94
Bronstein, 131, 180, 187
Buchman, 156
Burstein, 181

C

Chaikel the butcher, 56
Chaim Yeshayahu the teacher, 56
Chaim Yossel, 133
Chaim, the bathhouse attendant, 56
Chaya Leah of Kolonsk, 116
Chechik, 91
Cherna the widow, 56
Chernichov, 20
Chernomoretz, 4, 182
Chernomoritz, 61, 171
child by the name of Teddy, 35
Christian, 69, 120
Cohen, 183

D

Danieli, 141
Danzig, 182
David, 50, 51, 120, 121
Dinas, 127
Dinhan, 117
Dinovitz, 58
Dondik, 56
Dostoyevsky, 3
Dreyfus, 21
Drison, 182
Dubnow, 7, 38, 42
Dvorszetsky, 34
Dvorszetzky, 34
Dworzhetzky, 6

E

Eibeschitz, 42
Eichmann, 6, 9, 34, 40, 44, 45
Einhorn, 42
Eisenberg, 12, 13, 16, 51, 56, 61, 62, 117, 126, 131, 135, 161, 162, 163, 164, 165, 171, 172, 177, 178, 179, 180, 187
Eisenstadt, 19, 187

Epstein, 184
Erem, 78
Ethels, 127
Ezriel the son of the mute, 134, 135

F

Feigel, the wife of the gravedigger (Avraham David), 119
Feinschmid, 184
Feldman, 47, 56, 62
Feldstein, 184
Filipovich, 81
Filipowitch, 74
Finkelstein, 99
Frank, 6, 34, 36
Freiman, 184
Friedman, 36

G

Garbuz, 172, 181, 187
Gebirtick, 42
Gedaliah [last name missing], 62
Gieskin, 7
Gilbert, 42
Gittel, the "speaker,", 94
Gittelman, 115, 181
Gladkov, 78
Glick, 83, 89, 129, 150, 168, 170, 171, 172, 173, 174
Glicks, 46, 47, 48
Gloiberman, 182
Gluck, 181
Godiner, 7, 34, 37, 47, 49, 50, 56, 63, 64, 67, 70, 71, 102, 117, 130, 131, 157, 164, 181
Gogol, 3
Goldberg, 181
Goldschmidt, 168
Gorki, 3
Gotlieb, 4
Gottlieb, 181
grandfather Meir Yankel, 139
Grandmother Sheina Sarah, 132
Grober, 44
Gronya the wife of Chaim the bathhouse attendant, 117
Grub, 153
Grunyas, 127
Grushka, 47, 181
Grushkin, 47
Grushko, 119
Gurion, 110, 175

Gurshtel, 4, 7, 15, 16, 19, 24, 27, 47, 56, 58, 59, 60, 61, 62, 137
Gurstal, 84, 109, 110, 115, 117, 129, 189
Gurstel, 73, 98, 129, 133, 154, 171, 172, 175, 181
Gurstel-Gurion, 175

H

Hegelman, 182
Heine, 8, 39
Hersh, 41
Hershel the secular studies teacher, 126
Herzl, 21
Hillel the Custodian, 145, 146
Hillel the tailor, 145
Hillel the Tailor, 140
Hilllberg, 41
Himmler, 40, 43
Hitler, 2, 5, 8, 9, 10, 11, 27, 31, 32, 36, 37, 39, 40, 41, 43, 46, 47, 48, 49, 65, 88, 98, 104, 115, 131, 132, 136, 142, 146
Hochenberg, 35
Hodel, the daughter of Avremel the bricklayer, 123
Hoffman, 36
Huberband, 42

I

Ilivitsky, 111
Isaac Shalom Yudel's son, 114
Itskovitz, 180
Izuk, 116

J

Josef the Ritual Slaughterer, 24

K

Kagan, 48, 56, 59, 61, 62, 63, 116, 127, 158, 183
Kamadeyev, 56, 59
Kamadiev, 185
Kamadiyeev, 117
Kaplan, 42, 147, 185
Karchmar, 4
Karliner, 169
Kartschmer, 185
Kasovsky, 185
Kat, 185
Katznelson, 42
Kaz, 185
Kegelman, 59

Kerensky, 142
Kez, 84
Khaikin, 182
Khilinovitch, 42
Khmielevska, 115
King Christian, 43
Kizelstein, 65
Kleingeviks, 185
Klitenick, 37, 46, 48, 84, 89, 90, 102, 112, 113, 117, 121, 127
Klitenik, 7, 56, 58, 60, 61, 62, 63, 64, 184
Kobrik, 56, 185
Kolodny, 185
Komadeyev, 5
Komdyov, 172
Korolitsky, 185
Kortchuk, 42
Kosovsky, 4
Kostrinsky, 185
Koszciol, 119
Kovalyevsky, 119
Kovolevsky, 118
Kravitz, 172
Kristal, 47, 185
Krupchik, 172
Krupnick, 56, 81
Kruptchik, 185
Kruptshik, 56
Kruptzik, 112
Krutchenko, 121
Kupa, 165, 187
Kupetz, 185

L

Landman, 4, 7, 29, 37, 47, 48, 49, 50, 51, 53, 56, 62, 82, 84, 89, 113, 117, 120, 129, 156, 168, 173, 183, 186, 188
Landmans, 127
Laufer, 53, 62
Lehrer, 42
Leifer, 47, 183
Leizer, 126
Lemel, 37
Lemmel, 7
Lev, 147, 183
Levin, 61, 183
Lieberman, 144
Likhfar, 4
Lipnishick, 171
Liss, 42, 183
Lozen, 172
Luria, 152, 169
Lutsky, 37, 56, 61, 88, 117, 183, 187

Lutzky, 7

M

Mader, 187
Mariankellers, 127
Mashiach, 56, 127
Mayakovsky, 3
Mazrier, 183
Mazrirer, 60, 61
Meidelov, 115
Melech Asher and his wife. Gronya, 117
Melnick, 158
Meltzer, 56, 60, 61, 62, 78, 116, 154, 184
Mengele, 8, 38
Meryankelicha, 79
Mickiewicz, 3
Miller, 5, 15, 16, 33, 67, 82, 101, 102, 121, 127
Minas, 127
Minkes, 112, 117
Molya, the son of Chaytsha Chana Pesha, 114
Mordechai, the shoemaker (Basha's), 56
Moshe's brother-in-law, Aharon Shia, 124
Moshiach, 159
Motshizky, 46
Mozrirer, 56, 90
Mushkas, 133

N

Nachman the baker, 114
Nachman the packer, 115
Nissel, 58, 114, 115, 120, 180
Nissel the boatman, 27
Nissels, 119

O

Oginski, 18
Oginsky, 17, 26, 27, 126
Olivitsky, 19

P

Paslovsky, 26
Pelach, 63, 64
Peretz, 69
Perlov, 184
Perlstein, 59, 184
Peshas, 115, 116, 117
Pickman, 184
Pikova, 35
Pilsudski, 54, 58, 62, 83, 133
Pindrus, 184
Piontek, 184

Potrebnik, 184
Prager, 42
Pushkin, 3

R

R. Aharon, a Stolin chassid, 169
R. Yosef, an enthusiastic elderly chassid from
Lyubshov, 169
Rebbe of Lyubesh, 139
Rebbe of Stolin, 139
Reuven, 132, 159
Reuvens, 73, 99
Ringelblum, 6, 33
Roseman, 86, 144, 187
Rosenbaum, 99, 132
Rosenberg, 5, 22, 185
Roshchinder, 62, 63
Roshchiner, 48, 51
Roshchintzer, 116
Roshchnitzer, 117
Roshtchintzer, 186
Rotkovitsky, 60, 174
Rotkovsky, 56
Rotlinger, 41
Rozman, 15
Rubacha, 56, 62, 63, 117, 121, 186
Rubakha, 4
Rubenstein, 16, 82, 185
Rubinstein, 15, 119
Rudkovsky, 106
Rutkovitsky, 185

S

Sanders, 7
Schneidman, 61, 62, 160, 174, 186
Schwartzberg, 30, 56
Schwarzberg, 186
Schwarzenberg, 73
Segalovich, 131
Sekuler, 15
Sender, 92, 93
Sender the tailor, 56
Senders, 37
Sforim, 132
Shakespeare, 3
Shalachman, 56, 59, 186
Shirer, 41
Shkalir, 172
Shklyar, 4, 186
Shlachman, 127
Shlichman, 172
Shlomka of Bobrovitch, 115

Shmerls, 133
Shmigli, 46
Shneidman, 74, 106
Siegel, 187
Sinevitz, 30
Singalovsky, 22
Sinkova, 35
Sklar, 105
Sklyar, 61, 120
Sokoler, 1
Sokolov, 42
Sotenz-Alfred, 172
Steinberg, 143
Stern, 42
Sternberg, 42
Stoliar, 184, 187
Stoliner Rebbe, 150
Stolyar, 61, 93, 95, 115, 118, 119
Stone, 187
Strauss, 186

T

Tchernichov, 122, 141, 142, 143
Tchernomertzes, 118
Telechaner, 145
Terespolsky, 182
the children of Feibel Chasha Leah, 116
Tolstoy, 3
Topsha, 79
Treibush, 182
Trigenskaya, 3
Tshizh, 60
Tshizsh, 182
Tsinovitz, 184
Tsirinsky, 59
Tureck, 19
Turek, 125
Turok, 146, 187

U

Ustinov, 2

V

Vainshtein, 4
Vichnes, 147, 155
Viehonoshcha, 56

W

Wallenberg, 11, 43
Warshavsky, 42
Wasserman, 182

Weinstein, 182
Weintraub, 169
Weizman, 114
Wiedman, 182
Wiener, 182
Williams, 45
Winnik, 182

Y

Yankels, 160
Yanova Rebbe, 140
Yechiel the painter, 138, 139
Yeshayahu, 56, 74, 126
Yoliek, 64
Yosef (Cherna's son-in-law), 183
Yosef Abba the blacksmith, 138
Yosef the Ritual Slaughterer, 26
Yoshchemka, 114
Yoshpe, 183
Yossel the blacksmith, 138
Yossel the ritual slaughterer, 138

Yuszick, 47
Yuzuck, 182
Yuzuk, 116

Z

Zadok, 115
Zadok, the son of Chaytsha Chana Pesha, 114
Zamber, 42
Zavel, 60, 115, 120
Zavel the butcher, 60
Zeitlin, 42, 70
Zelikovitch, 109
Zelikovitz, 175
Zerubavel, 78
Zilberstein, 58, 59
Ziskin, 92
Ziss, 111, 114, 117, 130
Zucker, 79, 81
Zuskin, 37
Zvodner, 132

www.ingramcontent.com/pod-product-compliance
Lightning Source LLC
Chambersburg PA
CBHW050412110426
42812CB00006BA/1871